Understanding Higher Education:
Alternative Perspectives

Chrissie Boughey & Sioux McKenna

This wonderful book will be a treasure for graduate students and scholars who seek to understand and theorise higher education in ways that support social justice. Rooted in the experiences of South Africa, the book uses social realism to argue for alternative ways of seeing higher education that can inform practice and policy in both the Global South and Global North.

Prof. Leesa Wheelahan, William G. Davis Chair in Community College Leadership, Ontario Institute for Studies in Education, University of Toronto

Professors Chrissie Boughey and Sioux McKenna have written a truly insightful, engaging and informative book on teaching and learning in higher education. Every vice-chancellor, academic and ordinary citizen must read this book.

Dr Sizwe Mabizela, Vice-Chancellor, Rhodes University, South Africa

This is an outstanding book, offering an exceptionally rich analysis of the impacts of neoliberalism on higher education in South Africa. It examines in vibrant detail the ways through which a market ideology has penetrated the education system, with devastating costs on faculty, students, and research. It also sheds light on resistances to the neoliberal transformation together with attempts to develop alternative perspectives. The book is an essential reading for anyone interested in neoliberalism, higher education, and the political economy of South Africa and beyond.

Prof. Fikret Adaman, Department of Economics, Boğaziçi University, Turkey

This important book offers a theoretically rich and engaging account of what is needed to ensure that university education is meaningfully accessible to all students. By examining these issues from the perspective of policies, students, curricula, and academic staff, it offers a systematic view of the challenges facing teaching and learning in higher education and the potential for positive change.

Prof. Paul Ashwin, Head of Department: Educational Research, Lancaster University, UK

A timely, insightful, and nuanced rendition of alternative perspectives on higher education. Boughey and McKenna have given local thinking the gravitas that will reverberate at the global level for many decades to come.

Prof. Emmanuel Mgqwashu, Director: Centre for Teaching and Learning, North West University, South Africa

This book provides an informative, illuminating and insightful critique of higher education. Its arguments change the way higher education is conceived of and conducted in African universities and beyond. This is a timely and most welcome research work that is theoretically grounded beyond the usual common-sense discourses on the subject.
Prof. Christopher Odhiambo Joseph (CJ), Dean: School of Postgraduate Studies,
Moi University, Kenya

Any academic text has to strike a delicate balance between the complexity of its content and simplicity in delivery. This book nails it! The authors provide us with significant insights into the contextual dynamics that are the world of higher education. This book is a compelling read for everyone involved in academia.
Dr Lillian Omondi, Department of Sociology and Anthropology, Maseno University, Kenya

If you wish to understand higher education today, especially in the Global South, this book is for you. Boughey and McKenna bring their extensive experience and astute analytical minds to bear on critical issues of teaching and learning to offer alternative perspectives that provide positive ways forward.
Prof. Karl Maton, Director of the LCT Centre for Knowledge-Building,
University of Sydney, Australia

Based on their rich experience as engaged lecturers and researchers, Chrissie Boughey and Sioux McKenna have exceptional abilities to critique the very system of which they are inevitably a part. They highlight why often seemingly self-explanatory systems are not effective in practice. Boughey and McKenna have written an accessible text that makes complex global challenges and problematic local realities comprehensible, whilst also outlining a vision for real change.
Dr Henk van den Heuvel, Director of the Centre for International Cooperation,
Vrije Universiteit, The Netherlands

This book offers a critical stance with which all higher education practitioners should engage given the rapid social and economic changes taking place the world over. This book is a must-read for academics across disciplines, academic developers, researchers, policy-makers, students and everyone concerned about universities and their role in society.
Dr Langutani Masehela, Head of Department: Academic Development Unit,
University of Venda, South Africa

This is a powerful and inspiring book sustaining the idea that for a just institution, teaching and learning is key.
Dr Nelson Mbarushimana, Director-General: Rwanda Basic Education, Rwanda

This book is an original and significant contribution to an important set of debates around the purposes and possibilities for contemporary higher education. Boughey and McKenna draw on an incredible breadth of expertise to tackle this analysis at a whole new level of sophistication. The core of their work is quite exceptional for its ability to take in the diversity of institutional cultures which comprise the South African higher education system, and then to develop their analysis across macro levels of funding and accreditation through to meso considerations of curriculum for students and staff development for staff through to the very micro details of lived realities of the people who find themselves in these contexts. An extraordinary contribution is their empathetic juxtaposition of the situations of both students and staff who find themselves culturally adrift in these institutions with huge hangovers of their colonial and apartheid pasts. Boughey and McKenna unsettle the common-sense arguments that tend to condition even the responses of university leaders, and they go further to debunk the misuse of educational theory. While their core contextual focus is South Africa, they offer careful comparisons of higher education systems across the continent, and internationally. This book is going to be a key resource for higher education scholars, wherever they locate themselves, and an important read for policymakers aiming to transform higher education systems to truly deliver on their promises.
Prof. Jennifer M. Case, Head of Department: Virginia Tech, USA &
Honorary Professor, University of Cape Town, South Africa

The authors provide a fascinating reflection on the discourses that dominate our higher education system. They use Social Realism to analyse the higher education system and offer an alternative for understanding students by challenging common-sense beliefs such as the notion of the untalented and unmotivated student. The book turns on its head the idea that universities are a meritocracy.
Dr Simpiwe Sobuwa, Head of Department: Emergency Medical Care & Rescue,
Durban University of Technology, South Africa

This book will occupy a distinct place for those grappling with research on teaching and learning. It will fill a significant gap because it enables teaching and learning practitioners to bridge the chasm between their observations and experiences on the one hand, and the lessons we can learn from scholarship.
Dr Matete Madiba, Director: Student Affairs, University of Pretoria, South Africa

Acknowledgements

We are grateful to a great many people who have contributed in various ways to this book.

In particular we would like to acknowledge our colleagues in the Centre for Higher Education Research, Teaching and Learning at Rhodes University. They undertake academic development work from a wholly social perspective and have contributed to our understandings of higher education in a great many ways. We would also like to thank our students, especially those postgraduate scholars we have had the privilege of supervising, who have introduced us to new ideas and theories and whose work has greatly enriched this text.

We thank our families for their wholehearted and tireless support of us, especially when our work leads to extended absences from home.

Special thanks are also due to our editor, Susan Blair, whose eagle eye spotted many of the errors we were no longer able to 'see' given our own proximity to our text and to our illustrator, Theresa Gordon, for capturing complex ideas in such an accessible way.

Published in 2021 by African Minds
4 Eccleston Place, Somerset West, 7130, Cape Town, South Africa
info@africanminds.org.za
www.africanminds.org.za

© 2021 African Minds

All contents of this document, unless specified otherwise, are licensed under a
Creative Commons Attribution 4.0 International License.

The views expressed in this publication are those of the authors.
When quoting from any of the chapters, readers are requested to acknowledge the relevant author.

ISBN (paper): 978-1-928502-21-0
eBook edition: 978-1-928502-22-7
ePub edition: 978-1-928502-23-4

Copies of this book are available for free download at:
www.africanminds.org.za

ORDERS:
African Minds
Email: info@africanminds.org.za

To order printed books from outside Africa, please contact:
African Books Collective
PO Box 721, Oxford OX1 9EN, UK
Email: orders@africanbookscollective.com

Table of Contents

Acknowledgements iv

Chapter One: Taking stock 1

Global change and higher education 1
The challenge for the Global South 7
Why look at South Africa? 9
What does this book aim to do? 12

Chapter Two: Making sense of experiences and observations 13

Doing research on teaching and learning 13
The nature of reality 14
Archer's Social Realism 22
Archer's morphogenetic framework 25

Chapter Three: Dominant discourses, policy challenges 29

The global and the local 29
The macro level 30
The meso and micro levels 37
Policy after apartheid 40
Curriculum and the global economy 41
Quality assurance 46
Funding higher education 48
Reorganising the system 50
The Higher Education Qualifications Sub-Framework 51
Conclusion 52

Chapter Four: Denying context, misunderstanding students 53

The power of the words we use 53
Students as decontextualised individuals 54
The misappropriation of theories on teaching and learning 58
The 'language problem' and how it lets universities off the hook 60

Reading and writing as ideological acts 63
Fixing the problem of academic literacy 67
Disadvantage as an explanation for failure 69
The university as a neutral space 71
Students as clients 73
Students as social beings, the university as a social space 75
Foregrounding students' epistemological access 76
Conclusion 80

Chapter Five: Reconceptualising curriculum, structuring access 82

What is curriculum? 82
The curriculum is conditioned by the structure of knowledge 84
The curriculum provides access to powerful knowledge 90
The curriculum is conditioned by social context 94
The curriculum is conditioned by institutional histories 100
Historical differentiation by race 109
Private higher education 111
The focus on programmes and modules 113
Extended curricula 113
Academic advising 116
Conclusion 116

Chapter Six: Resisting and complying: Academics responding to change 118

Academics and agency 118
The conditioning role of the discipline in academics' identity formation 118
The history of the system and the conditioning of individuals 119
New Public Management and managerialism 124
Staffing in a global structure 128
The emergence of compliance 129
Ever-increasing demands on academic life 130
Staff demographics 133
Concluding thoughts 135

Chapter Seven: Evaluating change, looking forward 136

Introduction 136
The landscape at T_4 137
A differentiated and developmental system 147

A Covid Postscript 150

References 155

1

Taking stock

Global change and higher education

Over the last 50 or so years, higher education across the world has seen enormous changes, many of which have emerged in response to globalisation and neoliberalism. So many writers have explored the implications of these two phenomena for higher education that yet another explanation might seem superfluous. This book, however, is particularly concerned with teaching and learning in universities, so we will risk repeating what others have said in order to explore the implications of these forces on this area of academic endeavour.

In its most obvious form, globalisation is concerned with the economic changes that have resulted from the development of transportation and communication links thanks to advances in technology. As we will argue in this book, however, it also has social and cultural implications, as a particular set of ideas have come to dominate thinking and action around the world.

Economically, globalisation involves producing goods using networks stretching across national boundaries. Possibly even more important, given that this book is about higher education, is that globalisation is about using knowledge to 'reinvent' the goods that are produced as a result of the global economy. The mobile phone provides a simple example of the idea of 'reinvention'. Many of us renew our handsets on a regular basis, possibly because of the contracts we take out with providers of cellular telecommunication or because we are enticed to buy new models. Typically, we 'upgrade' to a new handset even though our old devices may still be working perfectly well and serve our current needs adequately. The manufacturers of mobile phones, however, keep 'reinventing' their products so that updated models appear on a regular basis with 'new features'.

These new models are usually designed (or reinvented if we continue to draw on this metaphor) in locations noted for their concentration of highly qualified engineers and other experts such as Silicon Valley, just outside San Francisco. Manufacturing these designs will involve sourcing the raw materials needed to make them from countries which often do not have the capacity to refine what is found abundantly within their borders. Titanium, for example, is found on South African beaches but is sent to places

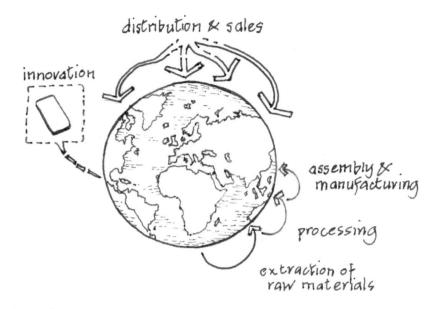

such as Australia for processing. Once the raw materials have been processed into a usable form, they are then shipped to factories that turn them into components that will go into products manufactured in another factory possibly in another country altogether, such as China or Korea. The supply chains involved in the production of a mobile phone therefore stretch across the globe and need to be managed to ensure that what is needed for the next step in the process arrives 'just in time' for it to carry on without any hitches or delays. The choice of location for a particular stage of the process is often related to the cost of labour.

Actually, manufacturing a mobile phone is but part of the process involved in keeping this global chain moving. Demand for new versions of particular types of phone has to be created by marketers. Distributors then have to get the phones into shops or, increasingly, into a van that a courier will drive to deliver them to individual customers. Calculations have to be done in order to cost finished products in ways that will ensure the maximum profit for shareholders in the companies that make them and, of course, the markets on which shares are sold and bought also have to be managed. And, in the background, advances in technology keep the wheels rolling on the entire process.

All this requires a high level of skill on the part of those involved in the global economy. The so-called 'Fordist' models of mass production dominant in the last century required large numbers of workers who would do the same job on a factory assembly line for most of their lives. The demand, therefore, was for 'low' and not 'high' skills. In contrast, in the new global economy, 'high skills' are needed for all the processes of invention, sourcing and distribution, manufacturing, marketing and finance that drive it.

The demand for high skills has obvious implications for universities. Of all institutions offering education and training, universities, in principle at least, have the potential to

equip young people with the highest level of skills. As the global economy grew, therefore, universities came to be constructed as sites for this kind of training in spite of the fact that many institutions of higher education had little experience of offering anything other than study in the traditional academic disciplines and a few professional areas such as law, engineering or medicine.

The idea of an economy 'fuelled by knowledge' has captured the attention of governments around the world, with the result that they have promoted growth in their higher education systems in order to accommodate more and more of the young people they hope will become 'knowledge workers'.

As young people flooded into universities in search of the qualifications that would equip them to work in the global economy, a number of things happened. The first was that student bodies grew in size. Suddenly a great many more universities were needed to accommodate the rapidly-increased student body.

As the student body 'massified' it became more 'diversified', as it came to comprise students from a wide array of social and cultural backgrounds rather than from the elite classes who had traditionally enjoyed almost exclusive access to higher forms of learning. This growth in numbers and the increased diversity brought with it attention to teaching and learning, the area of academic endeavour with which we are most concerned in this book.

The implications of the global economy were not restricted to a growth in student numbers and the diversification of the student body, however. Universities began to teach and research in new areas and different kinds of institution began to emerge. We may all be accustomed to the idea of the 'polytechnic' or 'university of technology' but, in the history of higher education, these are relatively new kinds of institution. Countries not only needed more universities to address the demand from prospective students and the goal of high skills for the globalised economy; they also needed different forms of universities to attend to all the different kinds of skills being identified.

Globalisation involves more than the economy as the increase in communication associated with it has also brought social and cultural change. Ideas and opinions flow across the world in minutes thanks to social media. Concerns about conspicuous consumption are not new, with Veblen raising this issue as long ago as 1899, however, social media, a key mechanism of globalisation, means that opulent lifestyles are readily constructed on film and in other media such as the Instagram accounts of 'influencers'. These lifestyles, and the ways of behaving and ideological valuing and thinking they embody, are adopted as 'norms' to which all are expected to aspire, even though the possibility of sharing in the riches they depict is relatively remote. The ease of communication associated with globalisation has spread not only ideas; it has also impacted on the use of English as the dominant language across the world.

For many young people, therefore, higher education is not only seen as a means to obtaining a well-paying job but also as a way of participating in the world depicted on computer and mobile phone screens. Historically, few young people followed a path leading to qualifications from universities as these were held to be the domain of the elite, and so most prepared for the world of work in other ways, such as apprenticeships and other forms of on-the-job training. In the globalised world, many of these opportunities have fallen away, with a degree or some other form of certification held up as the means through which to avoid low-paying, low-prestige jobs.

Globalisation is not the only force to have impacted on universities. The set of ideas collectively termed 'neoliberalism' has also affected them in profound ways. Neoliberalism entails a hegemony of market logic; that is the economisation of every aspect of our lives. The literature on neoliberalism typically focuses on free-market capitalism and, thus, the reduction of any form of control on economic activity conducted by individuals and companies. The deregulation of economic activity around most of the world has been accompanied by the privatisation of state entities, a phenomenon seen most clearly in post-Soviet Russia where so-called 'oligarchs' were alleged to have bought up oil companies and other entities previously owned by the state, often very cheaply (Hollingsworth & Lansey 2009). The laissez-faire approach to economic activity was accompanied by reductions in government spending, the thinking being that less 'interference' in the economy on the part of governments would result in the private sector taking over and providing services that had hitherto been state funded. Taxes on large industries and on wealthy individuals were reduced following arguments made by economists such as Milton Friedman (Friedman 1970) that this would allow for a 'trickle-down' effect which would lead to economic development that would eventually benefit all.

However, Madra and Adaman (2018) caution that neoliberalism needs to be understood from a much wider epistemic frame than simply a reduction in state power in favour of a free market. They argue that some governments, such as Erdoğan's Turkey and Correa's Ecuador, invoke entrepreneurial discourses and cost-benefit language in a manner which entirely exemplifies neoliberalism while at the same time deploying state power and non-market instruments (Madra & Adaman 2018). Neoliberalism can thus occur across varied political contexts and entails conceptualising human behaviour entirely as a form of cost-benefit analysis.

Neoliberalism, accompanied with other such ideas associated with globalisation, had an enormous impact on higher education, seen most visibly in the reduction of state spending on the sector. The thinking here was that, if knowledge was a commodity that successful students acquired, they could effectively trade their certified skillset in the global economy by selling their labour as 'knowledge workers'. Because individual students reap the economic benefits of such certification, they then should carry the costs of achieving it. Besides producing knowledge workers, the university was also seen, in this neoliberal thinking, to be in the business of selling their research in order to 'reinvent' existing goods. Because universities could then presumably sell such research-based products, they should fund their own development.

As state funding for higher education decreased, universities responded by raising the fees for tuition charged to students. At the same time as this happened, funding provided to students in many countries in the form of bursaries and scholarships was also reduced or, in some cases, fell aside altogether. This meant that all students, regardless of their socio-economic circumstances, were increasingly required to pay for their education. As a qualification from an institution of higher education was considered by many to be key to getting a well-paid job, the cost of obtaining these credentials was generally accepted. For many (including, e.g. Mintz 2019), the formulation of education as credentials has resulted in the devaluing of education, as young people enter universities not because of any intrinsic interest in what is being studied but with the instrumental purpose of getting a qualification that will lead to a job and a 'better' life.

As student bodies have grown and diversified, huge changes have also occurred in the learning experiences offered to them. Most young people across the world now follow outcomes-based or competency-based curricula focusing on the 'skills' that are claimed will ready them for the workplace. At the same time, the idea that they can be moulded to develop the 'attributes' it is assumed they will need as graduates has gained prominence. Students follow modularised courses where modularisation has often been supported by claims about the greater efficiency and increased flexibility of short courses that can be combined in myriad ways into larger units of learning.

Academics have thus been pushed to redevelop curricula to meet the demands of outcomes- or competency-based approaches and modularisation. In some cases, curriculum development has been in areas where the academics themselves have never taught, a phenomenon fuelled by the desire of the institutions at which they work to branch out and offer qualifications responsive to the global job market and thus attractive to students.

It is not only in relation to teaching that academics have faced increased demands, however, since the insatiable desire for knowledge in the global economy has resulted in greater pressure than ever being placed on the need to produce research. At many universities, offices for 'research development and innovation' have now been established and the monitoring of production at an individual level is commonplace. At the same time as pressure on academics has increased, the idea that an academic career involved a tenured position in which an individual could rise through the ranks from lecturer to full professor has been eroded by an increase in the use of short-term contracts to regulate employment. In South Africa, 66% of academics are employed on a temporary basis (CHE 2020: 47). As academics have been called upon to do more, therefore, the benefits they could potentially enjoy have become less.

At the level of institutional leadership, vice-chancellors and principals have faced particular challenges. Not only do they need to consider how their university or college can best contribute to a globalised economy demanding students with the skills called for by employers; they need to do this in contexts of financial stringency and, thus, achieve 'efficiencies' never before imagined. These are often in the form of targets and norms set by the state. Calls to 'widen participation' so that students from a wide spectrum of socio-economic and cultural backgrounds can participate in higher learning have been made as a result of concerns for social justice and not just from a position related to the need for increased participation in the global economy.

University leaders thus face the difficult task of balancing efficiency (i.e. the need to contribute to the global economy) with equity (in the sense of providing higher education to a wider range of students). In the private institutions of higher education, which have proliferated in many countries since demand for qualifications has increased, the need to make educational decisions most often confronts the need to make profit.

The call for greater efficiency has also resulted in the outsourcing of services to private companies, many of which can offer, for example, cleaning or catering at prices more cost-effective than the same services run by universities themselves. University leaders therefore find themselves dealing with the contracts related to the provision of services and of endlessly negotiating for lower prices in tender processes. Such outsourcing increasingly includes activities once considered fundamental to the academic project, through 'unbundling', whereby partnerships with private corporations import learning materials, assessment processes, online learning management and more (McCowan 2017).

One more area in which neoliberalism has impacted on higher education has been on the proclaimed need for greater accountability and transparency. The thinking here is that, if funding is provided by the public either through their taxes or through payments for services or products, then bodies providing those services need to be accountable for the way the money is spent and the quality of what is provided. As a result, universities have seen the introduction of national quality assurance systems alongside increased reporting on the way they administer and spend any funding they receive. The funding itself is often dependent on an institution developing a 'strategic plan' with goals and targets. Achievement measured against these goals and targets is then monitored on a regular basis.

Developments such as these fall under the umbrella term 'New Public Management', an approach to making public service organisations more 'business-like'. For universities, such developments have resulted in the introduction of a new level of management in the form of quality assurance offices, institutional planning divisions and so on. This has increased the number of administrative staff, a move often resented by academics who feel that staffing for teaching, research and community engagement is stretched to the limit (see, e.g. Edwards 2017).

In many respects, globalisation and neoliberalism have resulted in a model of 'the university' that is being followed across the world, regardless of the history of development of a particular country or the needs of its citizenry. This model of the 'global university' has been influential in other developments in recent years, including the protests that emerged in 2015 and 2016 at institutions of higher education across the world in countries as diverse as South Africa, the United States, India and Kenya. Many of the protests focused on rising tuition fees and the inability of students from social groups other than the most affluent to pay them. However, it was not only funding that drove students to remonstrate since there were also objections to the very nature of the universities and, more specifically, to curricula which alienated students from their cultural and social roots. Objections to the forms universities had taken across the world and to the curricula that structured students' learning experiences had their roots in decoloniality. These were underpinned by the argument that universities as they stood in many countries were 'imports' to foreign soil and that indigenous forms of education, historically practised in some of the most ancient institutions, had been marginalised and even eradicated (Tuhiwai Smith 2012).

The challenge for the Global South

What does all this mean for the complex reality of the Global South? Many countries in the South rely on the sale of commodities in the form of raw minerals and materials to drive their economies. The African continent, for example, has dominated the production of raw platinum, used extensively in electronics, for many years now. However, very little of the mineral refinement or component production happens on the continent. The ability to benefit more widely from the rich resources found on African soil is dependent on the knowledge and resources that can be used to add value, to refine, to use materials in manufacture and, then, to market and distribute finished products across the world.

In a report for the World Bank, Darvas et al. (2017: ix) have this to say on the subject in relation to sub-Saharan Africa (SSA):

> In 2016, economic growth in the [...] region reached the weakest pace in over two decades as a result of the low commodity prices that affect many economies in the region with strong reliance on mining and production of other raw materials. Against the backdrop of slow growth, it is even more important for SSA countries to diversify their economies, improve productivity, build value chains for agriculture, and improve both domestic and export markets. Because knowledge is the driver of productivity and economic growth, these goals require building human capital through more accessible, equitable, and better-quality education and training systems.

If we follow the argument made above, what is needed is enhanced capacity to engage with the globalised, knowledge-based economy as a result of the production of more graduates who can contribute to processes of adding value to the natural resources on which the continent can draw.

This is an economic argument. However, what is even more needed are graduates who are socially, politically, and not only economically, aware and who can contribute to the development of societies where the vast majority live in unfavourable living conditions.

For many, including Wheelahan (2010), access to the kind of theorised, structured knowledge that has historically dominated university teaching is about gaining access to 'society's conversation'. Access to certain kinds of knowledge is but one more way of seeing how the 'equity versus efficiency' tension plays out.

Unesco (2020) data for the entire African continent shows the current enrolment in higher education standing at just over 12% of the 18- to 24-year-old cohort. This is in comparison to the global average of 32%. Within these figures, enormous disparities exist. In Egypt, the figure stands at 33%, in Tanzania 4% and in Niger only 2%. With such small numbers of students entering higher education in many countries, there is clearly a need to ensure that the experiences offered to them are as good as they can possibly be and that the graduates who result can serve the needs of their countries and the societies in which they live in ways which are informed by broad economic, social and political debates.

Enrolments in higher education have grown on the continent with, for example, Darvas et al. (2017) noting that, in sub-Saharan Africa, enrolments counted fewer than 400 000 across the region in 1970, a number which had increased to approximately 7.2 million by 2013. Notably, this growth has taken place in a context of financial stringency. The 'Structural Adjustment Programmes' enacted by the World Bank and International Monetary Fund placed a number of conditions on receiving funding, many of which can be seen to have restrained the freedom of the university sector in the Global South to determine its own structure and purpose. Funding was particularly problematic when the decision was taken to withdraw funding for higher education in favour of the development of the schooling sector. This Global North policy can be seen to have had a number of deleterious effects on higher education in the South (Amutabi 2002; Atteh 1996; Nkinyangi 1991). According to researchers such as Amutabi (2002), this resulted in overcrowding in teaching venues and halls of residence and the lack of facilities as basic as seats in lecture rooms, as well as a generalised lack of academic resources including staff members.

In this context, there is a critical need for universities to consider what a growth in student numbers may mean for them. As long ago as 1973, Trow identified the achievement of a 15% participation rate in higher education as the point at which a system 'massifies'. Trow's focus in writing about 'massification', in what is now a classic piece on higher education, is not numbers. Rather, his purpose was to point out most forcefully that the challenge in a 'massified' system goes beyond accommodating large classes and managing large universities to include dealing with the diversity that numbers bring.

As we have already noted, universities have historically catered for a small elite; an elite who have been groomed for tertiary study thanks to all the experiences afforded to them before enrolment. These experiences are not limited to schooling but also encompass those afforded by the home of origin. As numerous ethnographic studies have shown (including, for example, Heath's seminal *Ways with Words*, 1983), the children of middle-class, educated parents are groomed for schooling literally from the day of their birth through talk and activities in their homes. These children enter school with an advantage which is then reinforced by their caregivers at home. Talk and activities in the homes of these children not only support learning in school but also challenge and extend it in ways that better prepare them for higher education. Local studies (see, e.g. Armstrong 2019) show how children from marginalised communities enter schooling without any of the privileged connections their classmates might enjoy.

While many countries are a long way from achieving a 'massified' higher education system, they still need to confront issues related to diversity as their higher education systems grow. A child born into a family in rural South Africa, for example, is unlikely to benefit from the advice and support of family members who have already attended higher education. The location of the family home itself and the poverty associated with it will impact on a young person's 'connectedness' to the wider world. In addition, the knowledge and practices this child would have accrued in her home of origin are then less likely to be acknowledged in higher education.

If we believe that higher education has the potential to contribute to the well-being of societies through the production of research and of graduates who can contribute to critical discourse and, thus, to democracy itself, the idea of widening participation is crucial. Even more significantly, this needs to be done in universities where reduced funding has led to poor-quality infrastructure and a scarcity of resources and where, we argue, dominant ideas about teaching and learning normalise a particular way of being and silence others by failing to take into account the diversity of students' socio-cultural and economic contexts.

Why look at South Africa?

This book looks at teaching and learning in higher education through a particular focus on South Africa. One could argue that South Africa is a special case given its iniquitous history of apartheid. It is indeed true that South Africa faced extraordinary challenges as it shifted to democracy but the argument made above, that the Global South as a whole faces issues of efficiency (i.e. the economic imperative) at the same time as engaging with those related to equity (the social imperative), was also true of South Africa. It was never a case of 'either/or'. Rather, policymakers had to attempt a complex balancing act as soon as it became clear that the end of apartheid was imminent following the release of Nelson Mandela, the country's first democratically elected president, from jail in 1990.

Apartheid resulted in the imposition of economic sanctions and the isolation associated with these. In 1990, South Africa faced an urgent need to join the global economy from which it had been excluded. The social imperative related to the exclusion of the majority of the population from decision-making, and to the processes, such as higher education, that allow extensive participation in the development of policy and social structures. The way in which this nation at the southernmost tip of the continent confronted this challenge is thus of relevance to those working in higher education systems elsewhere, especially, as we will argue, through a reflection on the many things that did not work out in the way they were intended by policymakers and institutional leaders.

In many respects, this book is an attempt to answer questions about what went wrong in South African higher education. The book draws on multiple research projects we have undertaken over the past two decades but in particular on a piece of research we did for the Council on Higher Education (CHE), the body established to advise the minister on higher education. The White Paper on Higher Education (Department of Education 1997, Section 2.69), intended to guide the transformation of the higher education system, notes that, although the primary responsibility for quality assurance must lie with institutions, a role existed for an umbrella body that would promote and coordinate efforts throughout the system. This role was assigned to the Higher Education Quality Committee (HEQC), a standing committee of the CHE. More specifically, the White Paper established the functions of the HEQC as including programme accreditation, institutional auditing and quality promotion.

In 2005, the HEQC embarked on the first cycle of institutional audits, producing a wealth of data related to public universities. As the audits came to a close, we were commissioned to produce a meta-analysis of teaching and learning which attempted to evaluate the impact of the audits on this core area of academic activity. In order to complete the research, we were provided with all the data produced as a result of audit processes: the reports in which each institution being audited had evaluated itself against audit criteria, the institutional profiles, or analyses of institutional data produced by the CHE, and the reports written by the panels appointed to audit each university.

Arguably, this work is the only piece produced to date on teaching and learning in the South African system that is based on such comprehensive data; data that not only included analyses of student performance and staff demographics, but also in-depth accounts on the part of institutions regarding the way they believed they had met the set of criteria developed for teaching and learning as part of the audit cycle.

In order to conduct the research, we needed to develop a framework to analyse the data we had been given. The framework we developed, based on Roy Bhaskar's (1979) critical realism and Margaret Archer's (1995, 1996, 1998, 2000) Social Realism allowed us to see that, although the higher education system had changed significantly in relation to teaching and learning in some respects, in others it had not (Boughey & McKenna 2016). Even more significantly, the use of the framework allowed us to see how the lack of change in some areas led to the failure to achieve equity or efficiency in the system. At the time we undertook the research, other studies analysing the performance of cohorts of students passing through the system (see, e.g. Scott et al. 2007; Lesteka & Maile 2008) had already identified the inefficiency of the system in terms of high non-completion and slow throughput rates. Those same studies had also shown that it was black South African students, who had finally been able to access the system in large numbers following the first democratic election, who bore the brunt of poor performance figures and, thus, that the goal of equity was not being achieved.

In many respects, therefore, the focus on South Africa in this book is relevant for all countries struggling with issues related to equity and efficiency. This is especially the case since South Africa has engaged with many reforms that other nations may now be considering. The development of national qualifications frameworks, for example, is being considered by many countries across the continent as we write, yet the introduction of the National Qualifications Framework in South Africa has prompted curriculum reform in universities that has not always been as positive as anticipated (see, e.g. Allais 2014), an observation we discuss in more detail in Chapter Five. In a similar vein, South African experiences of modularisation, or the breaking up of learning into small, itemised pieces which are accorded credits, or of the advocacy for 'Mode 2 knowledge' (critiqued by the likes of Muller 2001a; Kraak 2000), might inform similar initiatives elsewhere on the continent.

We also believe that our work on student learning in countries seeking to admit larger numbers of 'first generation' students, that is, students from families who have previously not been able to access higher education, has important implications for anyone concerned with making higher education more equitable through the enhancement of teaching and curriculum design. This work is informed by all the research we have conducted over the last 20 years or more on student learning from what we term a 'social perspective' that resonates with ideas of 'humanising pedagogy' (see, e.g. Bartolomé 1994; Salazar 2013). We believe this has the potential to provide insights into teaching and learning regardless of where it takes place, but especially in contexts where universities have long thought about teaching and learning as neutral and fair when, in fact, they have demanded ways of being and knowing that have privileged some over others.

The framework drawn from the work of Bhaskar (1979) and Archer (1995, 1996, 1998, 2000) allowed us to see what had changed, and what had not changed, in teaching and learning as a result of the first cycle of quality assurance work in South Africa (Boughey & McKenna 2017). In addition to this, the framework also allowed us to see how the reshaping of the South African system, like other higher education systems elsewhere, had been influenced by ideas from the Global North, and how institutions had responded to these ideas in ways which often worked against the intentions of policymakers.

As two academics working in a centre for teaching and learning in a South African university, we were also aware as we wrote of our own day-to-day work focusing on the development of staff in their capacity as academic teachers. We also draw on our work as reviewers for journals, where we note the increase in research on teaching and learning, particularly by academics with backgrounds in disciplines other than education or the other social sciences. These experiences have allowed us to note that a great deal of work in teaching and learning in higher education draws on relativist understandings of knowledge and knowing, as we will discuss in Chapter Two, whereby all knowledge about teaching and learning is seen to be fluid and dependent on individual interpretation. In contrast to such relativist approaches, the framework on which our research drew is realist in the sense that it assumes that there is a reality that exists independently of human action and thought. The philosophy underpinning the framework, Critical Realism, is enjoying increased interest in the world of educational research and we were drawn to the idea of demonstrating the way it could be used in relation to understanding the problems we had identified.

We have therefore described the framework in some detail, in Chapter Two of this book, to explain how it can be used in educational research. This is because we were drawn to the idea that demonstrating the framework in action as we analysed developments in

South African higher education from the early 1990s onwards might be of assistance to others working in the field. The remaining chapters in the book then aim to make the use of the framework overt as we work with our analysis.

What does this book aim to do?

Our book then, aims to do a number of things. First, it represents the attempts of two academics who have been involved in many of the national initiatives intended to transform higher education over the past 20 or more years in one country to answer the questions 'What worked?' and 'What didn't work?' in order to raise questions about the South African context in ways that might be of use to those working here and in other countries, particularly countries in the Global South facing similar rapid increases in student numbers and sector-wide reforms.

The second thing we aim to do is to demonstrate that we have used a theoretical framework to analyse a higher education system. As experienced supervisors of postgraduate students, we are particularly aware of how difficult it is to understand how theory can be used, literally, to 'see the world differently'. An analogy we often use in our own teaching is that theory is like a pair of spectacles. Without spectacles, you see the world in one way. Once you put on a pair of spectacles, and depending on which spectacles you choose, you will see the world differently. Some spectacles, for example, will allow you to see things in fine detail 'close up'. Others, for example those with tinted lenses, provide us with a particular view of things. We can wear many different kinds of spectacles but need to choose which we wear depending on what we want to see.

In this book we have chosen to wear spectacles with Social and Critical Realist lenses. We put on our spectacles and justify their choice in Chapter Two. We then look through our spectacles to present our analysis of the system. This is exactly what postgraduate students do when they embark on a piece of research and, in the book, we aim to show what this involves.

Finally, and this is probably the most important aim of the book, we want to argue for a different way of understanding students, of understanding the curriculum and of understanding the universities themselves. In order to do this, we have to cast aside our common-sense assumptions (something our theoretical spectacles allow us to do) and, literally, question much of what we have been led to believe. We have had to critically interrogate the way dominant ideas have shaped our thinking. This is our most important aim, as we believe that it is only by questioning common-sense assumptions and dominant ways of thinking that we will begin to understand what we can begin to do to make things better.

The book has required us to take a long hard look at much of what we have been implicated in for so many years. If it can persuade others to do the same, our hope is that our universities might begin to move towards offering students the kinds of learning experiences we believe they so richly deserve.

2

Making sense of experiences and observations

Doing research on teaching and learning

In recent years there has been a huge surge of interest in researching teaching and learning in higher education. Journals specialising in this area, such as *Studies in Higher Education* and *Teaching in Higher Education,* have increased the number of issues they produce each year given the number of submissions they receive, and numerous conferences now have the same focus.

Much of the interest in researching teaching and learning has come from disciplinary experts; people teaching in a wide range of subject areas in the universities. As we will discuss in more detail in Chapter Three, academics across the world are under increasing pressure to perform in all areas of academic work. It is no longer sufficient to simply be a good researcher. In the performance management and promotion systems of many contemporary universities, academics need to demonstrate that they are also good teachers and that they can contribute to community engagement, to the administration of workplaces and to the disciplinary communities to which they belong. The need to demonstrate competence in both research and teaching has led many to try to combine these two areas by researching their own practice as teachers.

This book is underpinned by research we have conducted over the last 25 years. As we indicate in Chapter One, one of the biggest pieces of research we have done was commissioned by the South African Council on Higher Education (CHE) and involved an analysis of the impact of the first cycle of quality assurance audits on the universities. In order to do this study, we used a framework developed from philosopher Roy Bhaskar's (1998, 2000, 2002, 2016) 'Critical Realism' and sociologist Margaret Archer's (1995, 1996, 1998, 2000, 2002) 'Social Realism'.

The work of Bhaskar and Archer was useful to us for a number of reasons which we will explain below. In this chapter we describe the elements of their work that we drew upon to develop the framework and the way we used it in the research commissioned by the CHE. We do this not only to allow our readers to judge the rigour of the work underpinning some of the claims we make, but also to demonstrate to others, who may be accomplished researchers in their own fields but new to research on teaching and learning, how we used the framework itself.

We begin by discussing some of the dilemmas which confront all researchers who seek to explore social life and involve human beings in their research studies.

The nature of reality

Many people embarking on a piece of research, particularly those without a background in the social sciences, focus on the distinction made between quantitative and qualitative approaches. As we aim to show, however, in many respects the quantitative/qualitative distinction is not very useful. What we really need to consider as we plan a piece of research is the nature of 'truth' or 'reality' itself.

The approach to scientific research that has dominated the Western world since the middle of the 18th century is known as 'empiricism'. Empiricism assumes that the absolute reality or truth of what is being researched exists independently of human thought and existence. The role of researchers is to 'discover' or 'uncover' this truth or reality and, in order to do this, they need to adopt an objective stance to ensure that they do not 'contaminate' or affect what it is they are trying to see and, thus, know. There is no difference between knowledge and reality in this approach. If you have the correct knowledge of a phenomenon, then you have accessed the reality.

Knowing, in empiricism, results from observation and experimentation. A scientist observes and measures very carefully in order to be able to describe. Alternatively, she might design an experiment that tests a hypothesis to find out if it is true or untrue. Research design often involves using statistics – either descriptive statistics that allow us to 'see' our data in a different way or inferential statistics which allow us to make generalisations or even predictions beyond the data sample we have analysed. As a result, empiricism research focuses heavily on quantitative approaches.

The alternative to quantitative approaches is often seen to be 'qualitative research'. Qualitative research often seeks to garner people's opinions or beliefs in relation to a phenomenon, using questionnaires or interviews, although it can also involve observation in the form of close description. But once the data has been collected, the question 'What does all this mean?' arises, as it indeed must do in any piece of research. This is because the data itself simply represents respondents' perspectives on or experiences of a particular issue or phenomenon. While perspectives, opinions or beliefs represent a certain kind of 'truth' at an individual level, problems emerge when attempts are made to extrapolate beyond the personal. As a result, we can end up with a piece of work that represents 'multiple truths' or 'multiple realities'. A researcher then has to work with the multiplicity of observations and reports of experience to arrive at a more overall position to report on.

This process of working with other people's observations and reports of experience involves the researcher interpreting what has been said or written. Given that what participants say in response to questions posed by the researcher are already the participants' own interpretations of a particular phenomenon or situation, the researcher's claims are then the researcher's interpretations of the participants' interpretations – involving what research handbooks call the 'double hermeneutic'.

When this sort of research is conducted, researchers are often careful to note their own positions and, thus, the potential for their own bias or fallibility as they engage in the 'double hermeneutic'. In essence, what they are offering is one view of the world, the situation or phenomenon, which could be challenged by other views. Their particular view is offered up to others with an account of the researcher's own position as a basis for interrogation or challenge. Such research is therefore grounded on the idea that realities are constructed, or brought into being, by individuals. Constructed accounts can acknowledge the influence of society. That is, they acknowledge that we are conditioned to see or experience in certain ways because of the environments in which we have grown up and live. This involves an acceptance of multiple views of reality in a position known as relativism.

Qualitative research does not preclude the use of numerical data. Typically, numbers are used in qualitative research to *describe* a situation rather than to *prove* the case. Numbers often involve the use of descriptive statistics which allow us to 'see' the data in new ways. These add depth to the analysis or interpretation by attempting to give an indication of how many people or how many situations it could apply to. Qualitative research conducted in this tradition tends not to be predictive – it describes and analyses what happens in one situation at one time from the researcher's perspective. Although causes and effects might be identified, the link between cause and effect is not generalised to other situations or other phenomena. The research is offered up to others to judge how it could pertain to the situations and phenomena with which they are working.

As we have indicated, this sort of research, rooted in relativist views of reality, is often contrasted with quantitative research, which typically is based on very different assumptions about reality and how we can come to know it. As we have noted, much quantitative research is conducted within the 'positivist' tradition that assumes an external reality independent of human action based on identifiable cause-and-effect laws. In contrast, much qualitative research is conducted from a relativist position that assumes that reality is constructed by individuals. But in many respects, the quantitative/ qualitative distinction cited in research handbooks is misleading since the real question that needs to be answered by researchers relates not to the nature of the data or data collection but rather to the view of reality underpinning both the research design and the kinds of claims being made.

The notion of an absolute reality independent of human thought and action is particularly attractive because, as Carspecken (1996) points out, the concept of multiple realities, and particularly the idea of multiple shifting realities espoused by postmodernists, can become 'ludic' or 'playful'. Ultimately it can lead to the question 'What's the point of doing research?' If all researchers do is present one view of the world, which is but one view among many on a reality that is ever-shifting and ephemeral, why bother to do research at all? Obviously, this is an extreme position and, as we have pointed out, researchers often offer up their understandings to others to see if they resonate or ring true in other contexts. Nonetheless, this sort of critique is still interesting and can perplex researchers.

Bhaskar's Critical Realism allows us to see beyond the limitations of both empiricism, with its assumptions that knowledge and reality can be conflated, and relativism, with its concept of constantly changing, multiple realities. It does this by positing a 'layered' or 'stratified' reality.

The first layer of this reality is called the Empirical (Bhaskar 2002). The Empirical is the layer of experiences and observations made, as its name suggests, via the senses. Experiences and observations are acknowledged to be multiple – to be made on the basis of our past histories – and, therefore, to be relative. We might all experience a single event in multiple ways. As Elder-Vass (2013) explains, experiences are social products because our experiences are not simply a set of cognitive sense-data; our experiences result from our interpretation of that sense-data through our own socially influenced conceptual framework.

The second layer, the Actual, includes the first layer of the Empirical and also includes events that occur in the world, some of which we may be aware of in the Empirical layer and some of which may go unnoticed. Our experiences and observations of the Empirical layer emerge from the Actual. The layers of the Empirical and the Actual are thus the world we know – the world we experience on a daily basis. Acknowledging the existence of the layers of the Empirical and the Actual allows us to account for the multiplicity of human experience and a world of knowing that is relative – that is, it may be different for different people at different times. However, Bhaskar goes beyond this in his identification of a final layer of reality, termed the Real, which includes all the events of the Actual layer and the experiences of the Empirical layer but also includes mechanisms from which the layers of the Actual and Empirical emerge. These mechanisms are intransitive and relatively unchanging. They are intransitive in that they exist and have power whether we are aware of them or not. Every event at the level of the Actual, and every experience at the level of the Empirical, emerges from an infinitely complex interplay of these mechanisms at the level of the Real.

Amongst other things, the term 'mechanisms' can be used to refer to physical phenomena such as a virus or a fungal spore. It can also be used to refer to social structures, such as gender, education, and so on, that regulate access to material resources. The existence of education, for example, is a social structure that can enable or constrain access to material goods in the world.

By using the idea of a virus being a mechanism we can see how the different levels of reality work. A virus may enter a person's body. The virus is real; it exists whether we know about it or not. The virus has the power to cause certain symptoms. Some viruses have the power to cause coughs and runny noses, for example. The fact that a certain virus has entered a person's body does not mean that the person will automatically develop symptoms associated with it, however. One person's immune system (another set of mechanisms) may work to contain the virus, with the result that that particular person experiences no change in her physical or mental sense of being. Another person's immune system may not be able to contain the power of the virus, however, with the result that certain symptoms emerge. Her nose may begin to run and she may cough. The

running nose and the cough can be understood as events which emerge from the interaction of the virus with other mechanisms in the human body. We can thus begin to see how the different layers of reality work.

From this particular example, which focuses on physical phenomena, we can also consider social phenomena. At the level of the Real we could begin to consider social structures like class, gender and race. Because of unjust societal structures, people's class, gender or race may mean that they have not had access to the nutrition needed to ensure that their immune system functions well or they may be more likely to suffer particular comorbidities. The interaction between society's construction of class, race and gender and access to nutrition and the development of the immune system and other medical conditions alongside exposure to the virus may well then lead to the emergence of certain events. A person's nose may begin to run or she might cough. A person from a different social group may never have suffered deprivation with the result that their immune system is functioning well. When the virus enters the body, the immune system blocks it with the result that there is no emergence of symptoms. Another person with other diseases linked to social issues may also contract the virus. When this happens, these other diseases make the impact of the virus worse...

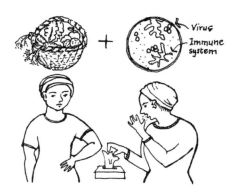

In this greatly simplified example, we have indicated only a few mechanisms at play at the level of the Real and events that emerge at the level of the Actual and have thus dealt with only two of Bhaskar's layers of reality. We can now add the third layer, that of the Empirical. People experience physical symptoms like a cough or a runny nose in different ways. One person might say 'Oh, it's only a cold', blow their nose and continue working as usual. Another might declare 'I'm so ill' and take to her bed, even though the symptoms are the same or very similar. When we try to account for these different experiences of symptoms such as a runny nose or cough, again we might bring the social into play. If a person has been raised in a milieu where enormous attention was paid to physical symptoms and the idea of needing to take care of the body was privileged, then it is possible that the runny nose and cough could be experienced differently to another person who had an upbringing where ailments were shrugged off. We can thus add the additional layer to our representation of these layers of reality.

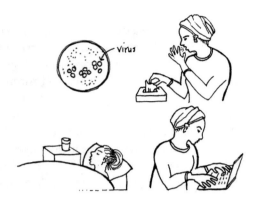

Key to Bhaskar's thinking is the notion of emergence. The runny nose emerges (or may not emerge) as a result of the interaction of multiple mechanisms at the level of the Real. The experiences of individuals then emerge as a result of the symptoms in interplay with ideas about physical health, and so on.

Although mechanisms have causal powers, they are not *strictly* causal. As we have explained in the example above, the fact that the virus enters the body as a mechanism with the causal power to bring about ill-health does not mean that symptoms will always emerge. The emergence or non-emergence of symptoms is related to the interplay and interaction of the virus with multiple other mechanisms. In Critical Realist research, we are therefore looking at the *tendency* of a mechanism to make something emerge. We will return to this point later.

The interplay of mechanisms at the level of the Real generally cannot be accessed directly using the senses. A scientist might be able to isolate and view a virus using a microscope but the interplay of a person's immune system or a person's set of beliefs about bodily health could not be observed directly. The idea that the full spectrum of mechanisms at play at the level of the Real cannot be accessed directly is important in Critical Realist research. A researcher can only work with empirical data, data that can be accessed via the senses, and therefore only at the levels of the Empirical and the Actual. In order to dig down and begin to explore the level of the Real, she has to use a number of tools, most notably those of abduction and retroduction.

Abduction, or abductive reasoning, involves using theory to see empirical data in a different way. Critical Realist researchers Danermark et al. (2002: 96) explain this as involving:

a move from a conception of something to a different, possibly more developed or deeper conception of it. This happens through our placing and interpreting the original ideas about the phenomenon in the frame of a new set of ideas.

In order to abduct, we therefore need to draw on explanatory theory. In the example above, we could draw on social or economic theories to try to explain the effects of social injustices related to poverty on the emergence of symptoms associated with a virus.

Retroduction involves moving from empirical data, from, for example, a description of experiences provided by a student, to positing the conditions which could have led to their emergence. A researcher thus asks questions such as 'What must the world be like for this to be possible?' in the context of an understanding that a deeper level of reality, the Real, exists and that this layer of reality involves a constant interplay of mechanisms.

The use of the tools of abduction and retroduction thus involve action on the part of the researcher. Any researcher is, of course, fallible and thus any identification and explanation of the interplay of mechanisms is open to challenge. The design of a piece of research needs to account for this potential fallibility. What is important, however, is the philosophical assumption of the existence of an absolute reality and therefore the adoption of a realist, rather than a relativist, position. There is an expectation that 'judgmental rationality' will be used to decide which is the strongest possible account of the mechanisms at play in the emergence of events and experiences.

The identification of three layers of reality points to the dangers of conflating what can be known through the senses (i.e. the Empirical) with what *is* (the Real). This conflation is termed the 'epistemic fallacy' by Critical Realists. What we know and understand is not all that there is to know and understand. While the diagrams and examples we have provided assist in making sense of a layered reality, they are simplified heuristics. It would be a mistake to see all mechanisms at the level of the Real as being of one kind. Similarly, not all events at the level of the Actual or all experiences at the level of the Empirical are of one kind. As Elder-Vass (2013) explains, a higher-level event may emerge from the interplay of a number of smaller events, that in turn emerged from a range of mechanisms at the level of the Real.

The idea of a layered reality can be difficult to grasp and at this point another example drawn from the field of higher education may be useful. In many countries around the world, as we will explain in more detail later in this book, the establishment of national qualifications frameworks have gone hand-in-hand with the introduction of the learning outcome and 'outcomes-based education/competency-based education'. In order to bring this into effect, a great deal of policy work had to be done. In South Africa, the Qualifications Act (Republic of South Africa (RSA) 1995) was passed and a set of regulations about what needed to be done to register qualifications on the National Qualifications Framework was developed. For the registration to be meaningful, the use of learning outcomes to describe learning in qualifications needed to be accompanied by the development of classroom practices focused on teachers supporting and guiding learners as they worked towards demonstrating outcomes.

A Critical Realist researcher interested in these new classroom practices would acknowledge the policy intended to lead to them. However, her assumption would not be that any changes she observed emerged from a simple cause–effect relationship as a result of the policy. By working with her data (she may, for example, have interviewed teachers or observed classes in a number of schools or universities), she would begin to identify other mechanisms which would interact with the policy levers and either promote or inhibit the emergence of new classroom practices. Structures such as gender, age, educational background, location and so on might come into play in enabling or constraining emergence. So too might the extent to which educators had been able to access workshops and other training events. The sets of ideas to which the educators subscribed would be likely to be a very significant mechanism. Some teachers, for example, might have held very firmly to beliefs about their role as 'teacher', which constrained them from adopting a new position as 'facilitator' of learning.

The schema above captures two levels of Bhaskar's layers of reality: the Actual and the Real. We now need to include the third level of the Empirical.

As the new changes were introduced, individuals experienced them in very different ways. Some were positive and excited about the possibility of change. Others were very negative. We can now begin to map this range of experiences and observations about the shift to outcomes-based education onto the framework.

A Critical Realist framework simply allows us to understand reality in a stratified manner and to understand that what we experience in many different ways (and which is thus relative) emerges from a level of reality that we cannot access directly. This level of reality nonetheless consists of mechanisms that are 'real' in the sense that they exist regardless of whether or not we acknowledge them or even know about them.

In order to do research on the emergence (or non-emergence) of new classroom practices, a Critical Realist researcher would need other explanatory or 'substantive' theory which could help them make sense of the mass of data and begin to identify some of the causal mechanisms at play. One researcher might draw from the field of education, another researcher might draw on other kinds of social theory. In a study which explored the introduction of a new curriculum in Swaziland, Liphie Pereira (2012) drew extensively on theory developed in 'New Literacy Studies' to explain why the educators in her study did not do as the policymakers expected when a new mode of classroom practice was introduced.

As we have indicated in Chapter One, theory allows us to 'see' the world in different ways. As with a pair of glasses, the type of lens will affect what we can see. We have to choose theory that will allow us to see what we need to see in order to answer our research questions. A Critical Realist framework allows us to adopt a position on reality, what we believe it is and how it can be known. We need other theory to work within this overall position.

The explanation of the Critical Realist philosophy in this chapter has stressed the idea of *emergence*. Events at the level of the Actual and experiences at the level of the Empirical both emerge from mechanisms at the level of the Real. Although it is possible to draw diagrams and figures such as those we have offered in the examples above, it is wrong to think of the layers as strictly separated and sequential. In practice,   the strata co-exist, subsume each other and work together simultaneously. This means that a researcher uses data to explore the world we know through the senses and then moves to the world we cannot know directly, the level of the Real. To most intents and purposes, therefore, Critical Realist research draws on the same methods as other research. We can know the Empirical and Actual through our interaction with others (by, for example, conducting interviews or using surveys and questionnaires) or we can observe the world closely simply by watching and recording.

It is also possible to draw on innovative methods. Behari-Leak (2015, 2017), for example, used 'photo-voice' in a study that explored the ways new academics were enabled or constrained as they tried to use the new understandings they had developed in a formal course on teaching at a university. Participants used photographs to construct a narrative detailing their experiences. What is important is that the methods access or generate the data necessary to explore the levels of the Empirical and the Actual in a way that allows the researcher to answer the questions she has set for herself. The Critical Realist framework provides a position on reality which then guides the research and allows the researcher to know what she is dealing with as she engages with data and begins to make claims.

As its name suggests, Critical Realism is 'critical' in that it follows a long tradition in orientations to research most obviously linked to a group of philosophers known as the 'Frankfurt School', who were concerned with social justice. Critical research aims to produce knowledge which will further social justice. As Bhaskar notes, 'the emancipatory potential of social science is contingent upon, and entirely an explanatory power' (1979: 2). If we can begin to explain the interplay of mechanisms at the level of the Real, we can begin to work with them to produce change for the better.

In linking the production of knowledge to social justice, our choice of Critical Realism as an 'underlabouring' philosophy for a book which seeks to provide an account of teaching and learning over time allows us to begin to account for change – what has changed and what has not changed.

The choice of Critical Realism was significant for other reasons, however, as we hope the explanation of the philosophy above has started to illustrate. Above all, it allowed us to adopt a *realist* rather than a *relativist* position in relation to our research by letting us explore the workings of phenomena that are real and relatively unchanging through the use of a theory that 'neither elides the referent nor neglects the socially produced character of judgments about it' (Bhaskar 2002: 203).

While Critical Realism has provided the 'underlabourer' by clearing the ground of deliberations around the nature of reality and its relationship to knowledge, it does not provide us with much by way of explanation as to the emergence of events and experiences in the social world, and for this we turned to Archer's work.

Archer's Social Realism

The value of Archer's work is that it allows us to look more closely at how social events and experiences emerge from the interplay of mechanisms over time. It does this through an examination of the relationship between people and social structures, which Archer refers to as 'the parts'. 'The parts' comprise structure and culture.

Structures distribute access to material goods. Education, for example, is widely understood as a social structure. It distributes access to material goods because success in education impacts on the sort of work an individual is likely to be able to secure and, thus, the amount of money she is able to earn in a lifetime. Gender is also a social structure, in that society uses it to allot roles to people and it can impact on the kind of work that is available. Structures not only distribute access to material goods; they also organise relationships in any society. Education, for example, shapes relationships between the 'uneducated' and the 'educated', even though this distinction is inherently invalid as the fact that a person has never been schooled formally does not mean they have not learned through the course of their lives. Gender, our other example, would work in a similar fashion in that it is used to organise relationships in society, many of which are oppressive unless challenged.

Alongside structure, 'the parts' also comprise 'culture', which is defined in numerous ways. In all of our research using a realist framework, we have defined culture using the concept of 'discourse'. A discourse is a set of ideas, beliefs, values, concepts and theories that are loosely bound together. Discourses can be identified in sign systems. Language is one such sign system. By analysing which words are used and the way they are used, for example, we can identify discourses in a stretch of text. Another sign system could involve the arrangement of furniture in a classroom or lecture theatre. By looking at who sits where and how this allows them to interact with each other, for example, we can see all sorts of ideas and values about power. From a Critical Realist perspective, the concept of discourses exists as a mechanism at the level of the Real, with specific discourses emerging in particular forms in different places and times and then enabling and constraining the emergence of events and experiences.

While discourse exists as an intransitive and relatively unchanging mechanism, the particular discourses at play in any time and place emerge out of that particular context. For example, in many countries of the world, a discourse of 'widening participation' can be discerned. Amongst other things, this discourse argues that higher education should not only be for the elite and that universities must open their doors to students from a range of socio-economic backgrounds. This discourse has emerged from changing social norms and values. The emergence of this discourse then enables the emergence of other events such as alternative admissions procedures. The emergence of the widening-participation discourse and of the alternative admissions procedures then enables a range of experiences and observations.

Some people decry the idea of widening participation, arguing that higher education is inherently only for a few with a particular intellectual 'bent'. Others welcome the idea. Students who are admitted as a result of measures intended to widen participation (which can be conceptualised as events emerging as a result of the discourse) may also report a broad range of experiences, with some, for example, feeling alienated by the universities to which they have gained access. In Archer's explanation of society as being the interplay between the people and the parts, all three ontological layers are always in conjunction: the Empirical, the Actual and the Real.

Over many decades sociologists have considered the relationship between 'the parts' and 'the people' in order to explore the extent to which people do indeed have the power to do what they want to do or whether they are constrained by the social and cultural conditions in which they live. Debates about the relationship between 'the parts' and 'the people', or structure and agency, have therefore focused on which has ascendancy over the other.

One view of the world, termed by Archer (2000) 'Modernity's man', privileges human agency over structure and has its roots in the Enlightenment, a period which focused on the use of reason to better the human condition. This view of the world is of 'man' creating the social world and, thus, of both structure and culture as emerging from the exercise of human reason. Archer also terms this view 'upwards conflation'.

The alternative perspective on social reality is termed 'downwards conflation'. This view involves the idea that 'man' is created by society – we are not free to act as we want because of the strictures of social structures and cultures. This view sees all human action and thought as being shaped by society. The idea that 'man' is a product of society has a long tradition in sociological thought and can be discerned in the work of theorists as disparate as Levi-Strauss, Durkheim, Marx, Lacan, Foucault and Derrida.

A third alternative, 'central conflation', is also evident in the work of structuration theorists such as Giddens, who see the systemic and individual aspects of social life as inseparable. Archer is critical of central conflation on the grounds that the 'parts' (structure and culture) and the 'people' (agency) are 'clamped together in a conceptual vice' (Archer 1996: 87). This then means that it becomes impossible to identify when or how agents are able to act to bring about change.

Archer's solution to her critiques of upwards, downwards and central conflation is an argument for 'analytical dualism', or the need for the *theoretical* separation of the 'parts' and the 'people' even though, in practice, they do not act independently. Archer goes on to argue that in order to understand the *interplay* between the 'parts' and the 'people' each has to be accorded distinct properties and powers operating at the level of the Real. This means that we can begin to speak about the properties of mechanisms in relation to the 'parts' – cultural emergent properties (CEPs) and structural emergent properties (SEPs), and also of agents' own personal emergent properties (PEPs).

The acknowledgement that structure, culture and agency all possess properties and exercise power is critical to the concept of *emergence*, which we discussed in relation to Bhaskar's work, since it is through the interplay of these properties and powers that events at the level of the Actual and experiences and observations at the level of the Empirical emerge.

Archer's later work focuses on the role of agency in particular. She argues that agency is exercised by means of what she terms the 'internal conversation' or 'reflexivity' (Archer 2007: 7). In making this argument she calls for a distinction between humans and other elements of the natural world in that humans can design 'projects', defined as 'any course of action intentionally engaged upon by a human being' (Archer 2007: 7). According to Archer, projects 'promote our concerns; we form "projects" to promote or protect what we care about most' (Archer 2007: 7). This means that agents, human beings, are also accorded powers, which are exercised in pursuit of projects by means of the internal conversation. These powers are exercised in relation to the powers and properties of mechanisms in the domains of structure (SEPs) and culture (CEPs).

In this book, then, when we trace the emergence of events related to teaching and learning from the early 1990s to date, we are looking at the ways in which key agents were put in place to address concerns about, amongst other things, efficiency, and we are looking at the ways in which they drew on the available mechanisms to achieve their personal projects. We look at how particular structures and cultures emerged or how they proved resilient to change. As we have pointed out, Archer's work forms part of a conversation with other sociologists regarding whether the 'parts' condition human action in such a way that the powers of the 'people' to create a world of their own making is curtailed, or whether the opposite is true, that the 'people' have power over the 'parts'. Archer's contribution to this debate is not only the concept of analytical dualism, that is the idea that structure, culture and agency can be analysed separately, but also the accordance of personal powers and properties to people (PEPs). Although people use these PEPs to pursue the concerns and projects they have identified for themselves, they are conditioned in the way and to the extent they use them by their previous experiences. For example, previous conditioning will impact on the extent to which an individual may exercise her PEPs by subscribing to a discourse, or not doing so. Some individuals, then, may be more disposed to taking up and engaging with some discourses because of previous experiences. Others will be more disposed to refuting the same discourses in order to protect their personal projects.

This brings us to the point that CEPs and SEPs are not activated autonomously. Rather, it is only through the exercise of agency, that is an individual exercising their own PEPs, that they are activated. Archer (2007) elaborates on this point by using the example of swimming. Following her thinking, water is accorded the power to make us float. That power, however, would never be exercised if we, as agents, did not enter the water, take our feet off the ground and allow ourselves to float. This particular power of water would remain dormant. It would still exist but would be dormant until we entered the water and tried to float. Agency is therefore necessary to activate the properties and powers inherent in the 'parts'.

If we now move to higher education, we can use Archer's thinking to see how agency works. We could, for example, conceptualise a student as having a concern about her position in society and her life chances and those of her family as a result of this position. Her personal project might then be to get a qualification in order to better this. In order to pursue this project, the student would need to draw on 'the parts', both social structures and the set of beliefs, values and so on that constitute the cultural system. The student would exercise her personal powers and properties in relation to the educational system to complete her schooling and, in relation to various other structures (including possibly alternative access procedures), to gain access to a university. She would draw on beliefs in the cultural system related to the value of getting a qualification and also on those related to what constitutes 'good' learning to succeed at school. These ideas about what is 'good' or 'successful' learning might serve her well in school but perhaps be of less use in university. Perhaps, at her school, there is an idea that learning is about memorising sets of irrefutable facts and seeing the text as sacrosanct and above critique. These ideas might have served her well in achieving the marks required for entry to university and thereby furthering her personal project. Once she gets to university, though, she may find that she has to draw on very different understandings of what constitutes 'good' learning if she is to succeed. She may find that the ideas and practices that she brought with her no longer serve her very well at all.

At a more micro level, the student might draw on the structure of technology in order to carry a cell phone and might then choose to use this in her learning. She might be exposed to a supportive WhatsApp group and a useful set of YouTube videos that gradually give her access to different ways of understanding what constitutes successful learning. The point of all this is that the student is consciously exercising her own personal powers as an individual to draw on structures and cultures to pursue her project of getting a qualification and bettering her chances in society.

We began our discussion of Archer's work by noting her insistence on the ability to separate the 'parts' (structure and culture) and the 'people' for *analytical purposes*. Archer follows through with the premise that the interplay of agency with structure and agency with culture is 'temporarily distinguishable' (1996: 66). As a result, it is possible to determine what happens over time with regard to structure, culture and agency in order for events and experiences to *emerge*. Archer's claim is therefore that we can examine the 'historicity of emergence'. She then goes on to describe what she terms the 'morphogenetic framework' as a methodology that allows for an analysis of the interplay of structure and agency and culture and agency over time.

Archer's morphogenetic framework

Archer's morphogenetic framework not only allows us to analyse the interplay of structure, culture and agency over time; it also allows us to account for why the emergence of change, 'morphogenesis', happens or does not happen. A state of no change is termed 'morphostasis'. According to Archer, morphogenesis/morphostasis occurs in endless cycles.

The first period of any cycle is termed T_1 or a particular point in time, and describes the conditioning structures and cultures that are in place at its beginning. As we noted in the preceding section of this chapter, individuals are understood to be shaped by cultural and structural conditions which may enable or constrain the way they act. For example, a student born into a home where both parents are medical doctors may well be conditioned to pursue a career in medicine for herself not only because of the ideas and beliefs she has been exposed to but because she has been introduced to the way the medical profession itself is structured. And it is not only individuals who are shaped and conditioned by the contexts that pre-exist them. The potential for change to occur in the social system or the cultural system is also conditioned by what happened in the past.

In this book, we are interested in the way teaching and learning in higher education has functioned over the last 20 years or so. As we explained in Chapter One, students' experiences of higher education over this time have not all been positive. Using the morphogenetic framework therefore involves analysing the conditions in place as the period in which we are interested began.

As we indicated in Chapter One, we use South Africa as a 'case' which we present to our readers so that they can make judgements about whether or not our analysis applies to their own contexts. The South African case begins in 1990 as apartheid, the political system which had dominated the country since the middle of the century, came to an end. To use the morphogenetic framework, we need to consider the way apartheid and related ideologies such as colonialism shaped the cultural system in order to see how they enabled or constrained new ideas, beliefs or theories as they were introduced. In the same manner, we would also need to analyse the way the structures of apartheid or colonialism enabled or constrained change as efforts were made to reconfigure the systems. In South Africa under apartheid, the higher education system was structured along racial and linguistic lines. Geography also played a part as different kinds of institutions had been located deliberately in different parts of the country. As attempts were made to produce a new institutional landscape in South Africa in the early 2000s, through a series of mergers and incorporations, it is possible to see how the old apartheid structuring constrained the development of the 'new' universities. Social divisions along the lines of language and ethnicity in many other countries on the continent have similarly constrained post-colonial development in higher education.

Once an analysis of the structural and cultural conditions at T_1 has been completed, the next step in using the morphogenetic framework involves analysing the interaction that takes place in a given time period, termed T_2 to T_3. In this period, agents interact with structure and culture. The final phase in the morphogenetic cycle is termed T_4 and is the period at the end of any one cycle. This is the point at which it is possible to assess the extent to which morphogenesis has, or has not, emerged.

The diagram below illustrates a morphogenetic cycle. Archer indicates that the cycles function across different time periods. For example, changes in the domain of structure may occur more quickly than those in the domain of culture.

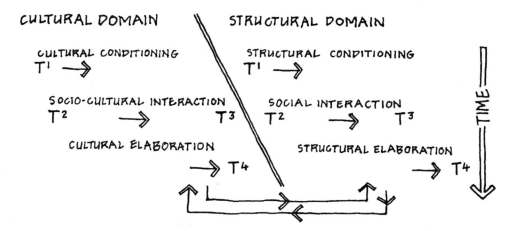

Structural & cultural configurations generating morphogenetic cycles in society.
(Archer 1995)

In this book, we attempt to look at how structures and cultures related to teaching and learning in higher education were conditioned at T_1, and how they have been elaborated or reproduced in the period since then.

Archer's morphogenetic framework can also be applied to agency. In order to do this, some more exploration of the concept of agency using Archer's ideas is needed. Archer identifies two groups of agents: *primary agents* and *corporate agents*. Primary agents are accorded very little power and influence by the social structures and cultures within which they find themselves. According to Archer, they are 'collectivities sharing the same life chances' (Archer 2000: 263). A group of working-class students may thus be primary agents in a particular university context where the structures and cultures constrain their social being. In pursuit of change, primary agents can transform themselves into corporate agents. They would do this by exercising their powers of reflexivity to pursue a shared project and by drawing on the cultural and structural domains. Archer (1995: 258) defines corporate agents as groups:

> who are aware of what they want, can articulate it to themselves and others, and have organized in order to get it, can engage in concerted action to re-shape or retain the structural or cultural feature in question.

In the history of South African education as well as in the histories of other countries, there is no shortage of examples of groups of students transforming themselves into corporate agents. In South Africa, in 1976, schoolchildren in Soweto, a large township to the south of Johannesburg, came together to protest about the policy which required both English and Afrikaans to be used as languages of teaching and learning. This can be seen as an example of a group of primary agents transforming themselves into corporate agents as a result of their objections to a discriminatory policy. The protests in universities across the world in recent years can also be seen as an example of corporate agents working to effect change. For Archer, collective action is a property of agency, although the power to exercise this action is enabled or constrained by the cultural and structural systems in which agents are placed. Primary agents have a vested interest in developing the property of collective action to improve upon their life chances and also to allow them to participate in decision-making (Archer 1995).

Certain individuals can also be characterised as *social actors*. Social actors are defined as occupying roles which themselves have properties and powers. These powers are enacted by individuals, but they are not reducible to the characteristics of the individuals who occupy the roles. The role of vice-chancellor, for example, can be seen to have such properties and powers even though a vice-chancellorship could be exercised in many different ways depending on the individual occupying the position.

We have elaborated on Archer's theory in some depth because, as we noted earlier, it allows us to explore the social world more thoroughly than would otherwise be possible. The rest of this book is structured in a way which allows us to demonstrate our framework in action.

In the next chapter, we focus on structural change in the case of South African higher education by exploring the way policies and other levers have been used to shape the system. As we have explained, however, Archer's concept of analytical dualism is intended

for purposes of analysis only. In reality, the 'parts' of structure and culture are in constant interplay. Structural change emerged as a result of the interplay between ideas and theories and the introduction of policies and funding formulas. We will nevertheless try to keep our analysis as clear as possible and will constantly refer back to the terms and ideas we have introduced in this chapter.

3

Dominant discourses, policy challenges

The global and the local

As we have pointed out in the introductory chapter, this book is an attempt to answer questions we asked ourselves about changes in the higher education sector over the last two decades. As two individuals with a specialist interest in higher education, we were very aware of problems that plagued the system. Dominant discourses have focused on the inefficiency made evident by student performance data (see, e.g. CHE 2020; Bunting et al. 2014; Scott et al. 2007 for South Africa; and Cloete et al. 2011 for eight flagship universities across the continent). The data also reveal continuing inequity between social groups. In our own country, black South Africans, the group the work on 'transformation' had intended to serve, bore the brunt of the poor success, throughput and graduation rates to a much greater extent than their white peers. We were also aware that constructing the problems of the system using the relatively abstract concepts of inefficiency and inequity served to mask the very personal experiences of many thousands of students.

The very hard questions we were asking about what had gone wrong in higher education were all the harder because of the work we had undertaken at both national and institutional levels on initiatives aimed to contribute to 'transformation', and our specialist interests in higher education also allowed us to see that much about the situation in South Africa was not unique.

Statistics from other systems allowed us to contextualise the problematic performance data in South Africa. In Australia, for example, research (Edwards & McMillan 2015) has revealed completion rates for students from low socio-economic backgrounds as standing at 69% and for indigenous students at 47% in comparison to the 78% of their more privileged peers. The same research showed that one in five indigenous students had dropped out of Australian universities before completing two years of study. In the United Kingdom, research has shown that socio-economic status impacts on the higher education participation rate overall and particularly at high status universities (Crawford et al. 2017). Similar statistics showing that students from lower socio-economic groups attend and thrive in higher education in far lower numbers than their more privileged peers can be found in the United States of America, France, Korea, and Brazil (Altbach et al. 2009;

Walpole 2003). Interestingly, the cultivation of a 'sense of belonging' amongst students has been identified as key to addressing high attrition rates (see, e.g. O'Keeffe 2013) and a number of large-scale projects have been initiated to this end (see, e.g. Tomas 2013).

The idea that students fail to complete because of their experiences of 'not belonging' in universities around the world resonates with the expressions of alienation made by many South African student protesters in 2015 and 2016. There would appear to be evidence, therefore, that developments in higher education at a global level have led to the emergence of similar phenomena in a number of locations.

This chapter begins with an analysis of T_1 which we identify as the period before 1990, a period which 'conditioned' the South African higher education system and put in place certain enablements and constraints. In this chapter, as we begin to use the framework outlined in Chapter Two, we consciously draw on the 'bigger picture' as developments in South Africa have been conditioned by those at a global level and we are beginning to see similar phenomena emerging from them. In this analysis of T_1 we move from identifying mechanisms conditioning all the policy work and other development that took place at a macro (global) level to a meso (national) level and finally to the micro (institutional) level.

The macro level

Until the middle of the last century, almost every higher education system across the world was an elite system catering for a very small group of students from specific social backgrounds. In Britain, for example, only about 5% of 17- to 30-year-olds were in higher education in 1960 (Finegold 2006). The number of institutions in any higher education system was relatively small and those who managed to enrol in a university largely came from privileged backgrounds. The serving of a relatively homogenous elite meant that the cultural systems of the universities were fairly stable. Assumptions about who was being taught could remain unchallenged, as higher education largely served the status quo by educating those whose backgrounds prepared them, to a large extent, for higher education, with the result that they knew what to expect from a university and what the universities expected of them.

Following the Second World War, moves towards the political left and the election of socialist governments in the United Kingdom, and a number of other countries, saw attempts to widen participation in higher education, alongside the emergence of a human rights discourse across the world (Mettler 2005). This opening up of universities led to the establishment of a new kind of institution, often developed outside major cities and with more vocationally focused programmes. The new universities were in part built to accommodate a group of students who had previously been excluded. The extent to which these students gained what in South Africa has been termed 'epistemological access' (Morrow 1993, 2009) to the universities (rather than merely opening their doors in a process of 'formal access') has been problematised by many. Maton (2004), for example, explores the experience of the 'wrong kind of knower' in British universities as they widened access in the 1960s. While similar shifts happened in many other countries, the focus on the United Kingdom example is particularly pertinent because the colonial histories of many countries in Africa has often tied us to their political, economic and social patterns. We will return to this issue later in the book but, for now, simply want to point out that the widening of access in the latter half of the 20th century is an example of the way changes in higher education systems emerge from broader political, economic and social shifts.

As a number of thinkers have pointed out, one such political, economic and social shift that has impacted on higher education most heavily is that of globalisation. Mann (2013: 11) explains globalisation as

> the extension of distinct relations of ideological, economic, military, and political power across the world. Concretely, in the period after 1945 this means the diffusion of ideologies like liberalism and socialism, the spread of the capitalist mode of production, the extension of military striking ranges, and the extension of nation-states across the world.

Possibly the aspect of globalisation that has exercised the most influence on higher education, however, is what economist Manuel Castells (1996, 2001) has argued is a 'new economy'. Central to this 'new economy' is the role of knowledge, thanks to its focus on the 'reinvention' of existing goods.

Castells (2001: 52) describes the centrality of knowledge and of the use of information and communication technologies in the 'new economy' in the following way:

> Productivity and competitiveness are, by and large, a function of knowledge generation and information processing; firms and territories are organized in networks of production, management and distribution; the core economic activities are global – that is, they have the capacity to work as a unit in real time, or chosen time, on a planetary scale.

Globalisation and the 'new economy' were enormously significant for higher education largely because of another discourse that came to be known as the 'high skills thesis', closely associated with the likes of Ashton and Green (1996) and Finegold and Soskice (1988). The high skills thesis argues that economic prosperity is dependent on a highly skilled workforce and 'joined-up' policy that will allow a nation to benefit from globalisation. The need for a highly skilled workforce then resulted in increased emphasis being placed on the role of the universities in producing it.

The high skills thesis has not passed without critique, with Kraak (2006: 9) pointing out that:

> The reality of high skill production is that it actually only occurs in a few sectors in the leading advanced economies, including: information technology; biotechnology; pharmaceuticals; aircraft manufacture; machine tools; the high skill end of financial and business services; and the high professions in the civil service, law and medicine. In other sectors, low skilled based work continues and even grows.

There is also considerable debate regarding the extent to which the high skills approach is appropriate for developing nations with some, including Kraak (2006), arguing for a 'hybrid' approach that seeks to develop and utilise a mixture of skills that can be drawn upon in different economic contexts. Regardless of these critiques, the power of discourses that privilege the high skills thesis has had profound implications for universities across the world, particularly with the rise of what has come to be called the 'Fourth Industrial Revolution', or the belief that the increased availability of technology will fundamentally change the nature of political, social and cultural life. While many universities subscribe to the need to drive such technological changes, others have argued that the Fourth Industrial Revolution will increase inequality and constitute a form of recolonisation (De Sousa Santos 2019).

Early implementers of the high skills thesis included the United Kingdom and Australia, with both countries seeing growth in their higher education systems from the late 1980s onwards. This growth was achieved by establishing new universities, often by awarding university status to institutions which had formerly been more vocationally orientated (as later occurred in South Africa). In the United Kingdom, for example, institutions known as 'polytechnics' and which had previously awarded a range of vocational and technical qualifications achieved university status thanks to the 1992 Further and Higher Education Act. A further group was created out of former university colleges. A similar picture can be painted for Australian higher education. To return to our Critical and Social Realist framework, what we can see, then, is the interplay of a set of discourses about globalisation, high skills and the knowledge economy operating in the domain of culture with a set of structural arrangements (acts of parliament, policies, funding and so on) which led to the emergence of new universities and increased enrolments. The establishment of new universities and the enrolment of increased numbers of students can then be conceptualised as emergent events. It is easy to see how a very diverse range of experiences and observations can result from the process we have outlined. The experiences of staff and students are well documented in the academic literature and we will draw on these later in this book.

As value was placed on higher education as a means to achieve economic prosperity, another discursive shift occurred. It does not take much to move from understanding the value of knowledge within an economy to placing a value on knowledge itself. This shift in thinking was accompanied by the fact that the universities, as knowledge producers, had the means of creating knowledge which could lead to profits in this new 'knowledge economy'. Rather than being a 'public good' and existing for the good of humankind, knowledge increasingly came to be understood as a commodity, a private good, with the potential to benefit those who had it or who could generate it.

This so-called 'commodification of knowledge' is then related to other discursive moves and to developments in the structural domain. If knowledge is understood to carry monetary value for individuals, rather than being a broader good in service of the public at large, then the need for the state to provide funding for the universities that produce it falls away. So, too, does the need for the state to fund the students seeking this knowledge

– if they will be the beneficiaries of this knowledge commodity, the logic goes, then they should pay for it. All this then leads to neoliberal discourses arguing for reduced state funding for higher education and students. These shifts in the world of ideas (i.e. in the cultural domain) then allow for developments in the domain of structure in the form of policies and new funding instruments.

Across the world, national policy moved to reduce state funding for universities and for students. In the case of reduced state funding for students, this shift reversed developments that had taken place from the end of the Second World War aimed at broadening access to what had been perceived as a public good, closely tied to national development and social cohesion. Such changes had included the provision of grants intended to allow students from lower socio-economic backgrounds to enter universities in pursuit of higher learning. The thinking now went that if students wanted to gain a qualification which would allow them access to the private goods achieved by competing in the global economy, they needed to pay substantially towards the cost of that qualification. As a result, responsibility to pay ever-increasing tuition fees began to be placed on students who either had previously only paid minimal fees or, in the case of those receiving state grants, had received a free higher education.

Associated with discourses promoting globalisation, therefore, we see an increase in neoliberal ideas in the form of a shift away from the 'welfare state' that characterised the period after the Second World War to the discourse of the free market, where individuals were expected to provide more for themselves in a process which became known as 'neoliberalism'. The development of neoliberal policies, through which state funding was reduced, also resulted in an opening up of opportunities for private enterprise. Private universities have always existed but the latter half of the 20th century saw a growth in private provision in many countries, including in countries across Africa (The Education Commission 2016).

In many respects, South Africa provides a contradiction to this. Because of the peculiar circumstances resulting from apartheid, social grants have greatly increased since the early 1990s as has direct funding of students in the form of grants from the National Student Financial Aid Scheme. However, in line with the global picture, South Africa experienced decreases in state funding of universities.

The reduction in state funding for universities not only required them to levy tuition fees but also to become more entrepreneurial and business-like as they managed their affairs. As a result, universities consciously began to seek opportunities to 'sell' the knowledge outputs they produced and often established specialist offices to assist researchers in doing this. The search for 'Third Stream Income', the other streams being tuition fees and state subsidy, also increased with institutions offering short courses and very actively seeking donor funding.

To return to our Social Realist framework once again, in the latter half of the last century, we can see the interplay of discourses that promote globalisation, the 'knowledge economy' and neoliberalism, with policies and funding frameworks reducing the responsibility of the state for higher education. This complementary interplay led to the emergence of more universities and to the enrolment of greater numbers of students who did, however, have to pay ever-rising tuition fees. Clearly, this then led to very different experiences on the part of students, parents, staff and other stakeholders in higher education systems. For example, a phenomenon widely reported in some countries (see, e.g. Neves & Hillman 2018) is the expectation that a university should provide value for money. Students' experiences of a university were thus often those of consumers of a product being sold to them. In many respects, universities have then responded to this by privileging tools to gauge 'student satisfaction' and, even, their perceptions of value for money. While globalisation, notions of the 'knowledge economy' and neoliberalism had their origins in, and privileged, the Global North, they have come to colonise the Global South in a number of ways.

Before leaving the global picture, or macro level at T_1, there is a need to note another set of discourses prevalent from the late 1970s onwards and associated in particular with the appointment of British prime minister, Margaret Thatcher, and the United States president, Ronald Reagan, and their adherence to their economic advisor Milton Friedman's notions of deregulation and the free market system. These discourses privileged an approach to the management of public services termed 'New Public Management'. Key to this thinking is the idea that public services, including higher education, need to be actively managed for efficiency by drawing on approaches developed in the business sector. The blending of economic principles related to the supposed desirability of the free market with principles of managerial supremacy led, in universities, to 'shifts in governance authority from the professoriate towards the university councils with compositions that resemble those of the private sector' (Nampota 2015: 123).

It is rare indeed to find a university without a strategic plan and an implementation strategy or one that has not engaged with activities such as quality assurance. These, and other structures and processes, emerge in part from the ideas of New Public Management, and have led to what Marginson and Considine (2000: 4) and others call the 'enterprise university':

> Established academic institutions including senates and councils, academic boards, departments and collegial rules have been supplemented (and sometimes supplanted) by vice-chancellors' advisory committees and private 'shadow' university structures.

New Public Management has been particularly influential in relation to funding frameworks, which are now often 'output dependent' in that the amount of funding an institution receives as subsidy from the state is related to its teaching and research outputs. Increasingly more abstract concepts such as learning and knowledge materialise as concrete elements that can be counted and rewarded, through metrics such as numbers of graduations and academic publications.

Associated with New Public Management discourses has been the emergence in higher education of what Whitchurch (2015) calls 'Third Space Professionals', who are individuals working in areas such as academic planning, quality assurance and so on, which were unknown in universities half a century ago, and who are often conceived of as being necessary for ensuring efficiencies in this neoliberal framework.

We have described globalisation as a set of relations which sees ideologies, goods and people moving seamlessly across the world, aided by information and communication technologies, sophisticated transport links, and a relaxation in protectionist policies, and fuelled by the high skills necessary to achieve this movement. Some universities have drawn on such globalisation discourses along with national policy to operate 'offshore' by opening campuses in countries other than the one in which they were originally established. The creation of 'education hubs' as a conscious strategy aimed at economic sustainability by some countries is part of this process. Dubai's 'Knowledge Village', a free-enterprise zone, provides a good example of one such hub, and anyone driving into the area sees universities operating offshore lined up like global chain stores in a shopping mall.

Another phenomenon, perhaps not yet commonplace in Africa, is the selling of 'accreditation' by universities in the Global North to a partner university in a developing higher education system. Effectively the 'accrediting' universities are selling their status as an institution in a more developed system to a partner in a new system. While such relationships are often costly for those seeking to share the Global North branding, they do not necessarily offer much in the form of quality oversight and support.

The understanding that higher education is a global enterprise coupled with the reduction of state funding that emerged from some of the ideas we have discussed in this section led to yet another phenomenon, that of universities chasing the enrolment of foreign students who were required to pay higher fees than locals. For example, the relatively low number of universities in countries in South East Asia and in China compared to their population size and the value being placed on higher education as a private good led many foreign students to seek places at Australian universities. Many Australian universities pursued these enrolments vigorously with consequences for teaching and learning and institutional cultures, which then became focused on the logic of profit (Marginson 2009; Marginson & Considine 2000; Marginson & Rhoades 2002). Compensating for reduced state subsidy by recruiting large numbers of international students makes universities particularly vulnerable to global economic downturns which result in few young people being able to afford to study overseas. If the university's raison d'être is making a profit, then it is without purpose when profits dwindle.

The impact of globalisation on higher education has had another significant effect in the growth of university league tables. The influence of ranking systems such as the QS World University Rankings, produced by Quacquarelli Symonds, a United Kingdom based company specialising in study abroad, and the Times Higher Education World University Rankings, amongst others, has pushed many universities into competing for a place in these international tables. Seeking a place in an international ranking system generally means privileging one particular aspect of institutional life (for example, research publications or the pursuit of an individual holding a Nobel Prize) at the expense of others (e.g. the widening of participation by students from lower socio-economic groups) (Teferra 2017). The criteria used by a particular ranking system mean, moreover, that some universities are simply excluded from such systems, a point made forcibly by Badat (2010: 245):

> The indicators and their weighting privilege specific university activities, domains of knowledge production, research types, languages, and university types. Thus, the natural and medical sciences are privileged over the arts, humanities and social sciences; articles published in English are favoured over those in other languages; journal articles are favoured over book chapters, policy and other reports. Furthermore, "comprehensive" universities and generally larger institutions with a wide range of disciplines and larger numbers of academics – especially researchers – are privileged over others ... The rankings therefore enable the self-selection of universities whose missions and academic offerings strongly match the rankings' performance measures.

This point is taken up by Marginson (2009), who claims that ranking systems 'inculcate the idealized model of an institution as a norm to be achieved and generalize the failure to achieve it'. And, of course, as Badat (2010) points out, the 'idealised model' on which the systems are based draws on universities in the Global North which, due to their location in Western capitalist societies, do not always offer sensible models for those located elsewhere. In spite of the many critiques of global ranking systems, universities across the world continue to play the game with consequences which are not always positive.

The meso and micro levels

The mechanisms at the macro level described in the previous section of this chapter play out in different ways around the world as they intersect with more context-bound structures and cultures at local levels. We now turn again to the meso and micro levels of our analysis of these mechanisms in the South African case study.

As South Africa moved towards democracy, conditions in the higher education system were very different to what they are now. From the 1950s onwards the higher education system had become increasingly structured on the grounds of race. Cooper and Subotzky (2001) provide what they term a 'historiography' of higher education in South Africa, which traces the development of the different kinds of institutions, effectively showing how race led to the creation of a number of different systems. Some institutions were reserved for white social groups while others were specifically established for black, 'coloured' and Indian groups, with each group experiencing very different levels of resourcing and varying degrees of freedom to conduct their own affairs without interference.

Historically white institutions were the best resourced and enjoyed the most freedom, not only in matters related to governance and the curriculum but also in relation to the way they could manage their financial affairs (Bunting 2006; Cloete et al. 2006). These institutions also tended to occupy prime locations in urban areas. Institutions intended for black social groups enjoyed far less privilege. Initially established only to train black people for roles in the apartheid state, the locations of many of these institutions were in rural areas.

The role allocated to historically black institutions of contributing to the socio-political agenda of the apartheid regime meant that tight control was exercised over governance structures by the state, usually through the state's appointment to key positions of individuals who were sympathetic to its ideology. The lack of freedom of movement within the Republic thanks to the 'Pass Laws' which limited the movement of black citizens meant that the historically black universities enjoyed a 'captive' student population regardless of the socio-economic status of homes of origin, a situation which was to change after 1990 when the relaxation of apartheid legislation meant that students with the means to do so fled to historically white institutions (Cooper 2015).

Finances of the historically black institutions were tightly controlled by the Department of Education and Training, in the case of those within the borders of the Republic, or by respective 'governments' for those established in the 'homelands'. 'Homelands' or 'Bantustan states' were established for specific racial and ethnic groups, with pseudo governments never recognised by the international community. Unlike their historically white counterparts, historically black institutions had to apply to the relevant entity for approval of expenditure, the appointment of staff and the levying of tuition fees. As we will discuss in more detail later, funding had to be spent within the financial year, with no possibilities for investment of any surpluses. The requirement that historically black institutions should request approvals of this nature and then apply a 'use it or lose it' process resulted in a lack of capacity to manage budgets which was to impact on their functioning once the requirement fell away following the end of apartheid (Bunting 2006; Moyo & McKenna 2020).

Under apartheid, therefore, structural conditions resulted in deep divides between institutions intended for different social groups. These divides contributed to the 'cultural isolation' of groups of institutions from each other, a situation which was exacerbated by the academic boycott of South Africa which meant that the country as a whole had constraints on its access to the wider world of academia. Cultural isolation was not limited to the historically black institutions since language also played a part. Historically white institutions were divided according to the language of learning and teaching, with the Afrikaans-speaking institutions more disposed to the apartheid regime than their English-speaking counterparts. In keeping with our realist framework, it then follows that the experiences of staff and students in the different kinds of institution also varied enormously.

At the historically white, English-speaking 'liberal' universities (Cape Town, Natal, Rhodes and Witwatersrand), staff enjoyed considerably higher degrees of freedom with regard to the way they chose to teach and research. These universities drew on discourses related to academic freedom to argue that teaching must be unconstrained and that decisions about who should be admitted were the prerogative of the institution itself and not of the state, though, as we will argue later, this only sometimes translated into these institutions actively defying the state. Institutional governance drew on traditions of collegiality which had long dominated European universities, with academics participating in structures such as faculty boards and the senate and, at departmental level, being led by professors appointed on the basis of their academic, rather than management, achievements. Administrative divisions were staffed with well-qualified individuals and, as a result, finances and other functions were well run. Appointments to key positions in the vice-chancellorate were largely free from the influence of the state.

At the same time as they claimed rights related to academic freedom, however, these same institutions drew down state funding in the form of subsidy which was considerably more, per capita, than that provided to those established for black social groups. A student enrolled at a historically white, English-speaking university entered well-resourced libraries, sat in well-equipped and well-maintained lecture theatres, was taught by highly-qualified, research-active staff and was likely to live in a comfortable hall of residence. In spite of, or possibly because of, all these privileges and freedoms, these universities never exercised the levels of resistance to the apartheid state which could have contributed to social and political change (Mamdani 1998; Maylam 2017).

At the historically white, Afrikaans-speaking universities, academics enjoyed considerably less freedom since these institutions had accepted the apartheid government's construction of them as 'creatures of the state' (Bunting 2006). This support for and adherence to state policies impacted on governance structures which, as a result, were relatively authoritarian in nature. As 'creatures of the state', they also tended to see knowledge itself as having an instrumental purpose, and criticality was not as valued as at their English-speaking counterparts (where it was evident in 'liberal' discourses if not consistently in action). The adherence of the Afrikaans-speaking universities to apartheid policy meant that these institutions were rewarded financially through donations from individuals and corporations which saw this as a form of investment. As a result, these campuses were some of the most well-developed in the country. A student enrolling at an Afrikaans-speaking university would, however, be unlikely to sit alongside a black peer. The English-speaking universities sometimes drew on the University Amendment Act (Act 83 of 1983) (RSA 1983), the so-called 'Quota Act', which allowed for the admission of small numbers of black students to programmes not offered at historically black institutions. The Afrikaans-speaking institutions generally eschewed this opportunity except at postgraduate levels where students did not have to come on to campus to attend classes (Bunting 2006).

The geographical division between institutions had an enormous effect on staff and students, which we will argue continues to this day. All historically white institutions were to be found in major cities, with the exception of Rhodes University, located in a small town in the Eastern Cape, and black universities were found in rural areas or 'homelands', with the exception of the University of the Western Cape (UWC) and the University of Durban Westville (UDW), established for 'coloured' and 'Indian' social groups respectively. As the 1980s wore on, both of these institutions rejected tight apartheid controls by admitting students from all social groups. This resistance to apartheid ideology attracted scholars from the political left, with the result that students enrolled at UWC and UDW would likely have experienced access to more critical thought than at many other institutions in the system. Their stance against apartheid meant that they regularly experienced brutality at the hands of the apartheid state. They were able, however, to benefit from funding from overseas donors such that these campuses enjoyed infrastructure that was more favourable than their positions in the apartheid order would suggest.

A further divide characterised the apartheid higher education landscape, and this related to the binary distinction between so called 'technikons' and the universities. Technikons were established to provide vocational education to different social groups. As such, their conceptual agenda was limited and they offered little in the way of postgraduate education or research. Governance within the technikons tended to be very authoritarian (White et al. 2011) and this control extended to the curriculum, with all technikons following the same curriculum for a particular qualification, developed by one 'convening' institution. As we will argue later, this lack of experience of working with the curriculum on the part of academic staff employed in the technikon sector, alongside the lack of research in the institutions more generally, was to impact these institutions as they acquired full university status in the early 2000s.

Technikons offered vocational training and students enrolled at these institutions would, in most cases, have been registered for a national diploma, rather than an institutionally developed qualification. Their programmes of study would have afforded them work-based experience and they would have been taught by staff who were experienced in business and industry but who might have been minimally qualified academically. Depending on the social group for which the institution was intended, the resources available to students would have varied enormously as would the qualifications that were available. Perhaps most significantly, the technikons would not have exposed students to the criticality associated to some extent with some other institutions.

At the meso (national) and micro (institutional) levels at T_1, therefore, structural and cultural conditions were conducive to enormous disparities and differences observable in events and experiences of both staff and students. While these distinctions took a particular shape in apartheid South Africa, it is worth noting Teferra and Altbach's (2004) overview of the effects of colonial education across the entire African continent. They indicate four characteristics: (i) there was limited access to higher education; (ii) the language of instruction was that of the colonisers; (iii) the curriculum was limited and was focused on providing the administrative and other skills needed to manage the colonies; and (iv) there were limited physical and ideological freedoms. As we have shown, all four of these characteristics were in evidence at T_1 in South Africa.

As the end of apartheid dawned, therefore, the ANC government-in-waiting was faced with the task of eradicating these numerous disparities in order to create a single, coherent higher education system that would serve all South Africans equally. At the same time, however, the government had to contend with the challenges of globalisation, and its impact on the economy more generally and on higher education in particular. The need to balance equity with efficiency is something with which policy had to grapple, and it is to this that we now turn as we begin to explore T_2 to T_3 in the framework which underpins the argument in this book.

Policy after apartheid

The new government that came to power in 1994 did so as a result of compromise. South Africa did not have a revolution and civil war that totally upended the status quo. Instead there was a negotiated agreement regarding human rights for all and that the goods of society needed to be shared more equally than previously. The new South African Constitution (RSA 1996) accepted responsibility on the part of the state for basics such as education, housing, healthcare and sufficient food and water 'within its available resources'. Early policy work following the first democratic election in 1994 focused on 'reconstruction and development', or more specifically on the alleviation of poverty and the shortfalls in social services experienced by the majority of the population. In order to do this, however, policymakers acknowledged the need for a stronger economy. By 1998, the need to engage with globalisation through the establishment of macroeconomic stability meant that state *responsibility* for the provision of basic services was reconstructed as the *facilitation* of basic provision through the wooing and protection of both domestic and international capital and by means of tight deficit controls and an almost total liberalisation of tariffs and capital controls in the Growth, Employment and Redistribution Programme (GEAR), which replaced the Reconstruction and Development Programme (RDP). The slogan that had characterised ANC politics during the early years of its rule, 'growth through redistribution', thus shifted to 'growth for redistribution', echoing the Friedman Doctrine noted earlier in this chapter. Economic growth and improvement of the conditions experienced by the majority were seen to be inextricably linked. This had implications for higher education.

Probably the most significant piece of policy in this T_2 to T_3 period was the 1997 *White Paper on Higher Education* (Department of Education (DoE) 1997), subtitled 'A programme for higher education transformation'. The White Paper identifies four purposes for higher education:

1. To meet the learning needs of individuals in order to achieve self-fulfilment;
2. To provide the labour market with 'high skills';
3. To contribute to the development of a critical citizenry; and
4. To contribute to knowledge creation, knowledge evaluation and knowledge dissemination.

These four purposes acknowledge the contribution of higher education to both the 'private good', that is for graduates to thrive in a society economically, intellectually and emotionally, and the 'public good', that is for society itself to prosper through higher education's contribution to economic growth and, importantly, the criticality deemed necessary in a new democracy.

Curriculum and the global economy

The 1997 White Paper set out a programme for higher education but, before it had even been published, other policy had already set South African higher education in a particular direction. The South African Qualifications Act of 1995 (RSA 1995) established the South African Qualifications Authority (SAQA) as the 'guardian' of a National Qualifications Framework (NQF). In establishing a national qualifications framework, South Africa was following other countries in the world that had already developed frameworks. In doing so, South Africa can be seen to have been responding to the agenda identified for higher education as a result of globalisation.

A national qualifications framework functions as a means of mapping qualifications on a structure. The reasoning behind qualifications frameworks arguably relates to what we have earlier termed the 'commodification' of knowledge and, in particular, to the knowledge possessed by individuals. 'Knowledge workers' are in demand in any country which seeks to participate in a globalised economy, especially as we enter the so-called 'Fourth Industrial Revolution'. Just as globalisation relaxed the controls on trade across national borders, qualifications frameworks seek to allow individuals to carry their learning across borders. Someone with a qualification gained in, say, Kenya might want to work in Australia or China. Their qualification would only have 'currency' in the foreign country if it could be recognised and 'measured' internationally. Qualifications frameworks seek to make this possible.

Individuals might also want to cross borders in order to further their learning. They might, for example, want to build on a master's degree attained in Rwanda by pursuing doctoral-level studies overseas in the United Kingdom either by actually attending a university in that country or by enrolling in a programme and studying using open- and distance-learning. By describing and measuring the learning achieved at a particular level, a qualifications framework makes study and employment across borders possible.

While qualifications frameworks might contribute to economic development and efficiency, in South Africa the need for a framework was also based on arguments related to equity. During apartheid, the majority of South Africans had been denied access to formal education of any quality. This does not mean, however, that such individuals had not learned in the course of their lives. The qualifications framework therefore aimed to be able to measure, map and record learning acquired informally, through a process known as the 'recognition of prior learning'.

If a qualifications framework is to be able to describe learning in order to meet the goals discussed above, it needs a 'language' of description that will be understood globally. It is at this point that the concept of the 'learning outcome' enters the story. Learning outcomes, sometimes called 'learning competencies', describe what learners will be able to *do* in order to achieve a qualification. What learners are able to do needs to be observable in order to be measurable and, therefore, accredited. Although outcomes can encompass knowing, the argument is that the knowing itself cannot be observed. As a result, outcomes need to be expressed as manifestations of knowing.

This sort of thinking took the focus away from knowledge per se to the skills that could be demonstrated as a result of knowing. In doing this, learning outcomes served the sort of thinking associated with the new mode of economic production in an era of globalisation. Stephanie Allais, in South Africa, was later to term the process of implementing the National Qualifications Framework 'selling out education' (Allais 2014) because of the way knowledge came to be neglected. The 'neglect' of knowledge is a point to which we will return in Chapter Five of this book, so the discussion at this point is somewhat cursory. Nonetheless, it is important to introduce ideas about knowledge in a chapter focusing on the higher education context.

As we have already described, the 'new economy' associated with globalisation is dependent on the constant reinvention of existing goods. The reinvention of, say, a T-shirt to ensure it is made from sustainable materials might require knowledge of the polluting effects of chemical processes involved in dyeing fabrics. It might also require knowledge of the actual construction of fabrics from, say, bamboo. This requires theoretical knowledge involving understandings of what takes place at a molecular level. In order to develop this knowledge, other kinds of knowledge are necessary. Learners must know about molecules per se, before they can understand the way different molecules can combine to make new ones. This kind of knowledge is referred to by sociologist Basil Bernstein (2000) as 'hierarchical' knowledge, in the sense that it is cumulative, with each new item of knowledge building on what went before it.

The *practice* of actually dyeing the fabric involves a different kind of knowledge, however, since it involves applying knowledge of chemical processes to dye or print on a piece of fabric. In order to do this, an individual might not need to master the entire hierarchical structure of knowledge. Rather, they might only need to know enough of the chemistry to be able to dye a particular kind of fabric successfully. The focus would be on the process and the successful outcome of the process of dyeing or printing rather than on the knowledge underpinning the process.

The construct of the learning outcome was privileged in discourse in South Africa from the mid-1990s onwards as the qualifications framework was introduced. Since then, critiques of the learning outcome as a construct and also of the pedagogical approach of outcomes-based education have abounded. We will deal with some of these critiques later in this book but for now will focus briefly on critiques related only to the nature of knowledge.

These critiques, captured by the work of scholars such as Stephanie Allais (2014), mentioned earlier, and Leesa Wheelahan (2010), Jeanne Gamble (2014), and Paula Ensor (2014), argue that limiting learners to contextualised knowledge, for example, to just enough chemistry to know which dye to use on a certain kind of fabric, denies them the ability to move beyond that context. Access instead to an entire 'knowledge structure' would allow them to move beyond the context they have been working in to new contexts (Mtombeni 2018). Disciplinary knowledge, captured in the notion of a 'knowledge structure', is thus argued to be *powerful* knowledge, and the use of learning outcomes which specify particular contexts is seen to be ultimately disempowering because it limits learners to those contexts. This is discussed in more depth in Chapter Five.

Another key set of arguments relates to equity considerations and particularly to the notion of democracy. Bernstein (2000: 31) argues that abstract theoretical knowledge allows us to access the 'unthinkable, the impossible and the not-yet thought' and that, because of this, access to this knowledge is central to a democracy. In a similar vein, Michael Young (2007: 41–42) claims that theoretical knowledge allows us to 'to project beyond the present' to a future or alternative world, while Wheelahan (2010: 2) maintains that 'access to theoretical knowledge is important because it provides access to society's conversations about itself'. From these perspectives, if theoretical knowledge is not secured in the curriculum, the ability of higher education to contribute to the development of a critical citizenry, a purpose identified in the South African White Paper, is called into question. The development of the national qualifications framework and the privileging of the construct of the learning outcome from the mid-1990s onwards can be seen to have achieved exactly the opposite through the emphasis on skills and contextualised knowledge in pursuit of narrow outcomes related to economic production. The privileging of contextualised knowledge over conceptual knowledge could work against the very goal of economic development also identified in the White Paper. As we will show in later chapters, the influence of the learning outcome has been all-pervasive at many universities in South Africa.

A great deal of effort and energy was expended at South African universities to register all qualifications on the new national qualifications framework. In common with frameworks across the world, *qualifications*, described in the form of learning outcomes, are registered on the framework at a number of levels. The original NQF had three columns. One column was intended to describe 'general' qualifications based on learning grounded in the disciplines and which was theory-driven. A second column was devoted to vocational and professional qualifications with a focus on applied learning required by 'the workplace'. A third column, the middle 'articulation column', was intended to allow for movement between the two columns on either side. This meant, for example, that a learner who had qualified in the general track could move to vocational or professional learning by using the 'articulation column' to acquire a qualification which would facilitate the shift into professional or vocational learning. The articulation column was also intended to allow for the recognition of prior learning. In principle, a learner who had not been able to access formal learning but who had, nonetheless, learned could have her learning accredited using a qualification in this column and then move into another column to progress along a 'learning pathway'.

Once qualifications are registered on the South African NQF, a programme of study, which will allow learners to meet the outcomes describing the qualification, then needs to be designed. Qualifications are described using a 'nested' approach, which involves becoming gradually more specific about the area of study or qualification focus. This is achieved by first specifying the level on the NQF at which the qualification is registered and the number of credits[1] it carries. The qualification type, also called the 'descriptor', is then allocated. A qualification type would be, for example, a bachelor's degree or a diploma. The 'designated variant' or 'designator' is then added. A bachelor's qualification could then become a Bachelor of Science. The final level of description involves the area of specialisation. Thus, a Bachelor of Science in Geology or Forestry Management could be registered. This nested approach led to a large number of new qualifications being registered on the framework and was accompanied by the development of the programmes which led to them.

Many universities took up the discourses in policy documents related to producing graduates for the global economy by developing programmes with a specific vocational focus. This vocational focus appeared in the area of specialisation that might include subjects such as Tourism or Water Management. As this shift towards vocationalism proceeded, so concerns regarding the move away from 'powerful knowledge' were voiced (Muller 2009; Maton 2009; Shay 2013; Shay & Steyn 2014; Young & Muller 2013a, 2013b). In some universities, the move involved wide-scale reorganisation of traditional academic departments into schools or programme teams. This disruption to the way academic life had proceeded traditionally was very upsetting for some and impacted on the way academics began to perceive themselves and their work. This is a subject we will take up in more detail in Chapters Five and Six.

As new programmes were developed, curricula changed in other ways thanks to the introduction of modularisation. As part of the introduction of the South African NQF, the concept of the 'unit standard' had been introduced. Unit standards describe units of

---

[1] A credit is a unit of learning. Credits are measured by calculating 'notional hours' or the number of hours it is estimated it would take the 'average' learner to complete the learning. In many countries, one credit is assumed to take ten notional hours.

learning and can be grouped together to form a 'whole qualification'. For higher education, a 'whole qualification' was defined as comprising at least 120 credits. Unit standards, on the other hand, can consist of very small numbers of credits. As the NQF was introduced, the universities resisted the use of unit standards and insisted on the registration of 'whole qualifications' on the NQF because of concerns that such approaches would reduce coherence in programme design. There was a sense that university programmes are more than the accumulation of multiple small units of learning and that the whole is greater than the sum of its parts.

This decision to avoid the use of unit standards did not mean that learning was not disaggregated into smaller units, however, because as part of the process of registering qualifications and developing programmes, many universities moved towards modularisation. As a result of the process of modularisation, learning was packaged into smaller chunks that could then be combined into entire programmes. In traditional universities, rules for combination often require a mixture of foundational, core and elective modules. Modularisation therefore provides students with some choice and allows them to accumulate credits which can, in principle, be transferred.

As we have tried to show, the work on the NQF had important implications for universities not least because of the way it constrained understandings of knowledge. Structural and cultural conditioning during apartheid impacted on the way individuals took up this new thinking about knowledge as something that could be divided into small units and described as outcomes. Earlier in this chapter we indicated that, during apartheid, different kinds of universities enjoyed different kinds of freedoms with only a small group of universities resisting dominant thinking, and, even then, this was only by some groups in such institutions and only to some degree. Arguably, the historically black universities and the technikons were structurally and culturally conditioned into the greatest compliance to the state. As a result, once new policies were introduced at a national level, it was in these two kinds of institutions that the call for change at programme level was heeded most closely.

In our work analysing the history of the South African Academic Development movement (e.g. Boughey 2005b, 2007, 2010a, 2012a; McKenna 2003, 2012a, 2012b), the late 1990s were identified as a time when capacity to work with issues related to teaching and learning in higher education was eroded thanks to financial stringency experienced throughout the system as a whole. Academic Development, sometimes known as 'Educational Development', had grown during the early part of the decade as universities sought to accommodate the learning needs of black students who entered the system following the shift to democracy. This growth was seen in the establishment of posts, albeit mostly soft-funded, and in the creation of centres and other entities focused on providing support not only for student learning but also for staff development. Once the need for financial stringency started to bite, however, many posts were lost and, in some cases, centres and other entities were closed.

Unfortunately, this happened at a time when expertise in curriculum development and scholarship was most needed to question the direction the system was taking. Critiques of the use of outcomes-based education and the National Qualifications

Framework did emerge (see, e.g. Chisholm 2005; Jansen 1998; Muller 1998; Muller & Taylor 1995) but these were often focused on the schooling system. There were also some critiques of the implications of this shift for higher education (see, e.g. Shay 2013) but these came much later and partly as scholars of teaching and learning in higher education took up the work of Bernstein (2000), Maton (2014) and others. For the most part, and as the research noted earlier in this book was largely to show (Boughey 2009, 2010b; Boughey & McKenna 2011a, 2011b), universities responded to the need to recurriculate using the principle of the learning outcome in one of two ways. The universities of technology and historically black universities tended to be compliant and registered their whole qualifications and spent energy aligning programmes to notions of outcomes-based education. The historically white universities either used a very 'light touch' or, having complied with the need to register outcomes for 'whole qualifications', then proceeded to ignore pedagogical implications despite the plethora of policies related to teaching and learning being developed at that time (McKenna & Boughey 2014). Many of the policies emerging at this time related to the introduction of a national system of quality assurance.

Quality assurance

In developing a 'framework for transformation', the White Paper on Higher Education (DoE 1997) called for quality assurance in South African higher education. Quality assurance can be seen to be associated with the shift towards New Public Management at a global level noted earlier in this chapter, whereby public institutions are seen to need careful 'managing' to become more 'efficient'. The need for quality to be assured is also associated with an increase in the number of universities in national systems and with the growth in the number of private, 'for profit' institutions established as higher education increasingly became constructed as a commodity. As this happened, institutions established in one context often began operating 'offshore', sometimes as limited companies, as we have indicated previously, and the need became paramount to ensure that the offerings of a university established in, say, America, were of quality once moved to a very different context, say, Oman.

By 1997, the year of the White Paper, several countries had introduced quality assurance to their own higher education systems (Chidindi 2017). The International Network for Quality Assurance Agencies in Higher Education was established in 1991, and began with eight national quality assurance bodies as its membership; it now has more than 300 national, regional and professional higher education quality assurance agencies as member organisations. Thirty-four countries on the African continent currently have some form of national quality assurance body, with South Africa being amongst the first. South Africa's need for quality assurance identified in the White Paper was realised through the establishment of the Higher Education Quality Committee (HEQC) as a permanent standing committee of the Council on Higher Education (Council on Higher Education (CHE) 2001a) which had been set up to advise the minister of education on matters related to higher education, and also as a result of the White Paper. As in other countries, and following Harvey and Green (1993), the HEQC used an understanding of quality as involving 'fitness for purpose', although this dominant definition was also married with that of 'fitness of purpose', value for money and 'transformation', where the term 'transformation' was understood to involve 'developing the capabilities of individual learners for personal enrichment, as well as the requirements of social development and economic and employment growth' (CHE 2001a: 14).

The *Higher Education Quality Founding Document* (CHE 2001a) identifies a number of areas of responsibility of the HEQC, including the accreditation of providers of higher education to offer qualifications registered on the NQF, auditing and institutional review, and capacity development. The first phase of work, however, came to focus on accreditation and auditing, with the creation of an accreditation system and the completion of a first cycle of institutional audits between 2005 and 2012.

The institutional audit cycle was to impact on teaching and learning in South African universities in substantial ways. From the 1980s onwards, those working in the Academic Development movement had drawn on discourses related to equity as their work was focused on providing access to those long disenfranchised by apartheid. As policy requirements began to impact on the universities as the century drew to a close, a new role for Academic Development practitioners drawing on efficiency discourses began to emerge (Boughey 2007) as institutional managers realised that the capacity to support the demands of quality assurance and other policy requirements lay with Academic Developers. From the early 2000s onwards, new jobs were created in teaching and learning and quality assurance centres, often staffed by those who had previously worked in student support.

A second impact of the first cycle of institutional audits was the development of policies related to teaching and learning. In some institutions, the monitoring of the implementation of these policies was the responsibility of the quality assurance centres. In others, monitoring was much more diffuse and was characterised by a 'lighter touch'. If we draw on the framework on which we have based this book, it can be seen that the 'cultural domain' of the institution was very influential here. If the dominant culture was one where academics were 'trusted' to do what was appropriate because they were understood to share a common set of values, or where academics were likely to resist quality assurance by calling on 'academic freedom', the institution was much less likely to implement a strong quality assurance regime (McKenna & Boughey 2014). But if the institutional culture was very hierarchical and academics were seen to need tight management, there followed the formation of well-staffed quality assurance centres, the implementation of numerous quality assurance policies, and the close monitoring and reporting thereon being made compulsory.

Yet another impact of the first cycle of quality assurance work was the appointment of key agents responsible for 'managing' teaching and learning, in the form of deputy vice-chancellor-, dean- and director-level positions. This particular development was also related to the funding of higher education, the subject to which we will now turn.

Funding higher education

We have already alluded to some of the different ways funding was allocated to institutions under apartheid, noting that historically white institutions were much better funded than their black counterparts. It was not only the amount of funding that differed, as Bunting (2002) points out. Historically black institutions, both universities and technikons, received funding as a result of negotiating a budget with the relevant government department (or, indeed, 'government' in the case of the so-called 'homeland' institutions). Historically white institutions, in comparison, were subject to a standardised funding formula which meant that they enjoyed considerably more independence than their sister institutions.

The funding of historically white institutions was according to a formula developed in 1982, which took into account, amongst other things, student numbers, subject groupings and course levels. Once money was allocated to an institution using the formula, it could not be removed, and an institution was able to budget and build reserves accordingly. Historically black universities, on the other hand, were required to return any unspent funds at the end of a financial year, the consequence of which was a tendency towards 'fiscal dumping' in order to ensure that the allocation was completely spent so as not to impact on the following year's budgeting cycle. This also meant that an institution was unable to build financial reserves.

These disparities in funding led to a great deal of unhappiness with the result that, from 1988 onwards, versions of the standardised funding formula began to be applied more widely. As Bunting (2002) points out, although the application of the standardised formula brought historically black institutions more autonomy in the control of their financial affairs and, initially, benefited them as student enrolments were growing, the need to catch up with the backlog of resourcing meant that money was still scarce. Moreover, as student enrolments at the historically black universities started to fall away once universities opened their doors to all following the shift to democracy in the early 1990s, many historically black universities began to suffer real financial constraints as the decade wore on.

In 2004, a new funding formula for higher education was introduced (Ministry of Education (MoE) 2004). The National Commission on Higher Education (Venter-Hildebrand 1996), established by Nelson Mandela soon after taking up the position of the first democratically elected president of South Africa, had identified four principles for the funding of public higher education. These were that funding would need to employed (i) to allow for equity and redress in order to make the system more equitable; (ii) to make the higher education system more responsive to the needs of a developing economy in the context of globalisation; (iii) to ensure that the system met its goals at the least possible cost; and (iv) to ensure that the cost of higher education was shared between the state and those who would benefit from it.

The 2004 funding formula (MoE 2004) attempted to manage these principles through the increased use of incentive-based funding to steer the system. Key to the framework was the linking of funding to institutional- and system-level planning through the introduction of three-year rolling plans in which institutions and the Ministry would agree on, amongst other things, enrolment targets for different areas of study. Subsidy for teaching was linked to actual enrolments and was incentive-based in the sense that a part of the subsidy was withheld until graduation. This then meant that the longer an institution took to graduate a student, the less the subsidy that student would have accrued per annum. This partly incentive-based funding then contributed to discourses constructing the need for teaching to be 'managed' which had also emerged in relation to the introduction of quality assurance and which had led to the appointment of key agents working in this area.

Teaching was not the only area to be 'incentivised'. Thanks to the new funding formula, institutions were also to receive funding based on their research outputs. Postgraduate graduations and accredited publications were counted as 'outputs' and, as a result, came to be perceived as particularly lucrative across the system.

Historically, research and postgraduate supervision had taken place at a relatively small number of South African universities thanks to the way the historically black universities and technikons were constructed under apartheid. The incentivising of research in the new funding formula was intended to promote research and postgraduate supervision across the entire sector and, in turn, can be seen to be tied to the notion of the knowledge economy. It can be linked to the award of 'university' status to all institutions thanks to the reorganisation of South African higher education that took place from 2002 onwards. Once the formula was in place, all institutions began to promote the need for research and, effectively, to chase research output. As a result, key agents such as deputy vice-chancellors responsible for research and development came to be appointed and research and innovation offices were established at all institutions.

In order to increase research outputs, however, many institutions first needed to upgrade the qualifications of their staff who, particularly in the new universities of technology which emerged out of the former technikons, often had not even achieved master's degrees (Gumbi & McKenna 2020; Kraak 2009; Powell & McKenna 2009). As a result, South African academics came to face pressure from all directions as demands for 'increased throughput' of students were supplemented by demands for research outputs which often required academics' own research capacity to be developed. We will return to these demands and the impact on the nature of the academic workforce at various institutions in Chapter Six of this book.

Another element of the new funding formula was the use of 'earmarked' grants as levers for improvement and to achieve specific objectives. For example, teaching development grants and research development grants were initially introduced for those institutions not meeting 'output norms' in both areas, and even after these grants were extended to all universities, they continued to be calculated on the basis of institutional efficiencies. As with quality assurance, funding came to be used as a lever of the state to drive outputs in the system and to size and shape it to try to meet the demands related to both equity and efficiency.

Reorganising the system

When the newly elected government took office in 1994, the South African higher education system comprised 36 institutions split along the lines indicated in this chapter. As policy work began, one of the main aims was to produce a single system which would provide quality higher education for all South Africans, regardless of their social group, and which could serve the needs of the nation as well as of individuals. We have already described some of the main policy developments impacting on higher education: the SAQA Act, the introduction of quality assurance, and the introduction of the new funding formula in 2004. One further policy-related development was the National Plan for Higher Education (MoE 2001).

One of the most significant features of the National Plan was the goal of increasing participation in higher education from 15% to 20% over a 10- to 15-year period in an attempt to address inequity in participation. The assumption was that if the total participation rate was increased, then more black South Africans would gain access to higher education.

However, one of the main characteristics of the National Plan was its focus on the need to make the higher education system more efficient. Having 36 institutions split along the lines of race, language, institutional type and so on, with at least two institutions separated by nothing more than a wire fence, was clearly highly inefficient. Under apartheid, these 36 institutions had been funded by different government departments within the Republic of South Africa and different 'governments' if situated in the 'homelands'. After 1994, all came under the auspices of the Department of Education. Duplication and difference at the institutional level needed to be addressed.

The National Plan identified a number of needs in relation to the reconfiguration of the institutional landscape. These were the needs: (i) to reduce duplication in both programme- and service-delivery; (ii) to enhance responsiveness at both regional and national levels for programmes, research and community development; (iii) to help build administrative and academic capacity across the system; and, finally, (iv) to refocus the culture and missions of the different institutions. The refocusing of the 'culture and missions' of the institutions comprising the system was, of course, at the heart of 'transformation' as understood by many people (McKenna & Quinn 2016; Quinn & Boughey 2009). It is important to note that the concept of 'transformation' is strongly embedded in the relationship between the state and the higher education sector (Naidoo & Ranchod 2018). There is a strong focus in the South African National Plan on using higher education to serve national economic needs, just as there is in the plans of other nations on the continent, including that of Kenya.

In 2000, the Council on Higher Education made a set of recommendations related to how such reconfiguration could be implemented. The CHE proposal was that the system should be restructured to comprise three institutional types: (i) research institutions offering a full range of programmes up to doctoral level; (ii) a second group offering programmes up to master's level with doctoral-level programmes in a few niche areas; and (iii) 'bedrock' institutions focusing on undergraduate programmes. This proposal was widely contested by institutions who saw it as continuing the inequity of apartheid since most historically black universities had limited postgraduate offerings.

The minister did not take the advice of the CHE regarding institutional type, rather advocating in the National Plan a process of institutions identifying particular niches for themselves and working towards these using the system of three-year rolling plans introduced in relation to funding. He also appointed a working group to identify possible mergers and incorporations in the system, warning that the system was not regulating itself voluntarily as hoped and that he would need to exercise the full regulatory powers at his disposal in terms of the Higher Education Act (RSA 1997 Act 101) to effect change.

The 'Report of the Working Group' (MoE 2002), which eventually determined the shape of the system, was important not only because of the reduction of the 36 public institutions of apartheid into 23 post-apartheid institutions but also because of its identification of three 'institutional types'. These were (i) the 'traditional' universities offering a range of formative and professional discipline-based programmes; (ii) the universities of technology offering mainly vocational programmes at diploma level; and (iii) the 'comprehensive' universities offering a mix of discipline-based and vocational programmes at both degree and diploma levels.

If a higher education system in any country is to meet the demands placed on it by the state, industry, students and other stakeholders, it needs to be differentiated (Singh 2008). Because no single institution can meet all the calls made upon it, a sector needs to embody differentiation of type (as exemplifed in the case of South Africa above) and, within broad types, the identification by individual institutions of a particular niche for themselves. This niche would be made evident in an institution's mission and vision statements and the values and purposes it identifies for itself. More specifically it would inform its academic project.

The Higher Education Qualifications Sub-Framework

As indicated at the beginning of this section, one of the most important pieces of legislation impacting on higher education was the National Qualifications Framework Act. Work on the higher education portion of the framework began in the early 2000s, with a version gazetted in 2004 as the Higher Education Qualifications Framework, but it was fairly extensively revised and it was only in 2012 that the Higher Education Qualifications Sub-Framework (HEQSF) was eventually gazetted. The time taken to develop the sub-framework for higher education was largely due to deliberations and work on the nature of knowledge itself (see Muller 2009, as an example) which we explore in greater detail in Chapter Five of this book.

The publication of the HEQSF resulted in universities having to re-submit qualifications and the programmes leading to them to the CHE for accreditation. In the universities of technology in particular, this required a lot of recurriculation work in relation to bachelor's level qualifications. Previously, a Bachelor of Technology (BTech) degree had been available as a one-year 'top up' qualification on a National Diploma to 'convert' it into a degree. The new HEQSF abolished the BTech degree, leaving instead only the bachelor's degree which could be either generally or professionally orientated.

The need to implement the framework could have presented an enormous opportunity to engage with questions of knowledge – whose knowledge is included or excluded and to what ends the knowledge is meant to serve. But this is not what happened. The process of applying the framework happened alongside engaging with complex mergers and incorporations and was generally undertaken in a superficial process of compliance. That we did not use this as an opportunity to delve deeper into issues of knowledge and transformation is something that we have already lived to regret.

Conclusion

At this point, our framework requires us to consider the changes that have occurred in the policy landscape since the early 1990s.

As we hope our analysis above has shown, in the years since the shift to a democracy, policymakers have drawn on dominant global discourses related to the role of universities in our societies and economies, as well as to those related to the need for South Africa to develop an entire raft of new policies and frameworks to guide the higher education system. In Archer's terms, we could thus say there has been enormous change in the structural system through the development of policies and the implementation of mergers. At this point, we will not attempt an evaluation of the changes that have taken place. That will be left for the final chapter of this book. Instead we turn to reflect on how students have been positioned and have enacted their agency across this same time period.

4

Denying context, misunderstanding students

The power of the words we use

The words we use influence our understanding of the world and they affect how we interact with any person, animal or object. Despite the childhood rhyme that 'sticks and stones may break my bones but words will never hurt me', words are powerful and have real effects.

In Chapter Two we argued that discourses, which we have defined as 'clumps' of ideas that 'hang together' in words and other sign systems, have power as mechanisms in the realm of culture. Individuals draw on discourses to make sense of the world. For example, we might draw on a discourse of 'disadvantaged students' to explain challenges that students have with their studies. When the discourse being drawn on then complements other mechanisms, such as the availability of funding for student development, this can lead to the emergence of particular events, such as a compulsory support course for students identified as 'disadvantaged'.

As a result of the intersection of discursive powers with structures and the agency of people, the power of the discourse can be reinforced. In the example above, the intersection between the discourse of 'disadvantaged student' (realm of culture), the funding for student development (realm of structure), and the development of add-on courses by academics (realm of agency) all serve to reinforce the idea that students lack something fundamental due to their 'disadvantaged' status.

If, however, people draw on other discourses in the exercise of their agency, then this can result in dominant discourses being challenged. Academics may suggest, for example, that there are more complex explanations for student success or failure than 'disadvantage', and this might lead to a very different set of responses emerging.

Understanding that discourses have power means understanding that the ways in which universities speak of their student body has consequences. Across the African continent, there is evidence of both low student throughput and differentiated success along the lines of race, language group, ethnicity and social class (Cloete et al. 2011; Moremi 2018), so it is crucially important for us to have a sense of how students are understood within universities.

In this chapter, then, we look at how students have been discursively constructed over the T_2 to T_3 time span of the research that underpins this book and we consider how discourses have conditioned the events and experiences that have emerged. To return to our realist framework, it is important to note that the power of discourses is only activated when agents draw upon them. All discourses are rooted in social practice and we argue that it is incumbent upon us, as agents, to be conscious of the ways in which we draw on discourses in the exercise of our agency.

Across our research, including that which we undertook for the Council on Higher Education as described in Chapter One, we have identified a number of discourses by which students are constructed and by which students co-construct themselves. As indicated previously, while this data is South African and our research focuses on the emergence of events and experiences in the South African higher education context, we attempt to draw links beyond our borders where relevant. We begin by discussing the conception that has permeated almost all of the data we have looked at: a discourse that we have come to call the discourse of the 'Decontextualised Learner'.

Students as decontextualised individuals

In this discourse, students' success and failure is explained in terms of attributes inherent within them as individuals, such as intelligence, motivation and aptitude (Boughey & McKenna 2016, 2017). Students are understood as individuals who work hard or do not, are motivated or are not, are bright and talented or are not, and who are therefore in the appropriate course or do not really belong there. We acknowledge that students are, of course, individual beings, each with their own strengths and limitations, but it was clear that the dominance of this focus on the individual student's capacities entailed a significant blind spot to the bigger social structures within which students and the university exist.

Through the dominant discourse, the student is decontextualised from her social norms and practices, and her successes and failures are understood to be primarily or even exclusively a personal responsibility. The university, the society in which the university exists, the history of the country, the development of the curriculum – these are all hidden from view as the explanations for success and failure hone in on the individual.

In the data that we examined for the research on the institutional audits, one university explained poor student performance by arguing that 'students appear to lack motivation to study, having registered on the basis of having been awarded a bursary or merit scholarship'. If students have been awarded a bursary or merit scholarship to study at the institution, then presumably they have performed sufficiently well at school to enable them to meet the criteria for the award and, thus, have presumably been sufficiently 'motivated' to achieve this level of performance. The institution's report seems to suggest that, having gained access to the institution, the motivation somehow evaporates.

This sort of account locates motivation in individuals as an attribute that is either present or absent. No consideration is given to the role of social context in enabling and constraining the kind of agency that will lead to learning (Case et al. 2018; McKenna

2012b; Walker 2018). The university's alienating environment, peculiar cultural practices, and unclear expectations are not brought into consideration (De Kadt & Mathonsi 2003; Luescher et al. 2020). Interestingly, the solution proffered to the problem in this particular piece of data was to note: 'An area for improvement, therefore, would be to evaluate practices used for selecting motivated students'.

It is also not unusual in our experience to find that successful students are constructed as 'talented' – that is, as possessing attributes that are inherent rather than socially developed. If students are admitted to the university and fail, then it would seem that their talent was insufficient. The only fault that the institution bears lies in their initial assessment of that talent. Indeed, many universities have spent a large amount of money on developing access tests to help them do so.

This suggests that the problem lies in letting the 'wrong' students into the system. Given the relatively low participation rates in higher education in South Africa and beyond, as discussed in Chapter One, we need to consider that the students who do manage to access university study have often survived a dysfunctional schooling system and may have lived lives of financial deprivation. The ability of these students to overcome such circumstances to be amongst the few who access higher education is significant. One presumes that if talent was indeed an inherent attribute, these students must have it in bucket loads.

There is extensive literature calling for a stronger focus on the role of student agency to understand learning in higher education (Klemenčič 2017; Luckett & Luckett 2009), and there is a growing body of work that attempts to identify each student's strengths and weaknesses, through aptitude and other tests. Arguably, the dominant focus on students' inherent ability, described above, could be seen as a recognition of their agency; after all, the discourse of the Decontextualised Learner places the spotlight on the student herself – it looks at her strengths and weaknesses. This may at first glance seem a positive approach; however, it suggests that success rests on her actions regardless of the nature of the social space in which she finds herself and regardless of what might be the totally alien nature of the teaching and learning practices confronting her. The question of who or what it is that is 'appropriate' (or, more to the point, who is deemed 'inappropriate') is not dealt with. Such explanations for student success, that are focused primarily on decontextualised individual properties and disregard the realms of structure and culture, are an example of 'upwards conflation', a concept we explained in Chapter Two.

In talking about students, there is a continuum of possible ways of doing so. On the one end, there is this decontextualised understanding that the student body comprises simply a collection of individuals, each bringing their own inherent personalities and aptitudes. On the other end of the continuum is a focus entirely on the social, with the understanding that students represent particular socio-economic, historical, political contexts which they bring into the university, which in turn has its own social, historical, political context. Across all the data over multiple studies, we found there was a strong focus on the psychologised, individual end of this continuum and very little that took social issues from the other end of the continuum into account. This finding is echoed in the literature as Trowler (2008: xi) suggests that the lens used in much research on educational practices 'has been predominantly a psychological one, not a sociological one, focusing on the individual not people in interaction with each other and their environment'.

And where student success is repeatedly attributed to factors inherent in the individual, such as potential or cognitive ability, student failure is ascribed to a lack of seemingly neutral, a-social, a-political, a-cultural skills as a result of poor schooling or simply not being the 'right' kind of student. Across all the data we have analysed over the years, and in particular the work we did on the first cycle of institutional audits (Boughey 2009, 2010b; Boughey & McKenna 2011a, 2011b), there is ample evidence that students are largely understood in ways that are decontextualised from their histories and socio-economic realities.

Discussions about students are thus generally premised on the understanding that students can improve their lot through effort and will. They can 'pull themselves up by their bootstraps' and 'achieve the dream' provided they have sufficient motivation and aptitude. While histories of disadvantage may be acknowledged to be unfair, this discourse suggests that they can be fixed through hard work by the student. Importantly, this thinking assumes that the university is fair and open to all. The effects of this dominant discourse are everywhere, as will be discussed in this chapter.

The two ends of the continuum of ways of discussing student success – from understanding student success as a product of the individual student's inherent attributes at one end, to understanding this as emerging entirely from the social structures in which learning takes place at the other end – are examples of the two forms of conflation (upwards conflation and downwards conflation) that Archer (1998) warns us about.

On the one hand, we have upwards conflation where student success is understood to be entirely the result of characteristics inherent in the individual. On the other, we have downwards conflation where student success or failure is understood to be entirely the effect of social and cultural structures, with no powerful agency accorded to the student.

Neither end of the continuum of explanations really provides a nuanced account of student agency. Agency, or students' capacity to act (Luckett & Luckett 2009), is underdeveloped in both of these accounts. Extreme social understandings of student learning portray the education process as one whereby the student is inducted slavishly into a pre-existing knowledge domain with its own set of norms and

values, with no space for the student to adapt and critique such domains. And while the dominant account, that of the decontextualised student, accords the explanation for success to the student herself, it does so in a very flat and fixed version of agency. It is her motivation or cognitive ability or some other characteristic that explains her success. It is not about her developing and activating her agency to work with and against the structures and cultures of society.

By ascribing all power to students as the explanation for success or failure, without empowering them to enact agency, the data we examined places responsibility for student success or failure solely in the hands of the students themselves. One of the main attractions of this understanding of personal responsibility for success is that it has an absolving function. There is little consideration of how the institutional culture and discipline-specific practices might be underpinned by alienating values and norms which could counter some students' efforts to pursue their personal projects.

Without access to the peculiar cultural practices of the university or to the epistemological and ontological underpinnings of the disciplines within the university (a point we will elaborate upon in more detail in Chapter Five), it is doubtful that hard work alone can lead to success.

For example, in an article that discusses students enacting agency by studying together in peer-groups, Bertram (2004) notes the inappropriate and unproductive learning practices used by students when reading course material. Without access to the epistemologies of the target discipline, students called on rhetorical reading practices with which they are familiar from school (where the text is searched for keywords and concepts that match those in the question) rather than using the text to develop knowledge. Similarly, Case (2013) considers in depth the ways in which student agency is constrained by institutional structures and cultures. She argues that attempts to make sense of agency in isolation from sociological considerations are dangerous. In spite of the many warnings against a decontextualised account of student learning, this continued to be the default position across the T_2 to T_3 period.

The issue of talent as an explanation for student success becomes even more vexatious when held up against the fact that success rates are racially differentiated across all South African programmes from T1 in 1994 to date (CHE 2020). If it is indeed the existence or absence of talent in individual students that best accounts for success rates, then how do we explain the fact that white and Indian students perform consistently better than their black African and 'coloured' counterparts? Such discourses need to be vigorously troubled for the racist undertones they contain. In other countries on the continent, similar disparities can be found along the lines of social categories such as ethnicity, colourism or language group (Odhiambo 2016). In all these cases, the use of the notion of 'talent' as an explanation for student success needs to be interrogated for the ways in which this supposedly neutral explanation condones and reinforces social divides.

While it makes sense to have rigorous processes to ensure that the very limited spaces in higher education are filled by those most likely to succeed, we need to be wary of how we understand what it is that makes a student most likely to succeed in higher education. When we discursively construct the likelihood of succeeding simply as 'talent' or 'potential' or 'motivation' or 'cognitive ability', we hide the extent to which higher education success is a function of access to a particular set of literacy practices and dispositions validated and reinforced in a middle-class childhood (Case et al. 2018; O'Shea et al. 2019). This is an uncomfortable notion but one that has been repeatedly established through research around the world (Armstrong & Hamilton 2013; Guinier 2015; Mettler 2014; Walpole 2003).

Of course, we would like to think of higher education as a meritocracy in which everyone has a fair chance of success. We want to believe that it is the hard work of the individual, coupled with her personal attributes, that determines whether or not she gains access to the goods the university has to offer. It is upsetting to admit that it is the student's socio-economic background that most clearly correlates with university success. In addition, we do not want to consider the ways in which social structures such as race, ethnicity, and gender also function as mechanisms constraining students' chances of success.

That the university, through its current practices, plays a role in reinforcing the unjust social status quo is a bitter pill to swallow. Furthermore, it raises a number of challenges about how our pedagogy, curricula and institutional cultures could be re-structured to alter this. To acknowledge our complicity is to set ourselves the enormous task of addressing it.

Given that there has been a wealth of research countering the dominant decon-textualised account of students, it is important to look at why this has not been taken up. In South Africa, as in many other contexts, increased emphasis is being placed on using research from teaching and learning to enhance success rates. But all too often theories about learning and teaching are misappropriated to serve problematic and resilient dominant thinking.

The misappropriation of theories on teaching and learning

Where academics draw on theories of teaching and learning to pursue projects of their own, they also draw on the discourses available in their cultural context. The power of these discourses can be such that they lead to theory being misappropriated and shifted to serve the discourse. Theories are 'gathered into' discourses and, when this happens, the use of the theory can simply be incorrect.

As discussed in Chapter One, powerful theories can shed light on phenomena hidden by problematic dominant discourses. They can make the familiar strange and help us to see things we have taken for granted or misunderstood. Theories about students, curricula, and teaching and learning have the potential to offer us alternative lenses to look at issues like success and failure. It is therefore worth looking at the kinds of theories being brought to bear on our understandings of students and their learning. In doing so, we can also often see the way that they are being misappropriated in service of the discourse of the Decontextualised Learner.

While a quick review of the scholarship of teaching and learning literature demon-strates that a vast array of theories is being drawn upon, the effectiveness of such theories in providing appropriate lenses on the problem depends to a large extent on how such theories are taken up. And it would seem that we have a habit of taking potentially powerful theories and re-jigging them so that they reinforce our existing frames.

One example is the theory of 'student-centredness' which emerged in the 1990s as universities drew on this approach to try to attend to the needs of a far more diverse and massified student body. The call for student-centredness was a call to acknowledge students' identities and histories and to shift from traditional 'teacher-centred' approaches (Rogers & Freiberg 1994). It argued for a move away from focusing on what the teacher did to what the student did, who the student was, and what the student wanted and needed. This would seem to be exactly the right theory to shift the dominant Decontextualised Learner discourse.

Sadly, however, this 'student-centred' approach was often subverted to reinforce the Decontextualised Learner discourse (McKenna & Quinn 2020). To be 'student-centred' came to mean identifying the problems inherent within the student. The theory of 'student-centredness' was used as the basis from which to call for more thorough selection to make sure that the university gets the students with the necessary skills, and it was used to argue for remedial interventions that address the skills that the 'student-centred' approach had identified as lacking (McKenna 2013). Student-centredness may have emerged as a concept from an understanding that higher education has a role to play in achieving social justice but it is often misused to justify a focus on students' deficits, once again absenting the notion of the university as a social structure and the student as a social being.

The student engagement movement, which similarly promised a desirable shift in attention to the student experience, has also at times been appropriated. It has sometimes been brought into complementarity with the efficiency discourses of knowledge commodification, discussed in Chapter Three, to allow 'student centeredness to mean establishing what the student, as the customer, desires and then adapting the product, the curriculum, to suit them' (McKenna & Quinn 2020: 111). Reference to student engagement can also be found in a number of institutional policies and strategies and often entails a collection of metrics about students, with the understanding that these can be used to enhance efficiency in throughput in relation to the maximisation of subsidy.

Another example of a theory that has been misappropriated in our universities in order to complement the Decontextualised Learner discourse is that of deep and surface approaches to learning. The concepts of deep and surface approaches to learning were developed by Swedish researchers Marton and Säljö in the 1970s and were quickly taken up in research on teaching and learning around the world (Haggis 2009; Richardson 2005). But what began as an identification of how contexts enable different approaches to learning was corrupted into a consideration of why some students were 'deep or surface learners' (Boughey & McKenna 2016; McKenna 2012b). A theoretical approach that raised questions about mismatches between university and student practices thus became subverted to allow conclusions that students were doing the wrong kind of learning: 'surface learning', or, an even more worrying misappropriation, they were the wrong kind of learners: 'surface learners'. Importantly, the concepts of 'deep or surface learning' or 'deep or surface learners' were nowhere in the original theory and have never been validated since.

What the misappropriations of such theories have in common is a focus on the student in ways that are decontextualised from her social context, and a concomitant blind spot about the social context of the university and the structure of knowledge.

While we have given examples of misappropriations of theories thus far, it is worth noting that we also see evidence of the continued use of theories that have been repeatedly debunked (Hlengwa et al. 2018). Theories such as 'multiple intelligences' and 'learning styles' purport to focus on the student and her needs – surely an admirable intention –

but they do so in a manner that suggests that learning is a neutral process dependent on individual attributes and independent of social context. Not only is the social nature of the student and the university conveniently ignored by such theories, but the structure and history of the target disciplinary knowledge is also rendered invisible. As will be argued in Chapter Five, knowledge is no more neutral than are universities, students or academics. Teaching and learning theories that focus only on the presence or absence of 'neutral' attributes and skills in the student are convenient because they allow us to avoid the murky terrain of ideology.

It may seem that we are suggesting that academics or universities as a whole are intentionally or uncaringly in cahoots with a system of inequality, even selecting debunked theories or misappropriating theories to do so. But of course, this is not the case. Most people working in higher education believe in social justice and wish to be part of achieving it. However, mechanisms such as the discourse of the Decontextualised Learner constrain the possibilities for social justice in ways which are subtle and normalised and very difficult to identify.

There has to be an explicit intention to identify these discourses at work in order to reduce their influence within the system. Such discourses might be powerful mechanisms but we are not powerless to resist them. We have agency, and with agency comes a responsibility to question our common-sense understandings and, indeed, some of the academic literature on student learning. We need to challenge the ways in which theories are misappropriated to focus yet again on the learner's skills or deficits. We need to be alert to how such appropriations allow the academic department, the disciplinary knowledge, and the institution to be absented. We have to insert awareness of the extent to which our universities and institutional practices are deeply ideological and historical in nature and serve some students better than others.

This problem is of course not peculiar to any one country. Despite repeated calls over decades for us to understand the social nature of higher education (e.g. Dewey 1900; Freire 1970; Nussbaum 1998), most explanations of higher education success continue to ignore this. It is easy to understand why such individualised accounts have remained dominant: it is far simpler to develop remedial initiatives to address deficiencies in individuals than it is to look critically at the extent to which universities offer equitable access to powerful knowledge.

The 'language problem' and how it lets universities off the hook

Beyond the possession (or lack of possession) of personal attributes described above, another frequent and related explanation for student success evident across the research that underpins this book is that of language proficiency. Language has long been used as a political tool in South Africa and it continues to be an issue that raises great emotion. The debates about the use of Afrikaans as a medium of instruction in some South African universities continue as we write this book (see, e.g. Hibbert & Van der Walt 2014; Mkhize 2018; Prah 2017), and the lack of commitment to developing African languages for academic purposes, in the ways that the apartheid government spent millions of rands doing with Afrikaans, is frequently bemoaned. The privileging of some languages over others in the higher education system has created numerous injustices across the continent (see, e.g. Samuelson 2013). But hidden beneath many of these debates is another matter to do with the very way in which the phenomenon of language is understood.

Language is generally understood as a neutral phenomenon comprising grammar, syntax, vocabulary and punctuation used to convey ready-formed ideas and meanings between people. In this sort of understanding, ideas pre-date language. The ideas exist and are then encoded into language. The ability to convey those ideas to others or to 'receive' them from others is then dependent on an individual's ability to 'decode' the features of the language, that is, the grammar, syntax, vocabulary and punctuation. While this understanding of language has been widely refuted in the literature (see, e.g. Bangeni & Kapp 2017; Thesen & Van Pletzen 2006), it remains powerful and it has the added benefit of being politically expedient.

For example, way back in 1993 Bradbury noted that the 'second language' label in South Africa served as a means of avoiding difficult conversations about the intersections between race, class, and educational success. By attributing students' learning difficulties to their status as speakers of English as an additional language, it became possible to avoid engaging with the effects of the apartheid ideology of inferiority. Anyone can experience difficulties in understanding a language which is not theirs by birth, so it is far simpler to point to this issue to account for poor success than to consider how unequal social structures are reinforced within the university.

There are other reasons for the continued use of what we term the 'language problem' (Boughey 2002) as a key explanation of student failure. If language is the explanation for why some students fail, then it can be reasoned that a university's responsibility is simply to ensure that students have the requisite language competency to engage with their studies by putting appropriate admissions requirements in place. Perhaps, the university could take its responsibilities even further and offer add-on language courses focused on increasing students' vocabularies and improving their grammar. These language courses, usually offered by so called 'language specialists', exist outside the mainstream disciplines and focus on teaching generic versions of 'academic language' which are themselves highly questionable. The 'language problem' is thus seen to be something with which the university has to contend but not something in which the university is complicit.

As we have indicated in the discussion above, this sort of understanding of the 'language problem' draws on an understanding of language 'as an instrument of communication' (Christie 1985), a view that sees language as a vehicle for transmitting meanings constructed separately from the language. Language, in this understanding, is simply a neutral conduit whereby meaning is transferred. The neutral conduit is made up of generic grammar rules, vocabulary, etc. Problems that arise in misunderstanding are then because the student did not correctly encode or decode the message, hence the focus on teaching the code to the student.

Frances Christie (1985) identifies a model alternative to that of language as an 'instrument of communication'. This model, which she terms the model of 'language as a resource', draws on the work of linguist Michael Halliday (1985). Halliday sees language use as a system of choices. Language users make these choices based on their understandings of the context in which the language is being used. To make appropriate choices, the language user needs to know and subscribe to the value system being drawn upon in that particular context.

So, for example, the use of the passive voice in scientific writing is not an arbitrary practice. A scientist chooses to write 'Solute X was added to Solvent Y' as opposed to 'I made a solution by adding Solute X to Solvent Y' because of the valuing of objectivity in scientific research and, thus, the desire to conceal human agency. Because of the valuing of objectivity, language choices ensure that there is no evidence of the researcher herself in the writing. She has no gender or religion or race or age, indeed she is not visible in the research at all.

These and myriad other choices in language use emerge from the value systems of the context being drawn upon. When students are not familiar with academic contexts, even if they are aware of the rules of spelling, grammar and punctuation, they can still make inappropriate choices. For example, it is possible to refer to a young human being as a 'child', a 'kid' or a 'toddler'. Each of these vocabulary items is entirely appropriate in different contexts. In an academic context, the use of the term 'kid' would contravene the dominant value system that favours formality. Students frequently use inappropriate vocabulary in their writing as they have not fully accessed the value system of the new context. The same observation could be made of what many academics call 'WhatsApp language' in academic assignments. Students also sometimes err in the opposite direction, calling on a thesaurus of pompous words to mimic what they have identified as the elevated nature of writing in their discipline.

As another example of how language choices relate to values in the context, rather than 'neutral' grammatical rules, it is pertinent to consider how, throughout this book, we have used specialised terms related to our choice of theoretical framework. We have written on 'analytical dualism', 'mechanisms at the level of the Real' and so on. We had to introduce our framework in order to provide our readers with access to these terms.

The terms then allow us to make sense of the world in a very particular way. Obtaining access to a discipline entails being introduced to the epistemic position of that discipline and thereby to the language practices by which its truth claims are deemed credible. Language is thus understood to be central to taking on the meaning-making processes in specific disciplinary contexts.

Learning in a medium of instruction that is not one's home language greatly increases the difficulties many students experience, but we would caution that language, if understood as grammar and vocabulary in the medium of instruction, is a very small part of the acquisition of language as integral to academic practice, as we will now discuss further in relation to reading and writing, another area where theory has often been misappropriated.

Reading and writing as ideological acts

Social anthropologist, Brian Street, identifies two models of literacy (1984). The first of these models, the 'autonomous model', sees reading and writing as a set of skills involving the encoding and decoding of printed text. This model is one we are all most familiar with since it is intuitive given our experiences of learning to read and write at school. In the early years of schooling, we are taught the correspondence between symbols (i.e. the letters of the alphabet) and sounds and use this to learn to read words on the page and to spell words as we write. This aspect of literacy, which Street calls a 'technology', is critical to reading and writing. However, Street's work observing reading and writing as an anthropologist allowed him to identify that much, much more was involved than this technological proficiency, and this is what led to the development of his 'ideological model'.

The ideological model understands literacy as a set of social practices, that is, as a set of things people do with and around texts of various kinds. These would include a willingness to engage with certain kinds of texts in certain kinds of ways because of underlying values about what it is appropriate to do. It can even involve setting aside engagement with text altogether.

In a collection of studies that explored literacy practices in a range of marginalised communities in South Africa (Prinsloo & Breier 1996), Malan (1996: 146) has this to say about 'pension day' in Bellville South:

> Pensioners did not actually need to be able to read or write in order to receive their pension. One old woman in the queue told me that she was 'blind' (an image often used to describe themselves by people with little or no schooling), but when I asked her how she dealt with the pension pay-out, she said with great confidence: 'Very easy. Like anything else. What I don't know, I can ask someone who knows. If I hear about something, I go to those who can [read and write]. And now that person has to read to me what I want to know. That is how it works.' It did not matter to her that she could not even sign the form: '[I] just make a cross,' she said. 'Then they [the officials] chap, chap [they stamp the form].'

In this community, as in others in the study, engaging with printed text was readily negotiated.

Other South African studies show how in some social contexts engaging with academic texts is disparaged. O'Shea (2017) describes how students at a university read books and articles surreptitiously on their phones, as being seen to be an avid reader could result in allegations of presumed superiority and even that they were 'coconuts'.[2]

The ideological model therefore goes beyond understanding reading as a set of technical skills. It is seen to encompass sets of practices related to text which, ultimately,

---

2   The term 'coconut' is used disparagingly to refer to black people who are alleged to have assumed characteristics associated with whiteness.

are value driven. People engage with certain kinds of texts in certain kinds of ways because they see value in doing so.

The sort of thinking encompassed by the ideological model allows us to move beyond understanding literacy as a unitary phenomenon, involving everyone reading and writing in the same way, to seeing that many different literacies exist in the world. The much-vaunted 'academic literacy' is but one group of many literacies available in the world, and is based on sets of values about what can constitute knowledge and how that knowledge can be known in the academy. And, as we shall argue later, within the academy multiple literacies exist side-by-side.

The identification of literacy as a multiple phenomenon should not be taken to mean that we are advocating a relativist approach where 'anything goes'. Rather, our use of the Critical Realist framework, and other theories such as Legitimation Code Theory, allows us to see that different literacies perform different functions making some appropriate and others inappropriate to particular contexts. For example, literacies that draw on 'claim and evidence' structures have more explanatory power in the academy than opinion type literacies of social media and the popular press.

Another theorist, James Paul Gee (1989, 2008, 2012), takes Street's identification of the ideological model further in order to argue that being literate within a particular social context entails taking on a 'way of being'. In the case of the academy, this would involve understanding academic literacy as including everything from the ways in which one reads an academic article to how (and whether) one asks a question in a lecture theatre. In order to make this argument, Gee (2008: 154) draws on the concept of Discourse (always deliberately capitalised to distinguish it from other uses of the term). According to Gee, a Discourse is:

> composed of distinctive ways of speaking/listening and often, too, writing/ reading coupled with distinctive ways of acting, interacting, valuing, feeling, dressing, thinking, believing, with other people and with various objects, tools, and technologies, so as to enact specific socially recognizable identities engaged in specific socially recognized activities. Literacy is then defined as demonstrating mastery of a Discourse. When you have fully acquired a literacy, you have taken on these 'distinctive ways of acting'.

Gee's work is central to the argument we have been making in this chapter around the need to understand students as social beings as it brings the concept of identity into play. When students enter our universities, they are not simply required to learn new things. Rather, they become different people, they develop a new identity. We all have multiple literacies available to us, and we continue to take on new literacy practices throughout our lives as we enter new contexts, and thus we build multiple ways of being in the world. Taking on the literacy practices of the academy is thus understood as an issue of identity.

Part of an academic identity, for example, entails questioning what we read or hear and acknowledging that knowledge is always provisional and open to amendment in the light of evidence that challenges it. For many students, the challenges of taking on such practices can be intimidating, particularly if they have been encouraged to see the printed text as 'the word'. As readers, they are now being expected to question and, as writers, their role is not simply to repeat what has been said elsewhere but rather to make a series of knowledge claims about what they believe to be the case based on their reading of other texts or on data they have generated. The shifts required can be overwhelming regardless of whether students have done very well at school because schools generally require and reward different sets of practices. At a personal level, the need to shift and develop can leave students questioning who they are, all they have ever known and the entire world around them.

Access to the literacy practices of the academy is unevenly distributed. While academic language is no one's mother tongue (Bourdieu & Passeron 1994), taking up the peculiar ways of reading and writing of the academic disciplines is a simpler endeavour for some than for others. The ease with which the literacy practices of the disciplines can be taken up depends in part on the similarities of the practices expected in the university context to those practices that students bring with them from their homes, schools and other social spaces. In some homes, children are exposed from a very early age to the people around them reading and writing, and, more specifically, they are exposed to others reading and writing particular kinds of texts in particular kinds of ways – for example, reading out brief sections of a newspaper article and deliberating their agreement or disagreement with the argument being presented there. In this sort of environment, critical approaches to reading and writing may be normalised.

The key point about the ideological model of literacy is that literacies are context-dependent. Young people who have been exposed to and who have adopted the practices of literacies that are somewhat aligned to those valued in the academy are therefore privileged simply because of the circumstances of their birth and upbringing and not because of any inherent talent of their own.

What is very significant in all of this is that the university not only values certain literacy practices (which are then made difficult to access through the normalising of these practices as 'common sense'); it also ignores or sidelines others as 'inappropriate'.

As we have indicated earlier in this chapter, we would all like to assume that the university is a meritocracy and that success within it is determined by individual attributes and hard work (Sobuwa & McKenna 2019), and indeed this remains the dominant discourse. But research around the world consistently indicates that this is not the case (Armstrong & Hamilton 2013; Guinier 2007, 2015; Mettler 2014). The close relationship between middle-class literacy practices and those valued in universities, that we have discussed above, is one part of the explanation for the international correlation between socio-economic background and university success (Case et al. 2018; Walpole 2003).

As universities embark on widening access and ensuring equitable success for all students, we need to look directly at the gap between the promises of higher education to provide social mobility and personal advantage and the reality of its role in cementing social place and status (Clegg 2011). This means we need to reflect far more explicitly on the ways in which we might assume that our students already have certain literacy practices in place or what we can do to better enable access to these. Even more importantly, we need to reflect on why it is that students do not always do what we would like them to be able to do, and we need to be much more rigorously critical of the 'remedial' measures we put in place.

The social account of reading and writing we have provided here requires more than attempting to increase reading speed using computer-based programmes offered in 'reading labs' or instruction in the grammar and syntax of the language of learning and teaching. Such measures reduce the practices of reading and writing to their 'technical' aspects and ignore the social dimensions which are much trickier to address.

What we have tried to argue in this section therefore is that, while a basic competence in the language of instruction is indeed a prerequisite to quality higher education study, the dominant understanding of the 'language problem' is an incomplete and simplistic account of student difficulties in mastering academic literacies. To write a laboratory report successfully in Chemistry or an essay in Political Science or a case brief in Law is largely about understanding the disciplinary concepts, values and norms from which the particular language practices manifest.

There is thus a limited relationship between the language practices expected in the academy and the medium of instruction being used. Taking on the literacy practices of a discipline will be difficult for all students, regardless of their home language, but it will be especially a challenge for students whose prior experiences of literacy practices in any language have little in common with those being expected of them in the university. This is not to undermine the intricacies of learning in a language that is not one's home language; rather it is to disrupt some of the more simplistic understandings of this challenge. If students are battling to acquire the literacy practices of the discipline, having those literacy practices presented in another language of teaching and learning will not make this challenge go away. The understanding of language as simply a technical endeavour remained dominant throughout the T_2 to T_3 period under study.

However, having one's home language valued in the academy is about far more than easier access to knowledge practices. It is about identity and self-worth too, an issue which has only in recent years come to receive serious consideration in the South African academy but is also relevant across the continent because of the multiplicity of languages spoken and the dominance of the colonial languages in higher education.

The language(s) we speak are integral to our identities. Frantz Fanon (1961) argued that language is fundamental to cultural revitalisation and the development of agency. He argued that, because language and identity are so entwined, being denied one's language will have significant effects on one's mental health. Students who do not hear their languages on campus, or even worse, hear them being dismissed, are clearly not going to feel welcome at university. They suffer what Miranda Fricker (2007, 2013) refers to as testimonial injustice, whereby their very identity is not recognised.

More recently, and in terms of the framework we are using in this book, and only towards the end of the period we have called 'T_2 to T_3', many universities in South Africa have finally moved away from 'English-only' or 'Afrikaans-only' policies. In some cases simultaneous translation of lectures had been introduced as a means of opening up the use of, say, Afrikaans, to those who do not speak the language. However, unless the translators are themselves disciplinary experts, it is unlikely that they will be able to draw on the literacy practices of a particular knowledge area in their translation.

Preferable is the increased use of translanguaging, which is beginning to be implemented in various spaces in universities although this tends to be dependent on the understanding and the willingness of individual academics to exercise their agency in this regard. Tutorials are being held in multiple languages, students are being encouraged to use a mix of languages in conversation with each other to enhance access to knowledge, and academics are seeking ways to use multilingualism as a resource for teaching. Increasingly, albeit very slowly, indigenous languages are also being used as formal languages of instruction and assessment. We have argued that such approaches will not be a panacea to the ways in which the literacy practices of the academy can serve to reinforce social structures. They will not make higher education learning instantly accessible to all, but they will serve as a powerful part of a much more complex move towards social justice in the academy.

Fixing the problem of academic literacy

Unfortunately, in many universities around the world, the complexities of the relationship between identity, language and academic literacy practices are poorly understood. There is little appreciation that there is no such thing as 'academic literacy' per se; rather there is the academic literacy of Philosophy, the academic literacy of Paediatric Medicine, the academic literacy of Political Studies, and so on. In many cases, the theory of academic literacy has been misappropriated to support the very model it was developed to contest. Thus, we hear of 'academic literacy courses' that are generically offered to students who come from widely disparate programmes. There is thus no understanding that the academic literacy practices to which students seek access emerge from the values and structure of the target field.

Oftentimes the 'teacher' in such a general 'academic literacy' course is not herself a member of the target field and so is highly unlikely to be able to demonstrate the requisite literacy practices. In such courses, students are taught about issues such as topic sentences and essay writing devoid of disciplinary content and context. In complete contrast to its meaning in the research from which the concept arose, 'academic literacy' is often simplistically understood as being about English language proficiency (Boughey 2013; Boughey & McKenna 2016). In the data we examined from the institutional audits, one university in South Africa, for example, indicated that it offers modules in Communication 'that focus on enhancing English literacy'. What on earth is English literacy? What are the socially-embedded practices that are made explicit in such a course? Is it about becoming 'English' and learning how to make a decent cup of tea?

It is also worth observing that where such courses are offered, they generally have high pass rates. Students are usually able to meet the requirements of language competence in discrete 'academic literacy' courses focused on language structure, but there is little acknowledgement that they continue to grapple with the 'language problem' back in their mainstream classes.

Common-sense understandings of language and academic practices are not unusual but they are dangerous. They allow institutions to believe that, simply with the 'right' set of neutral, generic and transferable skills, students should succeed. Despite consistent evidence that such common-sense interventions are not addressing students' need for epistemological access, Moyo's (2018) study on the use of state funding to enhance teaching and learning in South African universities found that these approaches remain the dominant way in which billions of rands made available for the purpose of development are being used.

Alongside generic academic literacy courses, another intervention aimed at addressing the 'language problem' involves Writing Centres, which have become features of many universities. The ways in which such centres are structured and the kind of work they do is very uneven, and there are ample examples of tensions between those working in Writing Centres who may be informed by socio-cultural theories and those academics who may rely on decontextualised understandings of learning and who then direct their students to the centres to get their language problems 'fixed'.

Frequently, Writing Centres are described as supporting students across disciplines, with an assumption that writing is generic across disciplines, that it can be developed through instruction from non-disciplinary members, and that the curriculum itself requires no change. For example, in one institution in our study, the Writing Centre is said to 'identify, develop and support the literacies necessary for competency in writing', but one wonders if the tutors within such centres have themselves achieved the particular competencies required by the different disciplines. The plural of 'literacies' in this quotation is heartening as it seems to indicate an understanding that literacies arise not as a generic language structure but as discipline-specific practices emerging from particular ontological and epistemological positions. However, the idea of 'competency in writing' seems to indicate a notion that there is a standard form of academic writing that can be taught to students outside of the context in which it will be used.

There are alternative, more social understandings of the work of Writing Centres (see e.g. Archer & Richards 2011; Dison & Clarence 2017; Nichols 2011, 2016), where such structures work primarily to provide an audience for students – an audience that is probably not *au fait* with the literacy norms of the pertinent discipline but which has a strongly theorised understanding of how it is that literacies reflect particular sets of values. This audience can then ask questions of the novice writer that can assist them in becoming aware of the underpinning values and negotiating the concomitant literacy practices. These alternative approaches to the work of Writing Centres of necessity entail close relationships between the Writing Centre and the academics who have the disciplinary expertise and who assess the students' demonstration of this.

Other models of writing development such as Writing Intensive Courses, Writing Groups (Achadu et al. 2018; Thesen & Cooper 2013; Wilmot & McKenna 2018) and Writer-Respondent projects (Bharuthram & McKenna 2006, 2012) also engage with the development of writing in ways that acknowledge its social nature and its discipline specificity. Such approaches avoid notions of 'quick fix' whereby the student can improve their 'English' and learn a few academic skills and all will be well. Instead, such approaches are based on an understanding that knowledge practices need to be made accessible to students if they are to succeed and that the development of literacy takes lots of practice.

In sum then, the development of students' 'academic language' entails the acquisition of academic practices related to knowledge construction. Understanding language practices in the academy in theoretically informed ways is critical if development opportunities for students are to be made meaningful. What is not acceptable, given the enormity of the problems in our universities related to language and literacy, is a continued reliance on common-sense approaches.

Disadvantage as an explanation for failure

Thus far in this chapter, we have argued that the dominant understanding of students is one that is decontextualised from the contexts of students' lives and from the contexts of the universities. The dominant understanding of students is also simplistic in the ways in which language is seen to relate to such contextual issues. Another discourse dominant in higher education focuses on the notion of 'disadvantage' (see, e.g. Odhiambo 2016).

There is no doubt that there is a relationship between the structure of social class and access to and success in higher education. This is manifest in global data and in seeming unending efforts of governments across the world to 'widen access'. But in many countries, colonial history and issues of language make it difficult to distinguish the role of class from multiple other kinds of injustice, and indeed intersectionality studies suggest this is by definition an impossible task. In Rwanda, for example, we see examples of ethnicity continuing to manifest in the ways that class and educational access and success intersect (Russell & Carter 2018).

This chapter, using New Literacy Studies, has thus far argued that the ease with which students access the practices of the academy is in part related to the kinds of practices with which students have had prior experience, and in part related to how explicit the target practices are made through the course pedagogy. As long as our higher education system continues to privilege certain ways of being over others and does not make such ways of being explicit and readily accessible to all students, then social class will remain a major determinant of success.

When we speak of and act in relation to students, we often draw on discourses that construct them as deficient. Poor throughput and low graduation rates are seen to arise from a lack of student development. There is very little consideration that university structures and cultures might also have causal powers in this regard.

Schools, particularly those in rural areas, are described in the data related to the study underpinning this book as lacking facilities such as libraries and computer laboratories, which presents students with a 'legacy of disadvantage' of both 'poor English skills' and 'a lack of general knowledge'. The problems with the schooling sector cannot be underestimated in many countries across Africa, and the impact of poor schooling is clearly a major part of the complex issues faced in university teaching and learning. Many schools in South Africa are dysfunctional (Bloch 2009) and, despite a national curriculum, there is great variance in the everyday practices that are valued in different schools. The extent to which schooling systems are a causal factor in poor university throughput needs to be clearly acknowledged (Scott et al. 2007) although, as we will argue here, this idea also needs to be problematised.

Schools themselves are very different social contexts to universities and demand significantly different practices (Geisler 1994). Schools perform multiple functions and preparing students for university is only one of them, especially when we consider that only a small proportion of school leavers ever attend university in the case of the African continent (see, e.g. Darvas et al. 2017). While there is no doubt that some schools better prepare students for academic study than others, there are flaws in assuming that 'educational disadvantage' arises only from schooling. Social class and structural racism are also intricately linked to difficulties scholars experience at school and at university. The repeated identification of an 'articulation gap' between schools and institutions of higher education across our data, rather than between the university and students' wider social contexts, speaks to a particular view of the university as an unmovable social structure.

The effect is that as long as the university focuses on the claim that it is schooling's responsibility to prepare students for tertiary study, it is able to absolve itself of the need to identify and then make overt its own practices. The focus on the 'disadvantaged school' might therefore at times be indicative of unwillingness, on the part of the university, to reflect on what it means to teach and learn for epistemological access in higher education. Regardless of the types of programmes offered, the construction of students as deficient and 'disadvantaged' will impact on the type of teaching- and learning-related events which emerge in the university and on the experiences of both students and staff as they engage with those events.

One of the main ways in which the higher education sector has attempted to address the issue of disadvantage in higher education in South Africa has been through the implementation of Extended Programmes with an Integrated Foundation Phase. This DHET initiative has provided funding for an additional year of study, with the result that a three-year degree, for example, is stretched over four years. The additional year of study allows students to engage with extra developmental courses which do not count towards the credits needed for the qualification itself but which are intended to support students so that they are able to engage with the learning it requires.

The 'problem' is thus often understood to be inherent in the student who needs remedial support. This absolves those working in the 'mainstream' curriculum from having to make any changes to their pedagogy or content. This is exacerbated when the foundation work is undertaken outside the disciplines by lecturers who are not themselves active members of the target discipline.

When there are parallel routes, with some students being admitted into a 'mainstream' programme which in principle can be completed in a year less (even if in practice it very rarely is) and others being admitted into an extended programme which requires an additional year to complete, we also have the perfect set-up for a space of 'othering'. Such parallel programmes are underpinned by an assumption that those who are in the 'mainstream' programme are not in any need of the support offered to those in the extended programme, who are therefore 'deficient' in some way. We pick up the issue of Extended Curriculum Programmes in more detail in the chapter on curricula that follows.

What we have tried to show here is that a set of ideas that we have termed the discourse of the Decontextualised Learner has had a profound effect on what emerges in response to the need for both more access to and success in our universities. In terms of the framework we are using to organise this book, the discourse intersects with other mechanisms (including funding) to lead to the emergence of courses (that might be add-on generic skills courses) and experiences (e.g. perceptions of some students as inferior to others) which do not serve the system or the students within it very well.

The university as a neutral space

Yet another feature of the discourses constructing students that we are examining in this chapter is the absenting of the university's history, ethos and values. Had a social account of students been more evident, this would of necessity have raised questions about how the university values some ways of being over others.

One of the main benefits of the discourse of the Decontextualised Learner is that it allows institutions to understand learning as being autonomous of context. In the research which underpins this book, we found that learning is indeed primarily understood as a set of neutral skills, separate from history and culture. Skills such as note-taking, study skills and time-management skills, when coupled with specific decontextualised attributes in the student, such as motivation and potential, were seen to lead to educational success.

In the understanding of learning as a set of skills or competencies which are a-social, a-cultural and a-political, learning is understood to be open to all, provided that the individual exercises the agency to learn.

So dominant were these understandings constructing learning as dependent on factors inherent in the individual that the learning process was almost exclusively described in neutral ways entirely unrelated to the vast inequalities that surround us. If one understands that there are many ways of knowing and that knowledge itself is differentiated (as will be discussed further in Chapter Five), then learning cannot be seen to be neutral and decontextualised. Instead, learning and teaching are understood to be socially constructed, with academics teaching towards particular ways of knowing. This understanding recognises that there are multiple mechanisms from which such ways of knowing emerge.

All universities have clear data providing the demographic details of their students and their success rates and so on. And yet most institutional documents that we reviewed were silent on macro-level structures such as race and how this correlates with student success more broadly and their own institution more specifically. Racially-differentiated pass rates and other inequalities have not to date been widely used as the basis for deep reflection on transformation of curriculum or pedagogy. Such blind spots make it possible for some academics, even those who understand themselves as activists strongly committed to broadening access, to ignore their own role in maintaining the status quo through teaching in ways that constrain epistemological access. Arguments many academics make for change at a macro level in the higher education sector are rarely tied to micro-level practices such as the ways in which students are given feedback on assignments or are supported in developing their writing.

Understanding learning as socially embedded, as a cultural phenomenon, brings a different perspective to bear on the way in which institutional identity is conceptualised and the understanding of how it is experienced by students. The culture of the institution, the ethos of the university if you will, is an integral part of a social understanding of teaching and learning. The notion of a 'culture of learning' was at times invoked in the institutional documentation we examined, but this was largely to do with ensuring the physical environment was safe and clean and otherwise conducive to learning. Given the reality that many universities are unable to provide safe, clean environments conducive to learning (Soudien et al. 2008), concerns about such aspects of a 'culture of learning' are legitimate. However, in other examples, the term 'culture of learning' was used to refer to students' 'lack of work ethic', with institutions noting that they needed to develop a 'culture of learning' on campus in order to improve success rates. When the term 'culture of learning' is used to refer to a lack of effort on the part of students, there is little consideration of the ways in which academic institutions are themselves redolent with cultures of learning in ways which are not apparent to students.

One result of this failure to acknowledge that teaching and learning are socially, culturally and politically situated is students' feelings of alienation from the institutions in which they are studying. The identification of the discourse of the Decontextualised Learner along with the use of our framework allows us to explain these experiences which emerge from events (classes, assessments, requirements to write and so on) that themselves have emerged as a result of the interplay of the discourse with other mechanisms at the level of the Real.

The 2015 and 2016 South African student protests at T_4 have made it impossible to discuss the institution in ways that suggest a socio-political neutrality. But this is not to say we have yet made sense of how institutional cultures are maintained and practised. We have yet to fully grapple with the 'political dynamics of power that define the knowledge making project' (Kumalo 2021: 1). Nor have we grappled sufficiently with which aspects of these cultures are necessary for universities to be spaces of powerful knowledge-creation and which aspects are the vestiges of our colonial history.

In an understanding of the university as a cultural, social, political space, we begin to ask questions of our values and practices that were silenced before. In our teaching and interactions with students we begin to consider more carefully what inclusion looks like. As Jenni Case (2016: 31) has argued:

Who asks questions in class, and how can you shift these dynamics? Who comes to you after class to ask for help and how do you signal your availability? What happens when you get students to work in groups – how do you disrupt the patterns of dominance and submission that are too easily read off of society's rules? We can have a well-thought-through curriculum structure but if this doesn't reach down to an inclusive pedagogy and upwards to a welcoming institution, then it will not meet its intentions.

Thus far we have discussed the dominant construction of the student, that of the Decontextualised Learner, which absolves institutions from placing a critical spotlight on our institutional cultures, curriculum structures and pedagogical practices. But there is another conception of the student which we have noticed becoming increasingly prevalent and to which we now turn. This is premised on the notion of the university as a business and, in such a conception, the student as a client. Like the discourses we have identified above, this also serves to lead to the emergence of events and experiences which need to be opened to critique.

Students as clients

It is increasingly common for students to be referred to as 'clients' or 'customers'. This is perhaps unsurprising in the context of universities being understood as training grounds for the knowledge economy (Allais 2007, 2014; see also Chapter Three). In this understanding, students pay fees in order to get access to private goods that will enhance their social mobility. These private goods include knowledge, access to social networks and workplace skills. As we have also indicated in Chapter Three, the construction of higher education as a private good has allowed for reductions in state spending and an increase in tuition fees. This can then even allow for action, on the part of governments, to 'protect' students as consumers. In the United Kingdom, for example, a steep rise in tuition fees eventually led to establishment of an Office for Students (OfS), described as an 'independent regulator', which aims to ensure that every student, whatever their background, has 'a fulfilling experience of higher education that enriches their lives and careers' (Office for Students 2020). According to its website,[3] the existence of the Office is prompted by a discourse around value on returns since:

> Students invest significant time and money in their studies. Undergraduate and postgraduate courses involve commitments of several years. Many students take out substantial loans, to be repaid when they graduate and earn over certain limits. They need to know that their investment of time and money is worth it.

The construction of the student as a client complements a broader conception of the university as a 'technical institution' (Graham 2013) following a neoliberal agenda of feeding the market. This kind of framing of the university has ethical implications (Nash 2013). If students are 'customers', then the product for which they are paying can be considered in terms of its 'exchange value' (Harley 2017; Holloway 2010). In this framing, the certificate students achieve must be able to be exchanged for more than the original investment paid by the 'customer'. The exchange value might include having access to jobs that are more

---

3   https://www.officeforstudents.org.uk/about/our-strategy/why-we-do-it/

73

financially rewarding and allow greater degrees of autonomy than those available to those 'customers' who have not invested in tertiary education. In fact, in the context of high unemployment, the exchange value of a qualification may include access to employment of any kind. It is very difficult to counter this framing of higher education in such exchange-value ways, given most students' need for financial security and social mobility, but we would argue that the focus on the 'exchange value' of higher education, emerging from the discursive conception of students as customers, significantly narrows the 'use value' of higher education. In our

work, we found that constructing students as customers or clients who have paid for a service limits understandings of the student as critical citizen and fledgling scholar.

The implications of the 'student as customer' discourse are enormous and impact on the very purpose of higher education. The incursion of the discourse very quickly has pedagogical effects. If universities begin to construct students as clients and customers, it will be tempting to avoid offering courses that challenge students' worldviews. It will be tempting to avoid courses that are not of immediate relevance to the workplace. It is another step in the move to packaging knowledge as a product to be sold in the university marketplace.

This move was already evident in how student feedback was being understood and used in many universities across our data. In a few universities, our research showed that student feedback was being used to measure the performance of academics, thus suggesting that student satisfaction was a goal in the business sense whereby the customer is always right. Moreover, if we return to the framework underpinning this book, we can see that students' feedback, comprising their observations and experiences of teaching, is located at the level of the Empirical. While eliciting students' opinions is very important, we need to remember that what they say emerges from mechanisms located at the level of the Real. Treating what students say as 'truth' can therefore lead to a failure to explore how what they say emerges from the interplay of numerous mechanisms (Luckett 2007). As a result, some of the reasons for their dissatisfaction or unhappiness can go unaddressed.

Sadly, few institutions have policies on feedback which sufficiently acknowledge the need to triangulate information from different sources when making changes to the curriculum and to teaching. Perhaps even more worryingly, in the context of this chapter, few institutions have policies on the use of student feedback which allow academics to 'talk back' to what their students are saying from their positions as experts in the disciplines in which they were employed to teach. This has the potential to stymie innovation and to block change. Even more importantly, the practices related to privileging the student as customer can leave academics and other members of staff who are experienced and knowledgeable in their areas of work feeling disempowered and 'deskilled' as they are challenged by students who are only in the university for a short period of time and who actually understand very little about the nature of a university or academic work.

The use of a business (rather than academic) construction of quality is troubling, and emerges where the students are indeed clients and it is not the success of their educational journey that is monitored but the degree of their customer satisfaction. This sort of discursive construction of the student is resisted in much of the higher education literature (see, e.g. Badat 2016) but was evident in a number of institutional documents. In one institution, support for students related to registration, finance and even careers is offered under the auspices of a 'Student Service Centre' which is 'committed to client service excellence'.

This more recent emergence of the discourse of the student as customer is complementary to the Decontextualised Learner discourse that has been evident for decades. These various conceptions all allow the university to be constructed as a neutral space and to place deliberations about knowledge, power and identity in a blind spot.

With students positioned as passive and decontextualised learners, teaching is then discursively constructed as dissemination. Teachers, in this understanding, have the knowledge, and the purpose of their teaching is its transmission to students. Teaching is then constructed around a set of discourses involving the idea of 'getting the knowledge across' to students. This understanding is reinforced by the neoliberal constructions of education discussed in Chapter Three, which propose that the purpose of education is the transmission of skills and knowledge for a competitive labour market. Thankfully, alternative constructions of universities and students were also in evidence in the data, as we shall now see.

Students as social beings, the university as a social space

Thus far, we have focused on the dominance of the 'Decontextualised Learner' discourse, with a quick look at the emerging 'Student as Customer' discourse, and the implications of such discourses for teaching. But, of course, these are not the only understandings of students being drawn upon in our universities. We all draw on multiple and even conflicting discourses, and these have effects on what events and experiences emerge in the world. Reflecting back on our framework, we can see that the effects of such mechanisms can constrain or enable our agency but do not determine it. We have the power to resist structural and cultural conditioning; and, indeed, jostling for space in the data about students that we have grappled with over the years is a more sophisticated, theorised account of students and student learning, even if it has achieved little purchase and seems to repeatedly emerge and then quickly slip away (Niven 2012).

For example, in one institution's documentation examined in our research on institutional audits, in a section discussing the work of the Academic Development Centre, it was clear that teaching and learning were understood as deeply immersed in the socio-cultural context, and not as the neutral transmission of knowledge to a decontextualised individual. But the potential impact of the centre on teaching and learning was uncertain, given the existence of contrasting discourses across the bulk of the report. Within this same document, a section on 'Student Support Services' clearly drew on the Decontextualised Learner discourse and seemed to work against the impact of the Academic Development Centre. The report goes on to explain that student success is vested within the individual, who simply needs 'more effective study techniques'. Clearly, different stakeholders in the university were drawing on very different understandings to tackle the common concern of improving undergraduate pass rates.

In another institutional report, there was an explicit calling on the social context of the university and that of students:

> In order to recognise both the diversity and cultural capital of such students, there is an argument that mainstream curricula need to change to cater for all students. This model would require strengthened and adjusted curricula and is best described as bringing academic development off the periphery and into the mainstream.

However, even here this more radical discourse appeared only briefly and was slipped into a text replete with instances of dominant Decontextualised Learner discourses at work. For example, the quotation above was preceded by the statement that 'recruitment and selection procedures need to focus on identifying academically excellent students from an ever-widening base of feeder schools'. Academic excellence, it seems, is understood as something separate from social and cultural capital. It is worth noting that the academic development work done in some universities is mostly focused on students through extended studies courses and add-on support initiatives. And where it is focused on staff, this often takes the form of 'tips for teachers' rather than providing challenging spaces for reflection (Quinn 2012). The extent to which academic development work can challenge the university more broadly is thus limited. We will return to the development of academic staff as teachers in Chapter Six of this book.

In South Africa, writers such as Vilakazi and Tema (1985) have long accused universities of implementing student development initiatives that constructed the problem as being vested in the student and which allowed the establishment to continue untransformed. Our deliberations here, emerging from our research over the years, thus sadly do not constitute a new conversation.

Foregrounding students' epistemological access

Understanding the student as a social being, the university as a social space and literacy practices as socially constructed has profound implications for teaching. In contrast to the notion of teaching as dissemination of knowledge, discussed earlier, in a social understanding, academic teachers are not simply imparting knowledge, but rather they are inducting students into the norms and values, and the emergent knowledge-making and literacy practices, of the field. Each field inhabits different norms and values, and is geared towards producing different forms of knowledge for different purposes, and, as a result, different sets of academic literacy practices emerge. Thus, we have 'academic literacies' rather than a unitary 'academic literacy'. Teaching with this understanding requires a high degree of critical reflection on the norms and values of the field, and on teaching in ways that make these explicit to the student. This is what Morrow (2009) refers to when he argues that teaching is about supporting 'epistemological access'; that is, teaching in order to enhance the possibility for access to the disciplinary ways of making knowledge.

It is thus possible to turn the idea of teaching as an act of knowledge dissemination on its head and to argue that all acts of teaching at universities are about teaching students how to construct academic knowledge regardless of the level at which the teaching takes place and regardless of the innovation in that teaching.

Teaching students about the main theories in Sociology 101, for example, serves to map out the disciplinary terrain and induct students into an understanding of how knowledge is structured. Students are then tasked with using a quotation or reading from this map to write an assignment. This entails their taking a position and arguing for that position through a series of claims and evidence. What constitutes credible evidence might not be immediately obvious to the student, nor might the very notion of 'giving an opinion' or 'taking a critical stance'. But as they write the assignment, students are effectively taking the first steps in learning how to construct academic knowledge. In a Chemistry laboratory, students are being expected to take on a different set of literacy practices such as careful observation, meticulous documentation of steps in experimentation and so on. They are then expected to draw on the theory they have learned in lectures and from textbooks to make claims about what happened in experiments, each of which is backed up by the data they have collected in the reports they write on 'practicals'.

The pedagogical consequences of such an ideological understanding that language use is deeply embedded in the values and knowledge structures of the field are multiple. To begin with, it requires teaching that provides an explicit scaffolded induction into such language practices, which can be quite a challenge for the academics for whom these practices are often so normalised as to be invisible (Jacobs 2007, 2013). We need to be able to make what has become familiar to us strange so that we can point out to students how language practices work within our fields. This has significant implications for academic development, because practitioners in the field usually tasked with the job of teaching at foundation level or running additional tutorials might not themselves be familiar with the norms and values and emergent literacy practices of the field.

Induction into the target knowledge practices also entails providing multiple opportunities to practise the relevant manifestations. Depending on the literacy practices valued in the discipline, this could entail frequent chances for students to give presentations, design models, or paint artworks, but by far the most common will be regular opportunities to produce the form of writing expected in the discipline. Students not only need regular scaffolded opportunities to take on the discipline-specific writing practices, but they also need to be given the kind of formative feedback that inducts students into these 'ways of being'. This is a challenge in the context of large classes and heavy teaching loads.

It is easy to see the allure of constructing the 'language problem' as being related to sentence structure and punctuation and understanding reading and writing as a technical act. Such simplistic understandings allow for a solution to be provided separately from the mainstream curriculum in the form of add-on classes. Within an ideological understanding of language, on the other hand, developing the ability to read, write and speak in the ways required by the field now becomes something to be attended to within mainstream classes.

For decades now, so called 'language specialists' have been employed in universities to fix students' 'language problems' in add-on initiatives in South Africa (McKenna 2004a) and elsewhere, such as Namibia (Mungungu-Shipale 2016), Tanzania (Nyinondi, Mhandeni & Mohamed 2016) and Nigeria (Ndimele 2016). Addressing students' language-related experiences outside the mainstream classes allows universities to carry on without disruption. In many respects, this can be seen to be a self-serving industry. It provides employment for many people who might not otherwise be employable in universities given that they are not knowledge producers or experts within a university discipline or field. Such people are often employed on short-term contracts against earmarked funding (Boughey 2012a; CHE 2016; McKenna 2012a). Many do not see it as in their interest to pursue further qualifications, which would involve engaging with theory in more depth, given the precarious nature of their employment. As a result, practices which have been shown to have emerged from 'faulty' and un-interrogated understandings of students' experiences continue to proliferate. This situation is not helped by the fact that many of those appointed to powerful positions with the responsibility for 'managing' teaching and learning often do not themselves have a background in higher education studies or teaching and learning, and therefore they continue to draw on common-sense understandings as a basis for the initiatives they choose to promote (Moyo 2018).

As we have argued, 'Academic Literacy' courses that offer generic language skills; 'banal life skills courses' (Ginsberg 2011) that offer lessons on time-management and note-taking; and those kinds of Writing Centres that are set up to 'fix students' English' can all be seen to work in complementarity with the discourse of the Decontextualised Learner. Such initiatives are often presented as being 'transformational' in that they provide support for disadvantaged students, but rather than addressing the problems of high student failure and differentiated success rates, such interventions may actually exacerbate them. The common-sense discourses related to language and learning that underpin these structures work to further disempower students by pathologising them, while leaving the university and the disciplines within it beyond critique.

The social understanding that language use in the university manifests as field-specific literacy practices emerging from specific historical, cultural and political contexts has implications that go beyond the *how* of teaching and learning to raise questions about the *who* of teaching and learning. As we have argued, given the centrality of values and beliefs to the development of language practices, taking on the range of literacy practices expected for success can often involve profound shifts at the level of identity (Luckett & Luckett 2009). Students entering higher education will need to figure out the context and acquire the values and attitudes towards what can count as knowledge before they can truly engage with these practices (Case et al. 2018)

Perhaps even more importantly, teaching based on this understanding involves acknowledging that the shifts required of young people as they enter our universities can be enormously destabilising and can even lead to anxiety and depression. From this perspective, learning is not simply a cognitive activity but rather involves the entire being. Making sense of the context often falls into what is known as the 'hidden curriculum' (McKenna 2010), and this process can be enormously confusing and alienating for students (De Kadt & Mathonsi 2003; Luescher et al. 2020). Furthermore, because these literacy practices have been normalised for the academics steeped in the discipline, they might make judgements as to the students' intellectual capacity on the basis of whether the students have been able to crack the code.

The process of taking on the academy's literacy practices is often difficult at the level of student identity because the 'code' of target literacy practices is unspoken. It is difficult for academics to articulate this code and so it can easily be seen to be beyond question. It is very difficult to open up to critique that which you are barely aware of. It is only when the nature of the discipline-specific practices is made explicit, and access is scaffolded through multiple opportunities for engagement, that the underpinning values are exposed and are subject to critique. This has consequences for the decoloniality debate.

As we take on the responsibility for facilitating epistemological access, we need to question why certain practices are privileged in our lecture halls and examination processes while others are dismissed or ignored. And herein lies a tension that Janks (2000, 2009) calls the 'access paradox'. In scaffolding students' access to the dominant literacy practices of the discipline, we are reinforcing this dominance. In an age where we are raising questions about whose forms of knowledge are dominant and which knowledges are silenced (an issue we unpack in more depth in the next chapter), teaching in ways that enhance access to disciplinary practices thus requires a simultaneous consideration of other ways of being and doing. We need to not only make the powerful ways of being and doing in our disciplines accessible to our students, we need to teach in ways that create spaces for critique of these.

Teaching for epistemological access entails an 'ethic of care' (Leibowitz & Bozalek 2015; Tronto 1994; Zembylas et al. 2014) whereby we take fully into account the affective nature of education. If we understand teaching as the process of making knowledge practices explicit and simultaneously making spaces for challenging them, and if we understand learning as acquiring powerful knowledge and becoming a particular kind of knower, then this means that teaching and learning are deeply entwined with issues of identity. Understanding this entails understanding our responsibility to genuinely 'see' our students and to care for them and for ourselves as we undertake the complex process of knowledge creation and acquisition. Being aware of the affective nature of identity issues related to knowledge practices is essential to assuring epistemic justice whereby students are given access to powerful knowledge (hermeneutic justice) and are attributed credibility (testimonial justice) (Fricker 2007).

This understanding that teaching for epistemological access entails an ethic of care is not to be confused with teaching only that which is familiar and safe. Teaching has to provide access to more than what we already know. We want to be sure that our students are able to know more and to know differently as a result of our teaching. This is not always going to be easy. If students are not encountering challenging concepts, then they are being denied epistemic justice. Zembylas (2015) writes of the need for a 'pedagogy of discomfort' within this 'ethic of care'. He suggests that discomforting feelings are important in challenging dominant beliefs and habits which sustain inequalities. Ashwin (2020) argues that the current fixation on the economic value of higher education qualifications has distorted the transformation potential of our universities. Discourses privileging the economic value of going to university constrain the possibilities of individual transformation. Such transformation, he argues, requires discomfort. Ashwin's observations are particularly significant in the context, for example, of calls for 'trigger warnings' to be placed on books in university libraries and the silencing of some speakers at public events. Without discomfort, we cannot experience either personal or social transformation.

Conclusion

Discourses are powerful mechanisms in the domain of culture and are extremely difficult to shift. This chapter has argued that discourses drawn on to conceptualise students generally fail to take the social nature of learning and higher education into account. The problem of high student failure is considered mainly in terms of deficits in the student that the university then attempts to address by providing remedial interventions.

The dominant discourses used in universities to talk about students and to understand learning are problematic and partial. Furthermore, these understandings lead universities to implement student-development initiatives that do not directly tackle the social nature of learning but instead sustain the institutional status quo. Consideration of political, economic and social structures must be central to any reasonable account of student failure, but we found little evidence of this in the data we examined for the purposes of the study underpinning this book. We have argued that there are different ways to understand students and learning, which will lead to different kinds of teaching events and, hopefully, more positive experiences of higher education.

Elsewhere, in an article that reported on the 'meta-analysis' research that underpins this book (Boughey & McKenna 2016), we argue that the result of the first cycle of institutional audits conducted by the HEQC in South Africa between 2004 and 2011 was enormous change in the structural system of universities. All the institutions that were audited implemented structural changes as a result of the work of the HEQC. Teaching and learning centres were established or strengthened and there was enormous activity in the field of institutional policy development. At the same time, key agents were appointed to 'manage' teaching and learning and oversee the quality assurance thereof. While there was thus change in relation to structure, the domain of culture did not shift very much. What we saw was stasis in the ideas used to account for student performance data and feedback. These accounts, in the form of the discourse of the Decontextualised Learner, simply will not allow us to make sense of data. Our recommendation was therefore that any future work done by the HEQC needed to focus on enriching the theoretical stockpot of ideas used to account for what we could see in the performance data.

The HEQC did indeed embark on a cycle of quality work that took the form of a Quality Enhancement Project (QEP). The extent to which it stimulated different kinds of thinking about our students and what they achieve has yet to be researched. Our sense, having attended many of the events that were included in the project, is that this was not the case and that instead the reflections relied on a-theoretical notions of 'best practice'.

In many respects, this chapter is an attempt to challenge dominant discourses and enrich the theoretical stockpot by positing other ways of thinking about students and what happens to them in our universities. This depends on how the way we talk about students leads to things we do to students, to observations we make about them and in turn to the ways they experience higher education. The framework we have used for this book assigns power to every individual to choose from which mechanisms they will draw to pursue projects and concerns of their own. Those who are concerned with students and the way they experience higher education have the agency to consider the alternative constructions we have offered in this chapter.

5

Reconceptualising curriculum, structuring access

What is curriculum?

In the previous chapter, we looked at the ways in which social understandings of students and of student learning are frequently set aside in favour of decontextualised accounts. If students are often constructed in a-social, a-cultural ways, then what of the curriculum? This chapter engages with a number of issues pertaining to curricula in our universities.

Using the Social Realist framework that underpins this book, we try to show that we do not have complete freedom to do as we like when we design a curriculum. Our curricula are constrained and enabled by multiple structural and cultural mechanisms, which we attempt to outline in this chapter. But the curriculum is not entirely determined by such mechanisms. We are not powerless to bring about change. We do, however, need to have a nuanced understanding of the constraining and enabling mechanisms at play if we want sustainable and sound curriculum development.

Curriculum is a contested concept (Mamdani 2017; Muller 2009; Maton 2014) and is used in multiple ways in the literature. For some, curriculum means the syllabus, a description of course content. For others, curriculum is the structure of the programme, the details of how courses fit together and where credits are attained. In this chapter, we argue for a far broader conception than is offered by these definitions. We argue that the curriculum is the means whereby the 'goods' of the university, both public and private, are distributed.

Understanding the curriculum as a means of distributing 'goods' is particularly important in contexts where a qualification from an institution of higher education is often understood as a means of lifting an entire family, or even community, out of poverty. A curriculum distributes access to the kinds of learning experiences which will lead to the award of the qualification, and the qualification can be key to social mobility. At the same time, in countries with enormous disparities of every kind, the curriculum can distribute access to some kinds of knowing over others. It is perfectly possible for a curriculum to ignore the public good that can accrue from engaging with it by, for example, eliding all engagement with inequality.

Curriculum is 'the process of engagement of students and staff with knowledge, behaviour and identity in different disciplinary contexts' (Lange 2017: 32). It is thus understood as encompassing the what, the who, the how, and the where of teaching and learning. It includes both the planned curriculum and the enacted one. If we are to interrogate the form and function of the university in a meaningful way, we need to take all of these aspects into account.

In this understanding, curriculum comprises not just the subjects in a qualification, but all the aspects that make up a programme of learning. This includes consideration of what topics are being taught and what texts are being drawn on to tackle these topics. It also includes questions about who does the teaching, who does the learning, how the classroom is set out, who does the speaking in class, what behaviours, including reading and writing practices, are permitted and which are seen as inappropriate, and so on. In addition, it acknowledges that learning can happen outside the formally-planned curriculum, and that conversations in residences and experiences on the sports field also have consequences for student learning. And, as was argued in the previous chapter, this understanding of curriculum entails understanding students not just as a collection of the skills and attributes they bring into the university, but as people with rich histories, languages, norms and values, which may be more or less welcomed into the cultures and structures of our lecture halls, laboratories and libraries.

It is within this broad framing of curriculum that we have come in our own research to draw on the work of Maton (2014) to ask three key questions:

1. What knowledge is legitimated by the curriculum?
2. Which knowers are legitimated by the curriculum?
3. How are these knowledges and knowers legitimated in the curriculum?

These questions draw on an understanding that a curriculum is never neutral. It comprises choices of selection (what to include or exclude, who to include and exclude), choices of sequencing (what is foundational and what is elective, which concepts are prerequisite to others, and so on) and choices of pacing (how much time should be spent on what, in class and in assessment) (Bernstein 1981, 2000). Such choices are not made in a vacuum; they materialise from the histories of our societies, our disciplines, our professions, our universities, and ourselves as curriculum developers. Curriculum design thus emerges from multiple mechanisms, which results in it never looking identical across contexts, even in cases where the content may be relatively uncontentious. Mathematics 101 will be taught differently in Georgia and in Ghana. The style of teaching and the modes of assessment may vary even if there is general agreement as to what foundational mathematical concepts should be included in a first-year curriculum.

South Africa was one of the 'early starter' (Allais 2010) or 'first generation' (Tuck 2007) countries that worked towards developing a national qualifications framework. As we write, Kenya has developed a national framework, and a number of initiatives are afoot aimed at the development of regional frameworks on the continent. As we have noted in the section on curriculum in Chapter Three, a qualifications framework allows qualifications to be pegged at a number of levels using the constructs of the learning outcome and learning credit. The introduction of a qualifications framework requires those developing curricula to develop an understanding of the concepts that are used to make it work and the ability to craft outcomes for programmes which stipulate what it is that the successful learner will be able to do on completion and the assessment criteria that will be used to assess this.

However, such developments have the potential to be limited to changes in the structural domain. From national structures such as the CHE, SAQA and the NQF in South Africa, and similar bodies in other countries, through to institutional structures, such as the emergence of deans or deputy vice-chancellors of teaching and learning, teaching and learning centres and committees and so on, a great number of structural developments related to teaching and learning are put in place as a framework is developed. In contrast to this, however, we would argue that ideological deliberations about curriculum (in the domain of culture) have not occurred to any meaningful extent until very recently, most notably as a result of the student protests. Importantly, in South Africa at least, the structural changes experienced did not broadly engender critical engagements about the nature of knowledge itself. As Lange (2017: 33) argues:

> After the first decade of democracy, in the context of poor system throughput at undergraduate level, the preoccupation with teaching and learning policy moved to focus on the efficiency of teaching and learning, leaving out once again the engagement with knowledge from the agenda of work.

Key ideological questions have rarely provided the basis for discussions about curriculum, questions such as: How does the knowledge of the academy function as a public good? How is this knowledge made widely accessible? What purpose is this knowledge meant to serve? Whose knowledge is being validated? Whose knowledge is being excluded? It is our contention that we have to engage overtly with such questions in the domain of culture if the structural changes that have been implemented are to achieve their goals.

In this chapter, we reflect on the broader structural and cultural mechanisms conditioning curricula in South Africa, and how these have played out over the last two decades in the context of the introduction of the national qualifications framework. We begin with the issue of knowledge, an issue which we argue is ironically often absent in deliberations about curricula. To bring us back to the framework we have used throughout the book, this means we are asking about what happened during T_2 to T_3 and, more specifically, how the agents who were making changes to curricula were conditioned to make those changes as new policies were enacted.

The curriculum is conditioned by the structure of knowledge

Some disciplines and programmes, particularly those in the natural sciences, work more in the area of objective, empirical knowledge; others, more usually in the social sciences, are concerned with subjective, experiential knowledge. Yet others work with a fluid range of understandings of what can constitute knowledge and how it can be known. What is important, however, is that none are neutral; knowledge practices are always tied to the particular context of the discipline or programme. And, as discussed in the previous chapter, the literacy practices we expect of our students emerge in part from these contexts.

Across the natural sciences, humanities and social sciences, for example, the researcher is expected to develop an argument by making claims supported by evidence. Often, right across such fields, the evidence for the author's claims will be in the form of references to prior research. But the context of the field is key in determining which references would 'count' as credible forms of evidence for substantiating the author's claims. And the ways in which researchers from different fields draw on such references as evidence may differ fairly considerably too. In some cases, the researcher inserts the names of the authors she is citing – 'According to Mkhize (2017), ...' – whereas in others there might be a footnote numbering system to allow the reader to follow up on the credibility of the proffered evidence. This is more than a distinction of technical formatting. It speaks to the nature of the knowledge being produced and its relationship to the humans producing it. Sadly, generic workshops on referencing typically refer to the evils of plagiarism without making explicit the knowledge-production norms of the discipline (Mphahlele 2019; Mphahlele & McKenna 2019).

In some fields, the role of researchers in building the field and having to manage their subjectivity is hinted at through the inclusion of the names of those who have produced the research in the past. The subjectivity of knowledge produced in such fields is often made even more explicit through the use of the first person, as we discussed in the previous chapter, through sentences such as 'I then interviewed seven people from the Executive Committee'. In contrast to this, the objectivity valued in other fields may be symbolically indicated through the use of passive voice – '5ml were titrated' – or, where an active voice is used, through the anonymising of the researcher's identity – 'The researcher transcribed the surveys'. In this way, the claims are made in an objective manner seemingly untainted by human foibles of gender, class, nationality and so on. There are of course myriad other ways in which the different knowledge structures are manifested through different literacy practices, but what we see here in the example about referencing is that the disciplinary literacy practices are structured in very particular ways in line with the nature of truth and being (ontology), the means of producing knowledge (methodology) and the relationship between knowledge production and the researcher (epistemology).

There are various ways of categorising the kinds of knowledge validated within particular curricula, from the distinction between more objective and more subjective forms of knowledge, indicated above, to Biglan's (1973) concepts of 'hard' versus 'soft' and 'applied' versus 'pure' knowledges, and Kolb's (1981) 'abstract' versus 'concrete' and 'reflective' versus 'active' knowledges, and so on. In trying to make sense of the relationship between the curriculum, the disciplinary literacy practices, and the structure of knowledge, we have found the tools provided by Legitimation Code Theory (Maton 2014) to be especially generative. In particular, these tools address the knowledge blind spot of much of the sociology of education research by demanding that we attend directly to knowledge.

Legitimation Code Theory (LCT), as its name suggests, focuses on questions about what is legitimated in different fields. Having identified what is legitimated, it then becomes possible to ask questions about whose interests this legitimation serves. In order to do this, it draws on a premise that within different fields we use 'codes'. These codes validate specific forms of knowledge and specific types of knowers. It is not difficult to see how the possibility of identifying which different forms of knowledge and which types of knowers are legitimated is significant for widening access to higher education and, thus, to disciplinary knowledge.

LCT builds on both Bourdieu's (1990) argument that education reproduces social inequalities and Bernstein's work on the structure of different kinds of knowledge. In the academic arena, Bernstein (2006) showed that some disciplines can be considered to be hierarchical, that is, new knowledge builds on and subsumes prior knowledge, whereas other academic disciplines can be considered to be horizontal, that is, new theories emerge as new 'languages'[4] which sit alongside or overthrow prior languages. LCT allows us to look at how knowledge is built in different fields and provides various tools for doing so. By analysing what it is that is legitimated in a field, through LCT tools such as Specialisation, Semantics and Autonomy, we are able to make the processes of legitimation explicit and thereby enhance the likelihood of their acquisition. It is also through providing tools to crack the code of various disciplines, that LCT exposes such codes to critique.

LCT theorises that while every kind of knowledge has a particular structure, it also has a particular relation to the subject of the knowledge, the knower. So, it is not only *what* you know, it is *how* you know that counts. The extent of both the *what* and the *how* of knowing varies across fields. In some fields, legitimacy is achieved primarily through being a particular kind of knower, with a certain disposition and gaze on the world. Learning in such fields is largely about acquiring the appropriate gaze; for example, it may be that the gaze is one of social justice, or scepticism, or criticality, or feminism, or neoliberalism. But in other fields, the kind of knower you are is not particularly pertinent, and it is the relations to knowledge that dominate. Legitimacy in such fields is acquired through the demonstration of the knowledge, skills and practices of the field. Yet other fields may work with various other combinations of ways of relating to knowledge and ways of positioning knowers. Understanding how knowledge and knowers are structured within our curricula, Maton (2014) argues, is key to our being able to ensure access, to challenge dominant ideas and practices, and to transform the ways we teach and learn. We need to make sense of the nature of knowledge and knower if we are to understand the *what* and *how* of legitimation processes in our curricula, because these have significant implications for *who* gets to access the knowledge and be deemed a legitimate knower. A number of studies that we have supervised over the years have brought LCT tools to bear on curricula in various programmes and institutions and have looked at the ways in which particular

---

4   As we have already explained in Chapter One, one way of conceptualising a theory is that it functions like a pair of spectacles that allow us to see the world in a different way. Once we begin to use a theory, we need to take on its language, that is, we need to begin to use its specialist terms in order to describe what we can now see. This is what Bernstein means when he refers to 'languages' in the context of talking about knowledge structures.

forms of knowledge and particular kinds of knowers are legitimated. We briefly consider a few of these examples below.

Mlamuli Hlatshwayo (2019) looked at how knowledge is recontextualised from the Political Studies field into a curriculum in order to question where decolonisation can and should be undertaken. While much of the decolonisation debate has looked at the content of curricula, Hlatshwayo shows the need to interrogate the structure of the target knowledge and the extent to which it is a particular kind of knower that is legitimated within the curriculum. By explicating his process of undertaking such an interrogation, Hlatshwayo enables academics to construct curricula that are inclusive, open and socially just.

Thandeka Mkhize (2015) looked at the structure of the curriculum of the Certificate in the Theory of Accounting to question why so few black South African students qualify as chartered accountants. She showed that the basis of legitimacy in Accounting is primarily what is termed stronger 'epistemic relations', so the demonstration of legitimate knowledge, skills and practices is paramount, and there are very weak 'social relations', that is, the demonstration of having a particular gaze or way of being in the world is relatively unimportant. In LCT terms this means that Accounting is a 'knowledge code'. Mkhize goes on to argue that, because the structure of the target field is a knowledge code, this has constrained the focus in the classroom on the development of students as particular kinds of knowers. Her study suggests that the focus of legitimation in a heavily loaded, purportedly neutral, skills and knowledge curriculum has allowed an absenting of focus on the student and the development of privileged ways of knowing.

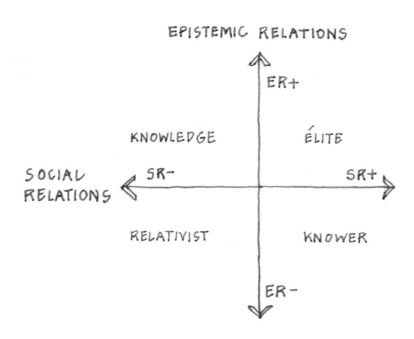

Karen Ellery (2016) looked at a Science access course and, similarly to Mkhize (2015), showed that, in spite of the focus on knowledge itself, being the 'right' kind of knower was also important to success. Ellery concluded that academics have to be able to undertake a rigorous analysis of what is being legitimated in our curricula if they are to provide students with access to powerful knowledge. LCT is thus useful not only for research but also as a tool whereby academics, for whom the discipline has often become obvious and familiar, can begin to articulate exactly what it is that is necessary for successful membership in the field.

Gabi de Bie (2017) looked at the merging of two subjects, Anatomy and Physiology, and showed how if curriculum developers do not have a strong understanding of the structure of the target knowledge, then curriculum decisions can be made for pragmatic reasons with troublesome educational consequences. Curriculum expertise is unevenly available across the sector but even in institutions where there has been a rich history of institutional autonomy and academics are steeped in the knowledge-making processes of the discipline, they may not have access to such expertise. Jacobs (2007, 2009) has argued that academic development practitioners may need to be supportive collaborators for academics in this regard.

Jacqui Lück (2014) used LCT to interrogate the Public Management degree and the Public Administration diploma. She found that there was an espoused concern with a particular kind of knower; this concern was expressed in the literature, in the workplace, and in her interviews with academics. This knower would be a public servant with a particular disposition and set of attributes, someone who would serve the public with compassion and with a focus on attaining fundamental human rights, someone who would be politically aware and understand the role of power in society. However, in what LCT refers to as a 'code clash', the curriculum was not focused on cultivating this kind of knower through developing this gaze; instead it was focused largely on the acquisition of a set of skills and practices unrelated to nurturing the target attributes. Lück found a clash between what was being called for by the public sector, which was a knower code, and what was being legitimated in the curriculum, which was a knowledge code.

Sherran Clarence (2014) used LCT to look at the teaching practices of both Political Science and Law in order to make sense of how students are given access to abstract and condensed knowledge in ways that allow for cumulative learning. She used the LCT concept of Semantic Waves to look at how students acquired the difficult ideas underpinning the fields of Political Science and Law. Semantic Waves entail a movement from knowledge that is context-bound, everyday, and not very dense, up towards concepts that are abstract, principled, and very dense in meaning, and then back down again. Clarence showed that unless connections are explicitly made between students' everyday experiences and the target abstract knowledge, then students can battle to engage with the knowledge of the discipline. She showed that focusing only on such everyday experiences would not allow access to the target abstracted knowledge – connections had to be made between these domains. Clarence also demonstrated the importance of connections being made between the various segments of the curriculum, which is fundamental to cumulative learning of the specialised knowledge of the academy. Unless students are shown how the various waves join up, they are unable to make the connections.

Anisa Vahed (2014) analysed the use of educational games and showed that while such activities readily increase student engagement (and student satisfaction), they will not necessarily enhance student learning if they are not aligned to the means of legitimation in the target field. Vahed argued that educational games (and other innovative pedagogies) have to align with and improve access to the particular structure of the target knowledges and knowers if they are to be effective as a means of enhancing learning and not just 'entertainment'. This is important because many pedagogical practices are advocated for implementation across fields as 'best practice' as if the structure of the target field is irrelevant and higher education practices are undifferentiated.

As with Vahed, Amanda Hlengwa (2013) concluded that pedagogical innovations are less likely to succeed if they fail to take the peculiarities of the specific knowledge and knower structures into account. Hlengwa researched service learning, a curriculated form of community engagement, which has been lauded as a means of connecting abstract academic knowledge to social concerns through engagement with communities. But she showed that this call for wide-scale implementation has at times failed to consider how academic knowledge differs considerably across fields (Hlengwa & McKenna 2017). Hlengwa does not argue that only certain fields should have service learning, but she clearly shows how the structure of the target knowledge and knowers can make it more straightforward in some fields than others.

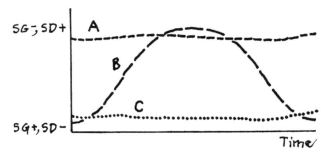

SG = SEMANTIC GRAVITY
SD = SEMANTIC DENSITY

THREE DIFFERENT SEMANTIC PROFILES:
A – A HIGH FLATLINE – COMPLEX, ABSTRACT AND UNRELATED TO CONTEXT
B – A SEMANTIC WAVE – MOVES FROM LESS TO MORE COMPLEX, ABSTRACT AND DECONTEXTUALISED, AND BACK AGAIN
C – A LOW FLATLINE – EVERYDAY, SIMPLE AND TIED TO CONTEXT

In these very roughly sketched examples of scholarly work using LCT, there is both a rejection of the understanding of knowledge as neutral and objective, separate from human concerns, and a rejection of knowledge as simply a replication of society's interests. In order to make the knowledges of our curricula more inclusive, we need to look directly at what knowledge is being legitimated, and we also need to understand that the specialised knowledge of the academy is itself a structure with its own powers. In these and many other studies, the understanding that our curricula are social and political, and that the literacy practices expected of our students are peculiar and cultural, is thus not left there. If such concerns were left there, it would be possible for academic knowledge to come to be 'perceived as being unable to make an epistemological claim to validity since it can only ever be an ideological device for maintaining positions of dominance' (Naidoo & Ranchod 2018). Combining the understanding that knowledge is social and represents specific interests with theoretical tools that focus on the structure of knowledge and knowers in the curricula has been a powerful means of critiquing the extent to which we enable social justice in our universities. We need to understand that knowledge is structured in part independently of how we acquire it, and knowledge fields differ in their internal coherence, their principles of cohesion, and their procedures for producing new knowledge (Young & Muller 2010: 15).

In all of our research, and that of our students, that looks at the nature of different forms of knowledge in different fields, there is an understanding that knowledge in the academy differs from knowledge outside it. The university, with its many different disciplines, subjects and programmes, attempts to engage with specialised knowledge in systematic ways. We now turn to this idea that academic knowledge in all of its disciplinary forms differs from everyday knowledge.

The curriculum provides access to powerful knowledge

Across all of the distinctions between disciplines and fields in our universities, what they (should) have in common is that they provide access to specialist knowledge. Specialist knowledge provides more than description; it provides explanations and it identifies principles and abstract concepts, and it is thus able to rise above the detailed specifics of context. It is therefore distinct from much everyday knowledge where principled explanations, for example, may simply not be available. We argue that this need to provide access to powerful, specialised knowledge[5] is an important conditioning mechanism in the design of a curriculum, and one which needs to be rigorously safeguarded. The knowledge offered by the university consists of 'specialised symbolic structures of explicit knowledge' (Bernstein 2000: 160) where meaning is integrated in cumulative ways rather than by its relevance to a specific context. Only through access to these integrated principles of meaning-making can students apply this knowledge to contextually-specific applications (Wheelahan 2009).

---

5   In this section, powerful academic knowledge is variously described as 'systematic', 'specialised', 'principled', 'theoretical', 'abstract' and 'conceptual'.

An example of one way of knowing which is not generally valued in the university is what we will call 'craft knowledge'. Woodworkers, for example, literally have the knowledge of how to work a particular piece of wood in their hands. They handle the wood, feel it, and examine its knots and whorls before they lift a tool to shape it. As they shape the wood, they continue to work with the wood in ways that are often not possible for them to articulate (Gamble 2001, 2014). Similarly, a football player may have expertise in kicking a ball in an arc into the goal. Being able to 'bend it like Beckham' might rely on a number of key laws of physics, but the footballer is unlikely to be able to articulate such laws, and is quite possibly unaware of them. While being a world-class craftsman or footballer and knowing how to perform these practices with sophistication is highly valued in the world, 'knowing' in this way is not seen to be academic knowing.

Academic knowledge is produced using rules about what can count as research and is evidence based. The process of producing academic knowledge is often discipline specific. Chemists, for example, draw on experimentation and anthropologists use ethnography involving close-up observation of people or groups of people. As we have shown, many of our students have used LCT to explicate exactly how different academic fields produce different forms of academic knowledge, but what the forms of academic knowledge have in common is that they are all specialised and underpinned by principles. While some forms of academic knowledge may have close ties to the 'real world' in which the knowledge will be used, and others will be more abstracted from that 'real world', all have in common that they are based on specialised principles and not simply context-based skills.

Arguments against the specialised nature of knowledge in the academy have come from many sources – from those with a strong skills discourse who expect the university to act as a training centre, to some decolonial scholars who see the removal of specialisation as the means to open the academy to other ways of knowing, to some postmodernists who argue that all knowledges are equally valid and who fail to distinguish between knowledge and reality.

This focus on the ways in which academic knowledge is specialised is not to say that knowledges outside of the academy should be ignored. Specialisation should never be a basis for denying respect or value to the non-specialist knowledge that people draw on.

> Specialist knowledge is 'powerless' in enabling someone to find their way about a house or city with which they are unfamiliar or helping a friend who has lost a child. The difference between specialised and non-specialised knowledge is a difference of purpose and ... a difference of structure; it is not a difference of value, except in relation to those purposes. (Young & Muller 2013b: 231)

We need to attend to the community and family capital that our students bring with them if they are to feel recognised in our universities and if the goods of the university are to be widely distributed and our students are to achieve full parity of participation (Fraser 1999, 2007). Indeed, we have repeatedly argued that key to access to the powerful knowledges of the academy is that connections are made between students' everyday knowledges and the specialised knowledge of the academy (Boughey 2002, 2007, 2012b; McKenna 2004a, 2004b, 2010, 2012b).

Recognising the specialist nature of knowledge of the academy is thus not a dismissal of other forms of knowledge, and nor is the awareness of the powerful nature of university knowledge a claim that the university is the only site of powerful knowledge. Specialised knowledge, which is able to transcend contexts and provide principled explanatory value, has been found in other places since the dawn of time. But our focus on the specialised, powerful knowledge in the academy is crucial, because any attempts at making higher education success more widely attainable that fail to take the abstract nature of such knowledge into account can have serious consequences for the students involved. Access to powerful knowledge is a matter of distributive social justice. Knowledge has to remain absolutely central to higher education (Ellery 2017; Shay et al. 2011; Wheelahan 2010; Young & Muller 2013a, 2013b), and we need to be cautious of limiting access to powerful theoretical knowledge out of a desire to broaden access.

The idea that the university serves to provide access to and steward 'powerful knowledge' is sometimes rejected because the idea of 'powerful knowledge' is conflated with the 'knowledge of the powerful' or the elite (Muller & Young 2014; Young 2007; Young & Muller 2013a, 2013b). Given our histories, it is unsurprising that many of the knowledges in the academy represent the concerns of the powerful and disregard those who have been marginalised. There is no doubt that the curriculum has been used 'as an ideological device for protecting privilege' (Naidoo & Ranchod 2018: 18). This has to change, as we will argue in more detail later, but critique of the 'knowledge of the powerful' should not be twisted into a call for the rejection of 'powerful knowledge', as complicated and contentious as the distinction may be.

There are a number of examples of attempts at making curricula more egalitarian that, to a greater or lesser extent, have served merely to reinforce social divides by undermining access to powerful knowledge. The focus on Competency-Based Education, and its cousin Outcomes-Based Education, across Africa and other parts of the Global South has largely been with a view to ensuring that access to higher education is made available to all and that graduates are given work-ready skills that enhance employability. These educational approaches look at the specific skills and processes that the graduate will need in the workplace and design the curriculum towards these (Millar 2014).

However, as Wheelahan (2010) and Jansen (Jansen 1998; Jansen & Christie 1999) argue, the focus on competencies and outcomes often denies access to more abstract, theoretical knowledge which is considered overly complex. In this way, well-meaning curriculum experiments focused on broadening access to 'useful' knowledge have served to reinforce social divides. They have reinforced divides between the Global North and Global South, because taking on these curriculum approaches is often a requirement for acquiring funding from agencies such as the World Bank. The thinking is that providing more 'practical' curricula focused on immediate context will be more accessible to learners, and will be more likely to address immediate social ills. Access to more abstract, principled knowledge is thus a desirable part of education in the Global North, but it is access to context-dependent knowledge that is the key focus of many curriculum experiments in the Global South.

Such experiments that carve away the powerful knowledge also reinforce social divides within a particular society. Middle-class students will, by virtue of their prior experiences, be more likely to access powerful theoretical and abstracted knowledge outside of any formal curriculum which is limited to immediate competencies in a specific context (McKenna & Quinn 2020; Wheelahan 2010). Thus, a curriculum that fails to provide access to powerful knowledge is likely to exclude working-class students from such knowledge more effectively than it will exclude middle-class students who will be able to access it through their home and other social contexts.

Ironically, the lack of access to more abstract theoretical knowledge limits the potential in places and amongst people where change and innovation is called for fervently. This is because theoretical knowledge allows us to imagine worlds that do not yet exist and to move beyond the contexts we know to those that the powerful knowledge allows us to imagine. Rata (2012, 2017) argues that access to such powerful knowledge is a precondition to education playing a role in building a democratic society.

Problem-Based Learning (PBL) is another example of a curriculum experiment that has in some places had the opposite effect from what was intended (Case 2011; Reddy 2011). The PBL curriculum is developed around specific problems that require students to draw from multiple disciplines to find solutions. It increases student engagement and enhances students' ability to move across disciplinary boundaries, and it makes clear the practical application of knowledge to real-world problems, all of which are clearly significant strengths.

However, in cases where a more radical version of PBL has been implemented whereby students are not first given access to a firm grounding in foundational theoretical knowledge, students can be seen to develop strong practical expertise in relation to specific problems without having access to the specialist principles underpinning such expertise. This then constrains their ability to tackle future problems.

All this means that we need to be vigilant about the ways in which seemingly progressive curriculum experiments intended to be more inclusive have sometimes disempowered the very students they were designed to serve. Wheelahan (2009, 2010, 2015) argues that theoretical, disciplinary knowledge must be placed at the centre of the curriculum, and that curriculum reforms that fail to do this will continue to exclude working-class students from access to powerful knowledge. Universities need to ensure that students gain access to the powerful specialised knowledges that are the 'goods' of the institution, and not just access to a set of outcomes deemed appropriate for the current workplace or to knowledge that is familiar and reinforces students' worldviews.

Arguing for the primacy of powerful knowledge in the curriculum is not to deny the ways in which social histories are implicated in determining whose knowledge is deemed powerful. As we will now move on to argue, looking at the role of social context in enabling or constraining curricula is central to social justice, but we urge curriculum developers addressing concerns about education replicating social privilege to do so in ways that firmly steward the right to powerful, specialised, principled knowledge.

The curriculum is conditioned by social context

Unlike teachers in schools with a national curriculum, university academics have fairly extensive agency to design their curricula, albeit conditioned by various mechanisms. One significant mechanism that conditions such agency is the location of universities in society. All through history, the structure and nature of the university has reflected the concerns of the society within which it has existed, and for most of its history this has been about serving the interests of the elite within that society.

Early universities were fairly explicitly tasked with reinforcing social divides (Graham 2013; Nussbaum 1998). They ensured that only an elite had access to the powerful, specialised knowledge offered within them. The early universities were deeply entwined with religious or state structures and functioned as important mechanisms of social control. From the Bayt al-Hikma in Iraq, to Al-Azhar University in Egypt, to the University of Karueein in Morocco, to the University of Bologna in Italy, early academies had deep ties to religious and state bodies in their form, function and funding, an observation that can sometimes be seen in their physical architecture as well as in the subjects they taught.

In the 16th and 17th centuries, universities became more secular, slowly separating from their religious agendas. At about the same time, new programmes more directly facing the material world began to be included in universities. The disdain for physical labour amongst the elite had previously meant that any subjects pertaining to practical work were seen to be distinctly beyond the role of the university, but as technological knowledge advanced and became more central to society, so it began to be seen as something worthy of serious study. Thus, it was that, by the 18th century, some forms of practical knowledge were introduced in universities. Gradually since then some practical fields, such as Architecture, Medicine, Engineering, and Law, have moved from just being tolerated in the academy to being accorded high status, and others such as Economics and Psychology have made a similar, though far more recent, move from the outskirts of the academy to the centre. Across this extensive time period, schisms began to appear between the Natural Sciences and Humanities (and their recent cousin the Social Sciences). The jostling for status between fields of study continues to this day.

Far more recent shifts to a so-called 'knowledge economy' have again brought major changes in the university. As we showed in Chapter Three, economic growth is increasingly premised on the notion of the reinvention of goods. Goods that may in the past have been sold primarily for their utility purposes, shoes for protection and warmth of the feet for example, are increasingly sold as personal branding, shoes as representing identity and lifestyle. This requires a constant reinvention of goods to ensure the consumer desires more and more of them. It has become abstract knowledge – in the case of our shoe example, knowledge of the anatomy and physiology of the foot and knowledge of psychology, marketing and sales, rather than the practical skill needed to sew a sole to an upper – that is in greatest demand in an era of hypercapitalism. Alongside this move, the Fourth Industrial Revolution has now brought with it a number of new fields of study as the lines between humans and technology blur and knowledge is seen to be a commodity that can drive such advances.

Out of the marketing, production and distribution of mass goods emerge major social and environmental ills. The ability to conceptualise and implement technology that pushes the boundaries of what we believe possible also brings social and environmental ills. These ills then need knowledgeable citizens to tackle them. As we develop the knowledge needed to produce more 'stuff' and to amplify the demand for it, so we create more and more problems of social inequality, unsustainability and pollution. Ironically, the university is tasked with attending to both.

The move to a knowledge economy has also led to demands for universities to accommodate a far bigger student body. As previously discussed, changes in the social order have driven demands for access by students from far more diverse social groupings. Whereas the university of the past primarily served the elite, in the second half of the 20th century, demands for equity around the world led to the university being conceptualised very differently. Obstructed by colonialism, such demands came later across Africa, with the issue of equity of access only really coming to the fore in the early 1990s in, for example, South Africa.

In Trow's classic 1973 article, which we drew on in Chapter One, he distinguishes between elite, mass and universal higher education. He argues that once participation reaches 15%, the system has shifted from elite to mass education. It is impossible to retain systems designed for a largely homogenous elite at this point and, most importantly, he argues that having a diverse student body requires fundamental shifts in the curriculum. As indicated in Chapter Three, participation in post-secondary education across Africa is less than 3% of the age cohort, by far the lowest participation rate in the world (Teferra & Altbach 2004).

In South Africa this figure is now about 22% (CHE 2020), with student numbers in public higher education rising from under half a million to a million in just over 20 years (with about a further 115 000 in private higher education institutions). South Africa has thus moved from a system deeply invested in furthering the interests of the elite, under apartheid, to a mass system which has to address the needs of a very diverse student body, and an increasingly diverse staff body. This shift happened faster in South Africa than elsewhere as the crumbling of apartheid brought particular moral imperatives to the broadening of access. It would, however, be a mistake of exceptionalism to think that the recent changes experienced in South African higher education are entirely peculiar to this context.

Massification is often understood to be about student numbers. Of course, increases in numbers have significant resource and other implications. The doubling of student numbers in our T_2 to T_3 period has placed enormous pressures on the South African higher education system. But, as Trow (1973) points out, the shift from elite to mass higher education is about far more than the need for bigger venues and more staff. Questions around what and who the university is for and how it should function are re-opened by these shifts.

Across Africa, as elsewhere, there has emerged a tension between conceptions of the university as a driver of economic growth and a provider of high skills for employability on the one hand, to the university as a socialising space for the development of critical citizens who can contribute to a sustainable and inclusive society on the other. Actually, such a crude dichotomy of conceptions of the university fails to illustrate the full spectrum of expectations placed on a massified university system or the various tensions between such conceptions. Understanding the multiple ways in which universities are conceptualised by society is necessary to understanding the constraints on curricula re-structuring.

A number of moves have been made towards ensuring wider access to the knowledges of our universities in response to the ways in which our curricula emerge from our (racist, sexist, classist, xenophobic) exclusionary histories. In this process of widening access, critical questions have been asked about how our curricula continue to privilege content that arises from the Global North and our reading lists reflect the power held by Western/white/male academics. This decoloniality lens has led not only to a critique of content; such deliberations are also opening discussions around the colonial vestiges of our pedagogical approaches, curriculum structures and forms of knowledge (Mignolo 2000; Ndlovu-Gatsheni 2013).

Organising a socially just curriculum has to begin with the 'present, existential, concrete situation reflecting the aspirations of the people' (Freire 1970: 95). Freire argued that as long as our education systems have no connection to our surroundings, they remain closed off from critique and change. Systems that are imported without regard to the knowledge and values of the context constitute 'cultural invasion, good intentions notwithstanding' (1970: 84). Nyerere (1967) argued that the education project across Africa was decidedly without good intentions; it had a deliberate agenda to replace traditional knowledge so that the population would accept their roles in a colonial society. This 'epistemic violence' (Spivak 1988) was central to the colonial project. Colonialism entailed more than ownership of physical resources and human labour; owning the occupied at the level of knowledge was fundamental to the project (Said 1978).

Moving from colonialism and apartheid to a just society has required us to look directly at issues of knowledge and power in the curriculum. We argue, though, that the focus on structural issues which has dominated much of the curriculum change so far (as discussed in Chapter Three) has not always brought with it a concern for such ideological deliberations in the realm of culture, though there have been repeated calls for this. In South Africa, for example, the 'Soudien Report' of 2008 stated that 'at the centre of epistemological transformation is curriculum reform – a reorientation away from the apartheid knowledge system, in which curriculum was used as a tool of exclusion, to a democratic curriculum that is inclusive of all human thought' (Soudien et al. 2008: 89).

Certain states, bodies, companies, organisations and institutions wield disproportionate power. The power struggles and the specific interests that always characterise codified knowledge led, in South Africa, to a curriculum that functioned as 'an ideological device for protecting privilege' (Naidoo & Ranchod 2018: 17). Recognising this means understanding that the curriculum must be 'transformed to reflect the lived experiences of African people, including recognition of their scholarly work which is often on the periphery' (Lange 2017: 10). There is much debate about how the knowledges in our universities can now be transformed in ways that address Western imperialism and the 'dissonance between a changing student population and universities stuck in a colonial frame both intellectually and aesthetically' (Lange 2017: 32). There have been calls to de-centre such knowledge and replace it with African indigenous knowledges, and there have been arguments that doing so will simply 're-colonise' such knowledges, which will remain at the margins and be associated with localised thinking.

While some insist that the only way to truly validate indigenous knowledge and indigenous ways of knowing is to replace what came before, others are clear that what is needed is to broaden our knowledge base by seeing the ways in which Western imperialism has limited our access to powerful knowledge from other sources. Challenging the dominance of Western knowledge in the curriculum is not just about introducing other knowledges, it is also about challenging 'the perception that legitimate knowledge can only be produced by the West, that Africans are incapable of knowledge production' (Shay & Mkhize 2018: 317).

But how can a plurality of worldviews get reconciled in our curricula? How do we overcome 'abyssal thinking', which normalises and privileges some forms of knowledge while rendering others invisible (De Sousa Santos 2007)? How do we challenge the 'knowledge of the powerful' such that we can make spaces for other ways of knowing – but in so doing still steward and safeguard 'powerful knowledge'? As we have argued thus far, powerful knowledge allows our students the means of making their way in the world and the means to imagine and contribute towards a better world, and this requires a move beyond everyday knowledge to abstract, principled knowledge. We have also cautioned that some curriculum experiments around the world designed to make a curriculum widely accessible have carved the powerful knowledge out of the curriculum, leaving the student only with highly context-dependent ways of knowing.

So how do we address head-on the ways in which the historical privileging of particular knowledges, thanks to the ways those with the power to contribute to curriculum change have been conditioned, has rendered other potentially powerful knowledges invisible? And how do we avoid, in the process, falling into a romanticism where knowledges from particular sources are, simply by virtue of that source, deemed valid? Or into a relativism where any form of knowledge is deemed equally legitimate in the academy? Our argument is that the academy has a social justice responsibility to give access to powerful, specialised knowledge that *differs* from the everyday knowledge available outside of it. But we have to acknowledge that our colonial histories have meant that there is a wealth of knowledge that has never been scrutinised for potential specialisation, or, to put it in other words, the academy's powerful knowledges have by and large been built only from the knowledge of the powerful.

Some of the current calls to decolonise the curriculum teeter on the edge of suggesting that everything of the past must go, as if the distinct disciplinary forms are simply political tools of oppression rather than emerging, at least in part, from epistemological differences related to powerful modes of thinking. Young (2013) cautions that the social justice agenda of entitlement to knowledge for all is being undermined by 'attacks on knowledge'. These attacks have led us into a 'post-truth era' where any form of knowledge is deemed equally legitimate and valuable regardless of the purpose to which the knowledge is being called, and where expertise and specialised powerful knowledge are dismissed as elitist.

Young (2013) argues that such attacks on powerful knowledge sometimes come from within the academy, and asks 'how do we explain that it is educationalists, mostly on the Left, those who support a more equal society in all spheres of life, who are so opposed to the idea of all ... being entitled to powerful knowledge?' (Young 2013: 112). He goes on to argue that achieving access to emancipatory knowledge is often challenging and alienating at first, and that attempts to ensure broad, critical access should not be thought to be a means of eliminating such complex challenges. In the interests of critiquing the blind spots of the powerful knowledge of the academy, we need to be careful that we do not deny access to powerful knowledge for many of our students.

We were recently told, for example, at a symposium that what is needed to broaden access is to 'remove the jargon' from our disciplines. While we would be the first to agree that there can be a pomposity to some academic endeavours, which needs to be firmly critiqued, the idea that the semantically-dense use of language in our fields can simply be rooted out is to misunderstand the ways in which the knowledge of the academy is powerful.

Specialised knowledge is produced within social contexts and this can leave its mark and can limit its scope, but the value of specialised knowledge has to be independent of such originating contexts. Without access to such powerful knowledge, our students will remain dependent on those who have it and will therefore not experience the freedom 'to think the unthinkable and the not yet thought' (Bernstein 2000: 187). 'Is this curriculum meaningful to my students?' must be balanced with the question, 'What meanings in the world does this curriculum give my students access to?' We need our curricula to provide access to meaning that is valued by our students, but we also need to ensure this allows them to make meaning in the world (Grant et al. 2018; Young 2013).

This focus on the need for specialised knowledge is therefore not to deny the 'masculinist, colonial bias of much knowledge production [which] leads to bad (social) science' (Clegg 2011: 100). But the critiques of such bias that could move us forward are often sunk under the myopic lens of particularly acute forms of standpoint theory, or vexatious forms of 'knower code' (Maton 2014), whereby it is argued that only members of a particular social group can ever access some knowledges, and indeed only those members have the right to do so. In this particular conception, truth becomes 'relativised to social group and made context dependent' (Clegg 2011: 100) and, as we have argued earlier, knowledge that is relative and tied down to a particular context neither is particularly powerful nor meets the criteria of specialised knowledge offered by the academy (though it may for a time enjoy some political currency).

Much of the critique of Western knowledge focuses on the humanities and social sciences, and is aimed at the ways in which the curriculum is designed to produce a 'rational' neoliberal individual cut off from the student's sense of self and the community capital they possess and value (Clegg 2011). The development of agency, which we have argued is so central to success in higher education, is constrained if the assumed goal is at odds with the ways of being which a student imagines as possible. Higher education has to develop students' capabilities as agents to 're-examine their valued ends … and reflect on what is of more or less ethical significance in the narrative investigation of other lives' (Walker 2008: 272). It is this point that the protests of 2015 and 2016 in South Africa brought home most forcibly, particularly given the personal testimonies provided by many protesters detailing their experiences of a loss of self-worth in their time at university.

This position requires an understanding of colonialism not as some historical project but rather as one implicated in the current world order. While the displacement of knowledges of the 'other' was absolutely central to the colonial project, the displacement processes continue to hold sway to this day (Kumalo 2021). Mbembe (2016: 30–31) shows the ties between colonialism and the current neoliberal agenda in our universities. He argues that the decolonising project needs to face directly the ways in which our universities are subject to a particular economic project in the so-called 'knowledge economy':

> universities today are large systems of authoritative control, standardization, gradation, accountancy, classification, credits and penalties. We need to decolonize the systems of access and management insofar as they have turned higher education into a marketable product, rated, bought and sold by standard units, measured, counted and reduced to staple equivalence by impersonal, mechanical tests and therefore readily subject to statistical consistency, with numerical standards and units. We have to decolonize this because it is deterring students and teachers from a free pursuit of knowledge. It is substituting this goal of free pursuit of knowledge for another, the pursuit of credits. It is replacing scientific capacity and addiction to study and inquiry by salesman-like proficiency.
>
> To decolonize means to reverse this tide of bureaucratization. Unfortunately, this is not what is happening … administrative staff carry greater pay and prestige than the rank of some senior lecturers … to decolonize implies breaking the cycle that tends to turn students into customers and consumers. These tendencies are inherent in an institution run in accordance with business principles: the students have become interested less and less in study and knowledge for its own sake and more and more in the material payoff, or utility, which their studies and degree have on the open market. In this system, the student becomes the consumer of vendible educational commodities, primarily courses credits, certifications and degrees. The task of the university from then on is to make them happy as customers.

Understanding coloniality as an ongoing project, revived in the form of neoliberalism, raises questions about the knowledge-production project of the academy, for the curriculum emerges largely from that project. For example, there is enormous profit in academic publishing, and many universities in the Global South cannot afford the subscription fees to various databases whereby academic knowledge is accessible at the cost of millions of rands per university every year. To see just how perverse this system is, one needs to understand that much of the research done on the Global South is via data collected here and then transposed to the Global North for analysis and publication in the same way in which gold and diamonds are taken in their raw form for turning into profitable final products in the North. Even where the data is analysed and written up in the Global South, we need to consider that the costs of the research process are then borne in the South, and the peer-review processes are undertaken without charge, but then after those in the Global South have 'completed all these stages of intellectual and other labour, the final products are sold back to us by the Global North in the form of books and journals' (McKenna 2017) which universities battle to afford. Access to powerful knowledge, so crucial to the curriculum, is thus constrained by the current world order in a number of ways. Academic publishing is but one example of hypercapitalism in the higher education sector.

Thus far in this chapter we have been arguing for the foregrounding of powerful knowledge in the academy while raising concerns about how colonialism (and its current embodiment, neoliberalism) have relegated certain forms of knowledge to the sidelines. There is undoubtedly a tension between re-centring knowledge and simultaneously asking questions about whose knowledge is legitimated (Shay & Mkhize 2018). There are no easy answers here, but there is a need for careful engagement with such tensions as we make decisions about the forms of curricula to implement.

Those working in universities are, of course, not entirely free to decide for themselves what kind of curricula to implement. As we have indicated, various mechanisms play a role in who teaches, who gets taught, what gets taught, when and how, and so on. The structure of our programmes is increasingly being conditioned by national accreditation and funding requirements as discussed in Chapter Three, and also, as discussed earlier in this chapter, the structure of the knowledge acts as a mechanism as to what needs to be taught, in what order, and how, and, furthermore, as has been discussed in this section, the curriculum is conditioned by the history of the society in which the university exists. Another significant mechanism is the university itself. We now turn to look at how institutional cultures and histories act as mechanisms that enable and constrain curriculum possibilities.

The curriculum is conditioned by institutional histories

There is a general consensus that having a range of institutional types in a higher education system is a national strength as this allows for various post-school educational trajectories. Furthermore, only a differentiated sector can meet the varied development needs of a nation and the many demands on higher education (Singh 2008).

In many ways the complexity of South Africa's history makes it a useful case to consider in conversations about differentiation. As discussed earlier in this book, there are two main forms of differentiation in the South African higher education landscape: differentiation of *type* and differentiation of *history*. Having a sector differentiated by type is common around the world but is almost always contentious because of hierarchies of status and funding that can emerge.

Under apartheid, the differentiation of type was that of technikon and university. Technikons, known elsewhere as 'polytechnics', focused on vocational education and training. This was considered to be a problematic binary divide that failed to allow student articulation between institutions and prevented collaboration between academics across the two types. There was thus a need for a reworking of South Africa's institutional differentiation by type once apartheid came to an end, in ways that would get rid of the binary divide and allow for a unified sector that could offer a broad range of qualification types, with a focus on different forms of knowledge, and which could allow broad access while enhancing opportunities for articulation across the sector. Around the world, similar shifts have happened to soften such boundary divides. For example, in the United Kingdom polytechnics assumed university status in 1992.

However, the process of re-imagining institutional differentiation of type was significantly complicated in South Africa by the other form of institutional differentiation that had bedevilled the higher education landscape, that of differentiation of history. As discussed in Chapter Three, this differentiation emerged from the apartheid logic of dividing racial groups and providing very different life chances for each group. The spectre of apartheid thinking permeated the structures of South African higher education so explicitly that the merger process outlined in Chapter Three was necessary after the move to democracy.

The discussion of institutional differentiation of type and history in a chapter on curriculum is necessary because the history and culture of a university are key mechanisms conditioning curricula; from who gets access to the university, to who teaches in it, to whether research is central to its endeavours, to what knowledge is legitimated, to how success is determined: all of these curriculum issues and more are enabled and constrained by the institution's identity. As indicated in Chapter Three, the very nature of the academic project is impacted by institutional differentiation.

Any mass higher education system has differences of resources and differences of mission, but it is important to consider the extent to which different kinds of 'dispositions to knowledge and knowing are cultivated in these different sites' (Clegg 2011: 98) if we are to understand how differentiation plays out across the sector and what the social justice implications might be. In the sections that follow, we look at how the forms of institutional differentiation, historical and present, have had an impact on curricula in South Africa.

Curricula in universities of technology

Curricula at universities of technology are, in many ways, constrained by their histories as technikons. Part of this history includes the offering of national programmes, rather than institutional ones. Under the apartheid government, technikons could only offer programmes that had been nationally developed through a convenorship system and approved by the state. This system saw a particular institution being appointed as the convenor of a qualification and taking the lead in developing it in discussion with those other technikons that were permitted to offer that qualification. The consistency of the technikon offerings was assured by the quality body, the Certification Council for Technikon Education (SERTEC). The change to becoming universities of technology was thus a complicated affair whereby these institutions began to enjoy some of the autonomy that traditional universities had had for many years. As a result of the convenorship system, technikons had generally failed to nurture curriculum development capacity and, significantly, the system had fostered a particular conceptualisation of curriculum as a fixed, pre-determined and neutral structure to be implemented from the top down (White et al. 2011).

The technikon's conceptualisation of knowledge was generally as a set of vocational skills that graduates needed for employment in a very specific workplace. The coherence across the content of the programme was largely achieved by what Muller (2009), drawing on the work of Chisholm et al. (2000), calls 'contextual coherence'. Contextual coherence indicates that the knowledge is selected and sequenced into a diploma curriculum in ways that make direct reference to the utility of the knowledge in the 'real world', which in the case of technikons was the world of work. In a curriculum in which contextual coherence dominates, it is the context in which the knowledge will be used that is the basis for the selection, sequencing and pacing of that content.

In contrast to this there is also 'conceptual coherence', which has abstraction and conceptual difficulty and a concern for the epistemological core of the discipline as the means by which coherence is achieved across the programme (Muller 2009). While all curricula will have aspects of both forms of coherence evident within them, one will always dominate. This is inevitable given that different curricula are designed to enable access to different forms of knowledge for different ends.

The dominance of contextual coherence in the diploma programme is thus no doubt appropriate. However, Muller (2009: 219) argues that generalisable innovation relies on conceptual knowledge, and so some conceptual knowledge needs to be 'a component of all forms of occupational knowledge, for epistemological, economic and social justice reasons'.

If the entire focus of the curriculum is on the acquisition of immediate workplace skills at the expense of access to the underpinning principled knowledge, then this does not allow for the development of capacity to address contexts and problems that cannot yet be imagined in the current world (Gamble 2001; Wheelahan 2010), that is, it denies access to the powerful knowledge discussed earlier. Maton (2009) and Ashwin (2020) argue that a core purpose of all higher education is to make spaces for young people to develop the capacity to engage with context-*independent* knowledge. For example, in a design programme, learning how to design for a specific space using a specific computer program is only useful for as long as that computer program is the one deemed best in the workplace or for as long as the space for which it is being designed retains its current form and function. But learning how to design spaces using a computer program where there is a strong focus on the principles underpinning the target, the space to be designed, and the tool, the computer program, can allow that knowledge to then be translated into new worlds.

If the shift from technikon to university of technology was to signify more than a name change, then the very relationship of the institution to knowledge had to be re-imagined (Du Pré 2009; Powell & McKenna 2009). What was needed was a careful balance between access to knowledge construction and the training of skills (McKenna & Sutherland 2006). There has been some careful research undertaken to consider what forms of curricula would foster the provision of conceptually rich applied knowledge that both includes and moves beyond simple workplace skills application (Shay et al. 2011; Winberg 2005; Winberg et al. 2013; Wolff & Luckett 2013), but there has perhaps not been sufficient uptake of this research, so that many university of technology programmes remain focused on immediate workplace skills, without necessarily foregrounding access to the powerful principles underpinning such skills. This then brings into question the longevity of relevance of what is being taught. We have argued that until this transition is accomplished, it will be difficult to position universities of technology as the destination of choice in the ways that such universities are in many other countries (Boughey 2010b).

This has social justice implications because research shows that, around the world, it is students from poorer backgrounds who are more likely to be provided with 'an externally focussed curriculum' (Clegg 2011: 93), and if such curricula have particularly weak conceptual coherence, such students will have limited access to powerful knowledge. This often occurs in the name of 'employability', whereby context-independent knowledge and access to underpinning principles is undervalued through a call for immediate workplace relevance (Nudelman 2018). This reinforces social divisions as students from middle-class families are less likely to be exposed to such curricula and when they are, they are often able to draw on their cultural capital to access the forms of powerful knowledge that the curriculum evades.

Because universities of technology qualifications very rarely have academic disciplines as such in their programmes, but rather have subjects based on 'regions' (Bernstein 2006), strengthening the conceptual coherence is a challenge. While traditional disciplines generally take the form of 'singulars', which have clear boundaries between what is included as knowledge in the discipline and what is excluded, 'regions' have very weak boundaries and draw from multiple disciplines. Regions also face the world of work and are concerned with real-world application of knowledge.

While regions are also found in traditional universities, they are typically what Muller calls 'stronger regions'. They generally have a stronger conceptual base and more stable ways of determining what 'counts' and how knowledge should be built in the field (Muller 2009). These regions often have professional bodies, such as the Law Society, the Engineering Council of South Africa (ECSA), the Health Professions Council of South Africa (HPCSA), and the South African Institute of Chartered Accountants (SAICA). In contrast to this, many of the regions that are the basis of programmes in universities of technology are what Muller refers to as 'weaker regions'. They generally do not have a strong conceptual basis, and there is often a sense that the boundaries of what can be included as content in the programme are not clearly drawn. Such regions often have very limited connection to the original singular disciplines from which they draw their knowledge, and thus it is that Marketing, Business Studies or Public Administration might draw from fields such as Mathematics, Sociology, Philosophy, Economics or Psychology, but they do so in a way that does not necessarily give students a firm grounding in the principles of powerful knowledge of such constitutive fields. While we have argued that developing conceptual coherence in such programmes is a fundamental social justice issue, this is made difficult by their lack of grounding in a particular discipline or strong region (Muller 2009).

The call for enhanced conceptual coherence is not a call for a shift away from a vocational focus (Garraway & Winberg 2019). There is a real need for a strong vocational-education sector which offers high-quality diplomas, and there have been regular expressions of concern about the inverted pyramid in South Africa in which more students register for formative and professional degrees than for vocational diplomas. The primacy of contextual coherence, however, should not be at the cost of sufficient conceptual coherence. And the two characteristics of being a region, that is, drawing from multiple disciplines and facing the world of work, are crucial aspects of what such institutions offer. Sadly, three recent occurrences in the sector have possibly reduced the differentiated identity of the university of technology. These are the demise of the advisory board, the reduction (or, in some cases, elimination) of work-integrated learning and the conversion of many diplomas into degrees. We turn to each of these now.

In the technikon era, the advisory boards of programmes were made up of various members of industry who provided feedback on the curriculum. This emerged from the valuing of close ties to industry. Contextual coherence in the curriculum requires a clear understanding of context, which was to some extent provided by the advisory boards in the past. As the criteria for staff appointment in universities of technology have changed, so there is no guarantee that the academic staff would have workplace experience or networks of industry experts (see Chapter Seven on staffing for more discussion on this). This has meant that in some cases the detailed understanding of procedural knowledge of the workplace has been reduced, making it difficult to ensure that the contexts being referred to in the university are indeed those of the current workplace. The now largely defunct advisory boards are thus arguably more important than ever.

Alongside the dismantling of the advisory boards in many university of technology programmes, came the reduction or elimination of workplace experience from the curriculum. When the institutions were technikons, most diplomas included up to a year of workplace experience in what was then known as 'cooperative learning'. There were a number of concerns about the quality of these modules, and it seems that often students were made to undertake very menial tasks in the workplace unrelated to their studies and that there was in some cases very little follow-up, besides the keeping of a logbook with minimal information, on the extent to which their learning in the workplace built on the knowledge being taught in the on-campus part of the curriculum. Significantly, the cooperative learning portion often became a bottleneck as many students were unable to find placements for such modules unless they had family connections in the relevant industry.

These concerns led to a tightening up in regard to what then became known as work-integrated learning (WIL). As a result of the introduction of quality assurance to South African higher education in the early 2000s, the Higher Education Quality Committee, the body responsible for this area, developed audit criteria and programme accreditation criteria (HEQC 2004). Institutions that wanted to include funded workplace learning in their programmes had to demonstrate the ways in which these aspects were curriculated, that is, how they were monitored, assessed and evaluated, and universities had to take full responsibility for the placement of students and the training of the workplace mentors. Sadly, such requirements, which would strengthen the quality of WIL, frequently meant that universities of technology elected either to greatly reduce workplace experience or to scrap it from the curriculum entirely. These shifts had a profound effect on the nature of knowledge being legitimated in the curricula at universities of technology.

The third development relating to the diminution of institutional differentiation in South Africa has emerged from the need to re-register qualifications on the Higher Education Qualifications Sub-Framework (HEQSF) developed in 2012 (CHE 2012). The HEQSF pegs the diploma at a level lower than the bachelor's degree and eliminates an old 'top-up' qualification, the one-year Bachelor of Technology, in favour of the introduction of an advanced diploma, also intended to last one year. The combination of the new qualifications framework with the formula used to provide subsidy to South African universities favouring the degree over the diploma led many institutions to redevelop degree programmes from those previously leading to diplomas.

Another curriculum issue that plays out in particular ways in the university of technology sector is the process of student selection and admission. The entrance requirements in the school leaving certificate are lower for a diploma than for a degree, though institutions can set their own requirements. Given the limited number of places available in the higher education sector, and the extent to which a university qualification is a major mechanism for social mobility, it is unsurprising that there can be fierce competition for spaces in programmes. But the desire to achieve a qualification, any qualification, can have some difficult consequences. While universities of technology have managed, in recent years, to reduce the number of 'walk in' registrations where students simply queue for hours (or days) for a particular programme and, when that course is declared full, move along to another queue, there is still not much evidence that incoming students are fully aware of the specific focus of the course for which they are registering. This varies greatly and some programmes undertake extensive information sessions and detailed application processes to ensure there is a good fit between the skills and goals of the prospective student and the focus of the programme.

Many academics report that the selection process for many students is purely on the basis of matric points and which programme has spaces available (Bass 2008; Gumbi 2017). Students often apply for a programme using fairly scant knowledge about the course but with a clear understanding that accessing higher education and acquiring a qualification is the key driver of social mobility (Case et al. 2018; CHE 2016). Such matters of career choice and a lack of academic advising impact on working-class students more than on others.

Diploma curricula are very explicitly focused on specific industries, industries about which incoming students may be only vaguely aware, and the programmes associated with them are highly structured. There is almost no space for students to discover what the course is really about as they progress and then to adapt their curriculum to suit their needs and developing passions. Once students have registered in a diploma programme, they are constrained by the rigid curriculum and their choices are to continue with their cohort in the predetermined subjects or to drop out.

The fixed-programme model with its prescribed course structures means that students are expected to move through the years as a cohort, and while individuals are sometimes able to 'carry' a subject which they have failed along the way, this is sometimes impossible because of very strict prerequisite rules. Given how limited the flexibility within a university of technology programme is and how central the development of the requisite professional identity is to success within such programmes, this partly explains the much higher drop-out and throughput rate experienced by universities of technology in South Africa (CHE 2020).

The focus of the diploma on a particular workplace might justify aspects of the very rigid diploma curriculum structure, with little space for electives or for moving between courses, because the knowledge needed for that workplace may be fairly prescribed. But we believe it is worthwhile thinking through the extent to which this rigid structure is also an inheritance from the old national convenorship system. Although some work has been done with regard to claiming particular knowledge spaces and pedagogical approaches in the university of technology sector, it is clear that much still needs to be done if we are to truly have the kinds of differentiation in higher education that can address the multiple needs for education at this level.

While curriculum changes have certainly occurred alongside the shift from technikon to university of technology, these have often been in directions somewhat at odds with how they were conceived in the national policy environment. The blunt instrument of the national funding formula used in South Africa drives all public higher education institutions in the same direction: towards the offering of degrees (not diplomas) and towards the offering of postgraduate qualifications. That we have academic drift (Kraak 2009) in our university of technology sector is therefore unsurprising. This is highly problematic if we are to achieve a differentiated higher education sector that collectively offers qualifications across the range of knowledges needed by an emerging economy, and which offers a range of options that fulfil the interests of a massified student body.

The plans institutions are required to submit to the Ministry of Higher Education and Training are meant to be the key mechanism whereby the sector as a whole is driven towards differentiation. However, a lack of political will to address the contentious issue of institutional differentiation, the blunt nature of the funding formula, and the individual qualification accreditation processes have meant a blurring of institutional differentiation has occurred rather than the anticipated broadening of differentiated options for school leavers.

Having looked at some of the ways in which the type of institution affects curriculum development in the university of technologies, we now turn this lens to the traditional universities.

Curricula in traditional universities

Traditional universities always enjoyed far more freedom in curriculum development in South Africa. They could select disciplines, departments, approaches to teaching and modes of assessment, though they varied in the extent to which such freedoms could be exercised. Historically black traditional universities were constrained by extensive control by the state, as was discussed in Chapter Three and will be returned to later. In the institutions that enjoyed such freedoms, there was a discourse of knowledge as negotiated and often contentious, as opposed to the idea that it was neutral, as was so prevalent in the technikon sector.

Traditional universities are engaged in all three fields of Bernstein's pedagogic device (2003b); these are the field of production, where knowledge is created; the field of recontextualisation, where knowledge is selected from the field of production and recontextualised into a curriculum; and the field of reproduction, where recontextualised knowledge is taught in an educational programme. Inhabiting all three fields has various implications for the nature of the institution. For a start, it means that academics are often greatly committed to their disciplines and the ways in which knowledge is made, alongside holding strong views about the implications of the nature of the discipline for what gets taught and how. Changes imposed from outside the discipline onto curriculum and pedagogy can be fiercely resisted by these academics, and those outside the discipline may struggle to identify the basis of such resistance. There is also the reality that a hierarchy of status is evident between the three fields, resulting in research, undertaken in the field of production, being valued at the cost of teaching, in the field of reproduction.

Having all three fields strongly evident in the traditional universities and embedded into their structures also brings a number of advantages. For example, students are often taught by research-active academics who are contributing to the boundaries of the fields in which the student is seeking induction. This is important not only for aspirational reasons but because it can allow for cutting-edge research to be integrated into the teaching and

FIELD OF PRACTICE	KEY STRUCTURE (THOUGH NOT ONLY STRUCTURAL MECHANISM)	TYPICAL SITES
PRODUCTION	KNOWLEDGE (AND KNOWER STRUCTURES)	PUBLICATIONS, CONFERENCES, LABORATORIES
RECONTEXTUALISATION	CURRICULUM	TEXTBOOKS, CURRICULUM POLICIES, COURSE GUIDES
REPRODUCTION	PEDAGOGY	CLASSROOM PRACTICES, ASSESSMENT

assessment processes. Furthermore, where there is good-quality teaching by research-active academics, students not only get access to the knowledge content but they are enabled to make sense of how knowledge is built, what counts as legitimate claims and evidence, and how such knowledge is communicated in the discipline (Boughey 2012b).

While the historically white sector of the traditional universities in South Africa had freedoms to undertake research and to develop curricula, which could be seen to be an enormous strength in fostering a strong academic project where the curriculum is imbued with conceptual coherence, there are a number of problems that emerge from its history. It would be a mistake to assume that the awareness of the socially constructed nature of knowledge and the autonomy to design curricula translated into these institutions using these powers to challenge the apartheid state. While challenges to the ideology and structures of apartheid did indeed come from universities, these were neither consistent nor always very effective (Maylam 2017), and in many cases, traditional universities played a significant part in maintaining the status quo.

The more research-intensive universities have what we call the discourse of the 'trustworthy and argumentative academic' (McKenna & Boughey 2014). These academics are trusted by the universities in which they work to 'do the right thing', with the result that their institutions tended to employ a very light touch with regard to, for example, quality assurance. Their sense of identity as academics also meant that they could, and did, resist any efforts to control them. Quality assurance processes designed towards strengthening curricula, for example, were often rejected on the basis that they constituted constraints on academic freedom (McKenna & Quinn 2016; Quinn & Boughey 2009). Often such rejection took the form of academic departments simply ignoring requests to engage in processes such as curriculum reviews.

While academics in research-intensive universities enjoy a far higher degree of autonomy in what gets taught and assessed in the curriculum than their counterparts in more hierarchical institutions, they have often spent 20 or 30 years becoming experts in a particular canon with specific literacy practices, and may well fiercely resist changes being called for from both the decolonisation advocates and the managerialist regime. In these institutions, then, and returning to our framework, it is possible to see academics drawing on a particular set of cultural and structural conditions in order to maintain the status quo.

Curricula in comprehensive universities

As part of the mergers and incorporations in the South African higher education sector, there emerged another new institutional type alongside the restructuring of technikons into universities of technology. This took the form of the comprehensive university, which, as we discussed in Chapter Three, is meant to offer the full range of qualifications. In some cases, the comprehensive university was formed through the merger of a technikon and a traditional university. Given the structural and cultural differences between these institutional types, outlined above, it is unsurprising that bringing them together to form a coherent university was a significant challenge. Perhaps the challenge faced by traditional universities expected to change into comprehensive universities without any history of offering vocational programmes was even greater.

The goals set for comprehensive universities were to increase access, to enhance articulation between career-focused and general academic programmes in order to promote student mobility, to strengthen applied research and to enhance responsiveness to human resource skills and knowledge needs (DoE 2004). One important observation to be made here in the context of other similar points we have made in this book is that there exists a misunderstanding that curricula content, approaches to teaching and learning, and forms of assessment are sufficiently generic across diplomas and degrees that academic staff can simply move between them. The success of the comprehensive universities in achieving the goals set for them is dependent upon the development of an appropriate academic and organisational model which can allow for its position as a hybrid institution. We take up this point in more detail in Chapter Six but for now will note that, following the finalisation of the Higher Education Qualifications Sub-Framework, there has been academic drift towards degree programmes, with the result that there is little evidence of the development of diploma programmes meant to make up the majority of the qualifications offered in comprehensive universities.

Historical differentiation by race

The terms 'historically black' and 'historically disadvantaged' have both long been used interchangeably in South Africa to denote institutions established for black social groups in the apartheid era, but neither is particularly precise. While the use of the term 'historically' in relation to 'disadvantaged' suggests that the lack of resourcing is a feature of the past, this is far from the case. Not only are such institutions generally located in less-accessible locations (Soudien et al. 2008), they also find it difficult to attract and retain staff (CHE 2016) and often suffer from poor management and leadership, seen in, for example, the number that have been placed under administration and consistently evidenced in a general inability to manage resources (Moyo 2018). The use of the term 'historically' in relation to 'black' is also a misconception as these institutions' current demographics show. During the advent of democracy, black students moved into the historically white institutions in droves because of the advantages they were perceived to offer (Cooper & Subotzky 2001). Very few white students chose to move into historically black universities to study at these institutions at undergraduate level, although a few opted to take up places in high-prestige courses offering entrance into the professions at postgraduate level, such as Clinical Psychology.

Even more important, in the context of the arguments we have been making in this book, is the fact that while the student bodies of these institutions retained their racial composition, they changed in relation to social class (Cooper 2015). As we argued elsewhere, children of the middle classes enjoy considerable advantages which mean they are generally able to perform better at school-leaving levels and are thus able to achieve the more demanding entrance requirements of the historically white institutions. Those black students who were able to do so quickly moved into the well-resourced institutions previously designated for white students only (Cooper & Subotzky 2001). This meant that the historically black universities now had very few middle-class students in their student body. This had enormous financial implications as the students that remained in this sector could rarely afford to pay fees, which as a result had to remain relatively low, but it also meant that very few members of the student body brought with them middle-class literacy practices (O'Shea et al. 2019).

As we argued in Chapter Four, the literacy practices of the university are no one's by birth but they are, nonetheless, more accessible to those who have been inducted into practices akin to those of the academy by virtue of their previous life experiences. Around the world, access to and success in higher education is closely tied to socio-economic background (Bathmaker et al. 2016; Guinier 2007; Reay & Vincent 2016; Walpole 2003). Logically, this observation would mean that the demographics of a student body should have implications for pedagogy and curriculum structure. The insistence on non-differentiation in many dominant discourses means, however, that what could have constituted fruitful opportunities for positive change in relation to the curriculum have been turned down.

The most obvious of these was the attempt to introduce curriculum change in a proposal made by the CHE in 2013 (Scott et al. 2013). This proposal argued for the need for four years to complete the 360 credits of the undergraduate qualification to be the norm. The learning required for the qualification would then be bolstered and supported by the addition of up to 120 additional credits worth of 'developmental' tuition. The proposal did not aim to lock all students into four years of study but rather offered opportunities for anyone to 'fast track' through the undergraduate programme in three years.

Objections to what quickly became known as the 'four-year degree' emerged in all sectors, including the unions, who saw the proposal as discriminating against black working-class students who would no doubt be amongst those 'required' to undertake an additional year of study. The benefits of being provided with the development and support needed to ensure a 'clean run' through a programme of study, without the false starts and changes of direction experienced by many students as they fail courses and find other ways to gain the credits needed for a qualification, were ignored and the proposal failed to find traction. These objections also failed to acknowledge the fact consistently revealed in cohort studies that the majority of students, even those in some of the allegedly best-performing universities, take four years to complete a three-year qualification.

More recent attempts to enhance teaching and learning, generally prompted by a concern about the overall performance of the system as a whole, in the form of the CHE's Quality Enhancement Project noted earlier, also failed to acknowledge that pedagogy needs to be tailored to context and that 'good' teaching is not generic but is rather related to who is being taught and who teaches as well as to the 'what' of content (Boughey 2011). Instead, the tendency within curriculum design is to understand 'teaching as teaching as teaching' or, as discourses culled from popular websites on teaching and learning in higher education might have it, 'learning facilitation is learning facilitation is learning facilitation'. Such a position completely misses the point that different students' previous experiences in respect of learning and different forms of knowledge will require different approaches.

The construct of 'historical disadvantage', as we pointed out earlier in this section, derives from the intentional lack of resources awarded to institutions identified for black social groups under apartheid (Bozalek & Boughey 2012, 2020). Arguably, events of recent years mean that historically white universities (HWUs) are now beginning to encounter some of the financial challenges faced by their sister institutions for decades given the decrease in state funding and student protests about the concomitant increase in tuition fees and the effects of the Covid-19 pandemic. In addition, the student populations in HWUs have changed in the last 25 years or so with the result that professors teaching in these universities now stand in front of students who are no longer the same as those they sat beside as undergraduates. They have different life experiences, more knowledge of technology and so on. As many academics have nothing on which to draw except their own experiences as learners to inform their own teaching, much of the teaching that takes place in these universities does not accommodate changes in the student body and especially students' learning histories.

Private higher education

An increase in the number of private 'for profit' institutions of higher education is noted in Chapter Three of this book as a feature of the global landscape. Such institutions are now a common feature of higher education systems across the continent and may include public institutions in other countries operating offshore as limited companies. Following the first democratic election in South Africa in 1994, attempts were made to control the growth of private higher education in the country. In many respects, these attempts were rooted in the perceived need to protect public higher education institutions in one of Africa's most advanced economies as it moved to the provision of quality higher education for all. Attempts to control the growth of private higher education can also be related to the need to manage the proliferation of institutions set up by 'fly by night' companies that failed to provide the education for which students had paid.

Private institutions were prohibited from using the term 'university'. Thus, Monash University, a public institution based in Melbourne in Australia, could only be known as 'Monash South Africa'.[6] The establishment of private institutions was controlled by regulations requiring approval and registration as a private provider of higher education with the Department of Higher Education and Training (DHET) and accreditation of all programmes in a rigorous process controlled by the Council on Higher Education (CHE).

Private higher education has proliferated across the African continent with more than 120 such institutions operating in Ethiopia alone. There were 102 fully registered private institutions of higher education and a further 34 with provisional registration in South Africa in March 2020 (DHET 2020). Kenya is identified as the first country in the East African regional to establish private institutions, and was followed by Benin, Senegal, Tanzania, Uganda, Ghana, Mozambique and Cameroon. While increasing numbers of institutions are 'for profit', most private higher education institutions on the continent beyond South Africa are owned by religious bodies (Tamrat 2018). The link between universities and religion in the private sector echoes early universities established around the world previously noted in this chapter.

Most private institutions are heavily focused on low-cost, high-profit, vocational qualifications in business and commerce, since programmes in areas such as engineering and medicine typically result in higher running costs associated with offering laboratory work. Curricula are often developed centrally by a unit of some sort, which also applies for the accreditation of programmes. The development of learning materials and assessment can also be centrally controlled, with the result that lecturers, many of whom are employed on short-term contracts, are typically involved in programme delivery and not in its design. Programmes in the humanities, the natural sciences and even the social sciences are not common. Where subjects such as English or Sociology are offered, they are usually conceptualised as 'service' courses supporting the achievement of learning outcomes that are heavily focused on workplaces. Much of what we said about the context-bound nature of curricula in the universities of technology therefore also applies to the private institutions.

There is no doubt, however, that in a system which does not have sufficient places to meet demand from students, private institutions have an important role to play. Efforts to control their growth and oversee their operations by bodies responsible for quality assurance therefore need to achieve a delicate balance between allowing for innovation and demand and ensuring that the learning experiences offered to students are of at least the same standard as those in the public universities.

In this section, and staying true to the framework we have used throughout the book, our argument is that social and cultural conditioning in place at all types of institutions in South Africa meant that the opportunities for curriculum change presented in the last 20 or so years have not been taken up as meaningfully as they could have been. Even more significantly, needs for change have often been 'set aside' because of the assumptions of those who have the power to act to bring about change. What we have seen is an overwhelming focus on structural change, on calculating credit values and assigning

---

6   Monash South Africa was later sold to private provider the Independent Institute of Education (IIE), a subsidiary of the ADvTECH group, and now has no links with the public university in Australia.

NQF levels and so on, at the expense of the critical engagement with the 'what, who, how and where' necessary for meaningful curriculum development.

The focus on programmes and modules

The focus on structure in relation to curriculum change is also evident in processes related to the development of programmes and modules. As we have already pointed out, the introduction of the NQF in South Africa resulted in a distinction being made between qualifications and learning programmes, defined as the set of experiences made available to students to enable them to achieve the learning outcomes for those qualifications. As these programmes were developed, the focus was very much on compliance with the formal requirements for registration in the form of credits and NQF levels.

Some institutions went a step further at this time by 'modularising' their curricula. This involved breaking down teaching and learning into smaller units (often as small as two or three credits) and then building these modules up into a larger programme. The problem with this approach relates to the lack of coherence that often resulted. We have experience of reviewing processes of modularisation at one university where academics were encouraged to develop modules independently. They then went about 'selling' these modules to programmes in order to ensure that their own jobs were secure. As this process unfolded, sufficient attention was not paid to the coherence or sequencing of knowledge in the programme. In this case, we can see the impact of market forces on the choices made by academics as they exercised their personal powers and properties in relation to curriculum development.

One of the biggest problems with the development of programmes and modules, however, relates to the lack of flexibility. In some cases, units of the programme are tightly locked together in sequential order, with the result that students who fail a module or course can be blocked from making further progress. As we have indicated, this is particularly common in the case of the diploma. If students fail repeatedly, they may then have to resort to starting a completely different programme (Case et al. 2018). This phenomenon can partly explain the low throughput and attrition rates in programmes repeatedly identified as problematic by cohort studies (see, e.g. CHE 2016) although programme structure is but one mechanism at play in accounting for the whole picture.

Extended curricula

As we indicated in the previous chapter, one response to the issue of poor retention and throughput in the South African system was the introduction of what are known as 'Extended Programmes with an Integrated Foundation Phase' but variously called 'Foundation Programmes' and 'Extended Curriculum Programmes'. In many cases these have been used as the means of broadening access to students who had not attained the scores on the school leaving examination required for entry to mainstream programmes. Extended programmes are thus in some institutions understood within the single notion of access, whereby access entails physical access to the university structures rather than epistemological access (Morrow 2009) to the discipline or programme culture. Or to put it another way, as has been pointed out by the CHE (2004), student equity can be understood from two perspectives: equity of access and equity of outcomes. Many universities describe their extended curricula from the first understanding only – enabling more students to enter the academy.

The use of the term 'Extended Programmes with an Integrated Foundation Phase', as the nomenclature suggests, was an attempt to drive institutions to understand such programmes as integrally embedded within 'mainstream' programmes. Indeed, without a focus on discipline-specific practices, it is clear that foundation provision would be simply an additional year of generic skills courses developed on the basis of the Decontextualised Learner discourse, and our research over the years has found this is sadly often the case (Boughey 2010a; McKenna 2012b).

In spite of the moves to make funding for these initiatives more secure, many staff teaching the developmental courses in extended programmes continue to be employed on short-term contracts. This often meant the appointment of people with very little experience in the field or discipline being taught. Such people were then tasked with enhancing epistemological access to a discipline in which they themselves may have limited expertise (Boughey 2005a, 2012a; McKenna 2012b). And because such contract staff are often seen as being 'outside' of the concerns of the mainstream discipline, it is unlikely that any lessons they might have to share from teaching on such courses would be fed back to disciplinary experts. Not only do these contract lecturers rarely attend staff meetings where issues of curriculum are discussed, but their lack of qualifications and research production in the relevant discipline may mean that they do not carry the credibility which would allow them to have a voice in such spaces.

A condition of the DHET funding is that extended curriculum students are admitted to programmes leading to an accredited qualification. However, in many cases, the entire extra year of tuition occurs at the beginning of the curriculum and is divorced from the learning that takes place in the rest of it. Add-on programmes of this nature are typically low on knowledge content and high on generic skills, which makes the acquisition of disciplinary norms especially difficult. In some cases, extended programmes are even offered on different campuses from their mainstream counterpart. As long as the programmes are geographically separate, taught by different staff and even managed entirely externally from the faculty, these programmes cannot draw on the disciplines to which students are seeking access.

An additional concern with the Extended Curriculum initiative is that it addresses a small percentage of students. The percentage of students entering higher education through such programmes has increased year on year but still sits at just 12% (Draft DHET Policy Framework for Extended Curriculum Programmes May 2017). As we have indicated, the programmes that exist are often targeted at students who would not normally gain admission to a university while, at the same time, those who have been accepted directly into 'mainstream' programmes having met regular admission requirements continue to fail in droves.

Over the T_2 to T_3 period, a number of different course types emerged to accommodate the 120 additional credits made available through this funding: (i) fully foundational courses; (ii) extended courses; and (iii) augmented/augmenting courses. These three different course types suit different purposes and meet different needs.

Foundational courses are just that. They aim to provide a foundation for students to move forward at tertiary level by developing conceptual knowledge and knowledge-making skills (e.g. laboratory-related skills in science). Fully foundational courses fit well in knowledge areas with a hierarchical knowledge structure, that is, in areas where lower-level observations and principles are subsumed into ever more overarching theories and accounts. Typically, these are characteristics of the natural sciences. In a hierarchical knowledge structure, a gap at the lower levels can mean that students become 'stuck' and cannot proceed any further with their learning until the gap is filled. However, the addition of an add-on foundation year at the front end of the programme is popular across many extended-curriculum programmes regardless of the nature of the knowledge, as this model is far easier to implement logistically and requires the least disruption to the mainstream curriculum structures. As is to be expected, there are difficulties in ensuring sustained success through the degree among students who have completed the additional year. Having made it through the 'foundation year', many students then fail in the mainstream curriculum. The fundamental flaw in the institutional construction of foundation provision within a student-deficit discourse had not been recognised; instead, problems that arise with success rates amongst these students were once again seen in the data for the research underpinning this book to be explained as the institution 'not having stringent enough admission criteria'.

Extended courses are courses where the length of time taken to complete the course is extended. This means, for example, that a semester-long course could be offered over a full academic year. Extended courses mean that teaching and learning simply proceed at a slower pace giving students more time to consolidate and develop what they know. Assessment is in step with the pace of learning so that, for example, by mid-year, only half of the work of the course would be assessed.

Finally, augmented/augmenting courses are courses into which additional tuition is inserted by offering extra contact sessions. If a course is offered through four contact periods per week, it could be augmented by offering up to eight contact periods per week. These additional sessions are offered either by the academic responsible for teaching the course (as in 'augmented courses') or, more usually, by staff members specially appointed to run them (as in 'augmenting courses'). Students enrolled in an augmented/augmenting course need to keep up with the work of the regular course. This means that if an assignment is due in the second week of the regular course, students doing the augmenting/augmented portion also need to do this assignment. In theory at least, augmented/augmenting courses require greater mastery of the literacy practices than extended courses because of the pace of assessment.

An extended programme could encompass all or any of three different course types discussed as developmental provision. This offered a significant opportunity for curriculum change. The kinds of social and cultural conditioning we have outlined earlier in this chapter have meant, however, that those academics with the power to effect change have often eschewed it and have, instead, delegated responsibility for advancing students' learning to others employed to teach the developmental credits which are not particularly well integrated conceptually into the programme. As this has happened, an entire industry of 'academic support professionals' has come into being, a point to which we will return in Chapter Six.

Academic advising

We have become aware, in our research on student learning over the years, of the extent to which students battle to manage their own progression through their programmes; missing assignment deadlines, losing certificates of due performance (DPs), and then failing courses. Students in big courses can often feel adrift and uncertain, and expectations by lecturers that these students will know what is expected of them because it is all 'in the study guide' are problematic. With the possible exception of high-status courses such as medicine, law and accounting, many students enter their programme without having a clear sense of what they have signed up for. This is perhaps of less concern in formative courses such as the BA or BCom, where there is a high degree of flexibility within the programme structure and students can negotiate their pathway in any number of ways (though even here there is much variation between institutions, see Case et al. 2018; Marshall 2018). However, in the university of technology system, we have seen that this can be a very problematic matter as students register for very specific vocation-focused qualifications without understanding what it is that a clothing technologist or dental technologist actually does (Boughey 2010b).

It is clear that academic advising is fairly ad hoc in South Africa and that often students are able to 'slip through the cracks' of a massified system (Case et al. 2018). While we will never be in the position of many North American universities, where the system of academic advising is integral to the structure of the university with every student allocated an advisor from the point of admission, we believe there is a gap in the South African higher education sector in this regard. Many universities do not have a very clear early-warning system where students are informed of forthcoming problems in their progress, though some universities are now implementing these. The First-Year Experience programmes at some universities pay careful attention to supporting students as they become aware of institutional expectations and structures, although, following the arguments we have made in Chapter Four, some efforts to do this can be problematised from the discourse of the Decontextualised Learner.

Conclusion

In this chapter, we have shown how curriculum, if broadly conceptualised as access to the goods of the university, is conditioned by a number of macro and more micro structures and cultures. In particular, we have emphasised that the structure of the target knowledge needs to be taken carefully into account in curriculum development processes. The academy is not simply a training centre providing workplace skills; it is a public-good institution developing and disseminating powerful knowledge which enables us to work across contexts and to address challenging problems. In our consideration of what constitutes powerful knowledge, we need to steadfastly and explicitly interrogate whose interests are being served and how 'knowledge of the powerful' might be allowed to masquerade as 'powerful knowledge'. We also reviewed the ways in which these complex issues intersect with institutional differentiation of both type and history in South Africa, with implications for higher education systems across the continent. The mechanisms enabling and constraining curriculum development that have been identified in this chapter are far from exhaustive, but we argue that many stubbornly persistent discourses in the cultural domain do not serve us very well.

Archer (1995, 1996, 1998, 2000) indicates that change in the domain of culture often takes far longer to achieve than change in the domain of structure. Furthermore, if discourses in the domain of culture do not complement the structural change, unintended consequences may result. Understanding the ways in which structural and cultural mechanisms condition curricula is fundamental to transformation; however, this does not mean that academic staff are unable to bring about change. In the next chapter, we look at academics, as the main agents of curriculum transformation, and we look at the ways in which they have exercised agency over the T_2 to T_3 period.

6

Resisting and complying
Academics responding to change

Academics and agency

Throughout this book, we have been concerned with the extent to which higher education has responded to the calls for change that have dominated the public and academic space from the late 1980s onwards. In this chapter, we turn to the academics in our universities in order to ask about the demands made on them and the ways they have been able to respond to changing contexts.

In order to do this, we draw on the concept of agency and, following the framework that has underpinned the rest of the book, acknowledge that academics, like all other human beings, have personal powers and properties which allow them to act in relation to the concerns they have and the projects they identify to pursue those concerns (Archer 1995, 1996, 1998, 2000). While individuals have the power to act, they are not completely free to do so as they are always conditioned by (but not determined by) the social and cultural structures to which they have been exposed. This social and cultural conditioning can enable or constrain depending on their personal projects and the power accorded to them by virtue of their position in society.

This chapter therefore begins by looking at the social and cultural conditioning emerging from the disciplines in which academics work, and then more broadly at those in place as the new social and political order in South Africa dawned in the early 1990s and academics began to be called upon to be part of the processes of transformation envisaged for the higher education system. Many of the mechanisms we identify will have relevance to academics beyond South Africa.

The chapter once again calls on many of the ideas and claims made in Chapter Three. However, the purpose of returning to these ideas in this chapter is to look at their impact on academics more specifically.

The conditioning role of the discipline in academics' identity formation

In much of this book we have made the claim that different disciplines make different forms of knowledge and disseminate these through different literacy practices. A simple look at a journal article from Somatology alongside one from Sociology alongside one from Semantics will quickly demonstrate that it is not just the theories and concepts that differ across fields, but the very nature of knowledge. We have argued that these practices emerge from the norms and values of a discipline and this means that only those who are well-versed in such practices are able to enable access for novices. But this argument has implications for more than epistemological access for students, it has enormous implications for academics' identities too. Henkel (2005) argues that an academics' primary affinity is in fact to the discipline of which she is a member rather than to the institution in which she is employed.

Becher and Trowler (2001) suggest that a great many social practices that academics hold dear relate to the discipline they are responsible for both building and safeguarding. Academics in disciplines with agreed upon methods for creating knowledge may, for example, enjoy far more collegiality than those where the very notion of truth is contested. However, it should be noted that increasingly academics work in fields, rather than singular disciplines and we have at times in this book used the terms 'discipline' and 'field' somewhat interchangeably, though it can be argued that fields draw from multiple disciplines. While coming to understand the role of the discipline/field in which an academic works is key to understanding what it is that they do and value, the extent to which academics share practices within a discipline varies and probably conditions their research practices more than it conditions most other aspects of academic work (Trowler 2014). Manathunga and Brew (2012) argue that shifts in higher education, such as those outlined in this book, mean that many academics now rarely work in singular disciplines, and this has consequences for their identities and affiliations.

What is no doubt needed is a 'more nuanced understanding of academic disciplines and their power' (Trowler 2014: x). Trowler suggests that many of the generalisations about disciplines work well from a distance but a close-up look begins to reveal extensive diversity between disciplines grouped together as 'cognate' and fault lines appear even within any one discipline. Becher's (1989) much cited metaphor of the university as comprising 'Tribes and Territories' offers useful broad brushstrokes to understanding how the nature of knowledge affects the practices of academics – why Physics academics engage in different practices to Philosophy academics, for example – but closer inspection requires us to take into account the effects of institutional structures and cultures within which the Physics or Philosophy academic works. As we have argued throughout this book, the particular histories of universities condition the emergence of any practices and may complement or contradict the effects of the norms and values of any particular discipline. Furthermore, changes in higher education globally, in particular its positioning as the producer of labour for the knowledge economy, has brought about significant shifts in the organising structures of the academy (Trowler 2014).

The history of the system and the conditioning of individuals

The social and cultural conditioning of the South African higher education system under apartheid has been outlined in this book. Drawing on Bunting (2006), this exploration shows how colonialism and the structural development of apartheid associated with it resulted in different groups of institutions with very different cultures and differing abilities to draw on the resources made available by the state.

Cooper and Subotzky's (2001) 'historiography' of South African institutions of higher education along with Bunting's (2006) work allow for more examples of the way the structural system impacted on the cultural systems of the universities under apartheid. Suffice to say at this point, however, that, as it became evident that a new political order was about to dawn in the late 1980s, different groups of institutions were characterised by very different cultural systems. In general, the historically white English-speaking universities had been conditioned to expect much more freedom in determining their own affairs both at institutional levels and at the level of the individual academic. The technikons and historically black universities, on the other hand, were culturally disposed to accept more management and steering from above, with the historically white Afrikaans-speaking universities being located somewhere between the two with regard to expectations of freedom.

If we look more deeply into this statement, we can gain greater insight into the notions of 'management' and 'freedom'. Bunting (2006: 40) argues that, by the early 1990s, the Afrikaans-speaking universities were 'instrumentalist institutions which were governed in strongly authoritarian ways'. He goes on to define 'instrumentalist' in this context as an institution 'that takes its core business to be the dissemination and generation of knowledge for a purpose defined or determined by a socio-political agenda'. The valuing of knowledge for its own sake and of the use of academic thinking to ask difficult questions in relation to society and its problems was thus not part of the cultural system. Jansen's (2001) personal account of his experiences at a historically white Afrikaans-speaking university also provides insights into the authoritarianism that prevailed. The institutions were extremely well run with controls in place at all levels but debate and contestation were not part of the cultural system, and committee and other meetings were often firmly steered by chairs to arrive at predetermined solutions to problems (Bunting 2006).

As we have indicated, the distancing of the historically white English-speaking universities from the apartheid government, on the other hand, led to the development of very different cultural systems. This does not mean, however, that the liberal approach they espoused was, in fact, as claimed. Numerous critiques of the roles of the historically white English-speaking universities during apartheid have been produced (see, e.g. Maylam 2017 for a rigorous history of our own institution, Rhodes University). Many would argue that the historically white English-speaking universities were as complicit in maintaining the apartheid regime as any other.

With regard to academic governance, universities largely followed a 'collegial' model derived from Europe where power rested with the professoriate. This meant that senate was a strong body, comprised, as it was, largely of professors who were powerful because of their positions as leaders of their disciplines and the departments that practised them. While discussion and debate were welcomed within this collegial structure, access to decision-making was limited as the model held power at 'the top' of the academic hierarchy, with the result that more junior staff and students did not have access to the spaces where the debate took place.

Over the last two decades, in many universities the head of a department post has become a rotating appointment. This means that other, sometimes more junior, staff also sit on senates and faculty boards because of their appointments at departmental and school levels. In the past many universities followed the 'Humboldtian' model by appointing professors as heads of departments and, thus, leaders of the discipline. The professors therefore enjoyed considerable influence in deciding what should be taught and what should be researched. Although the roles of professor and head of department are rarely conflated nowadays, the legacy of this model prevails. Professors still hold considerable power within the disciplines and, in South Africa, this is especially problematic because of the small number of black professors in the country. The CHE (2016), for example, identifies only 27% of professors and associate professors as being black in 2012.

Under apartheid, those historically black institutions that were located in the Republic of South Africa were largely staffed by Afrikaans-speaking academics loyal to the apartheid state (Bunting 2006). This ensured the kind of authoritarian cultural system that had characterised the institutions at which many of these staff members had been educated. Although black vice-chancellors were appointed as the years wore on, their senates continued to be dominated by the same group for some years and authoritarian institutional cultures continued to be the order of the day. Those historically black universities located in the 'homelands' were treated as just one more government department and this had a similar impact on culture. Tight controls on every part of academic life meant that the understandings of what it meant to work in a university were limited, although challenges to authoritarianism were prevalent from the mid-1980s onwards. As a result, many of these universities became sites of struggle with a concomitant effect on functioning.

As discussed in Chapter Five, given the mandate to produce graduates and diplomates skilled in specific work areas, it is not surprising that utilitarian views of knowledge and its dissemination dominated amongst lecturers in the technikons. The focus on the production of workers for the apartheid economy meant that little research was conducted in these institutions. Where research did take place, it was always directed at a specific industrial end. This overall framing of the role of the institutions impacted on culture in significant ways, particularly in relation to the way academics understood their own roles and responsibilities.

As apartheid came to an end and institutions of higher education engaged with the process of transformation to ensure that they were relevant in a new social and political order, staff were conditioned by the cultural systems that had sustained their institutions and, in addition, had to work within a system which might not always have been enabling of change. The way staff exercised their agency following the end of apartheid was also conditioned by the series of mergers and incorporations used to 'size and shape' the system in the early 2000s (see Chapter Three). Imagine, for example, the clash of cultural systems as a historically black campus located in a former 'homeland' was incorporated into a historically white Afrikaans-speaking university (as in the case of the University of the North QwaQwa campus and the University of the Free State), or the merger of a historically black English-medium university with a historically white Afrikaans-medium university (as in the case of the Potchefstroom University for Christian Higher Education with the University of the North-West, formerly the University of Bophuthatswana). Other mergers had the potential to be more harmonious as, for example, in the case of the historically white Afrikaans institution, the University of Port Elizabeth, merging with Port Elizabeth Technikon, although it is interesting to consider the impact on culture as two institutions focused on different forms of knowledge but both relatively used to tight control from management came together.

One criticism of the mergers and incorporations that took place in the early 2000s was that, with the exception of the University of Natal which merged with the University of Durban Westville, the historically white, more research-intensive universities were left unchanged. This meant that the cultural systems of institutions such as the University of Cape Town, Rhodes University, the University of Stellenbosch, the University of Pretoria and the University of the Witwatersrand were left to continue without the impact of staff from other institutions with very different histories. This allowed particular forms of colonial privilege to continue in these institutions. It is also interesting to note that no historically white English-speaking institution was instructed to become one of the comprehensive universities, all of which have their history in historically black or Afrikaans-speaking institutions.

After the end of apartheid, academics and other professionals working in higher education have increasingly moved between institutional types. As a result, it is not uncommon for individuals to take up positions in a very different kind of institution to the one in which they had previously worked, only to continue to draw on the assumptions and beliefs that held sway in their previous contexts. This can result in clashes that can be profoundly discomforting for the individual concerned, as the new context is often experienced as 'unwelcoming' with the newcomer being perceived as 'not fitting in'.

The clashes can also work the other way when an individual from a very different kind of institution moves into a powerful position as what Archer would term a 'social actor' in a new job. According to Archer, social actors draw some of their personal emergent powers and properties from the roles they occupy. So, an individual might move into a new role in a different institution, and draw power from that role but also exercise agency to draw on sets of ideas and ways of working from a very different context. The result can be a clash as a 'new broom' comes in to 'sweep clean'.

An example of this phenomenon could be a vice-chancellor being appointed at a university of technology after a history of employment at traditional universities, who may not understand the significance of close links with industry for both teaching and research. She might also not understand the extent to which many of the academics she now leads draw on identities as 'professionals' rather than researchers. In a similar vein, a director of human resources who moves from, say, a comprehensive university to a research-intensive institution may misunderstand the ways in which academic governance structures mean that faculty boards and senate are greatly interested in matters related to staffing because of their roles as stewarding the general academic project of the university. The director thus has to work with a very different workforce to those he experienced in previous institutions, a workforce that can then be perceived as 'difficult' (McKenna & Boughey 2014).

Finally, imagine a young academic who has been educated in a university of technology. As we have explained in Chapter Five, vocationally orientated programmes often focus on the knowledge and skills needed to achieve learning outcomes which are work-orientated. As a result, the underpinning principles are often not taught. In such a context, if theory is introduced in the process of teaching for outcomes, it is theory 'for' the outcome. If the young academic who has been exposed to this sort of teaching then arrives in a department in a research-intensive university where everyone is talking abstract theory unrelated to its utility, including in the staff room, it is not difficult to see how he may feel intimidated and, even, that this particular institution is 'not for him'.

The point of these examples is to stress the need to appreciate the impact of social and cultural conditioning on the way individuals, and groups of individuals (Archer's 'corporate agents'), choose to exercise their agency. We believe that many of the disputes that have arisen in our universities over the years are due to the kinds of clashes we have described here. While we need to work at the development of a coherent higher education system that is open to and provides quality education for all, we also need to acknowledge that we have a differentiated system. Usually differentiation of type is expressed in terms of the qualifications offered. However, our position is that differentiation is much more complex and subtle than this, and that we need to take this into account when we look at academics' experiences of universities.

Although we have focused on South Africa in this analysis, we believe the higher education systems in other countries are also characterised by divisions between different kinds of institution. In Kenya, for example, a distinction is made, amongst other things, between chartered universities and constituent colleges of universities. It is highly likely that the history of each kind of institution as well as its purpose will impact on its culture and the way it is structured.

Adding to the complexity, the social and cultural conditioning experienced by academics is not only related to the institution. Academics may find themselves being positioned in particular ways based on their race, age, gender, nationality, sexuality and so on. Monnapula-Mapesela (2017) points out the many ways in which the agency of academics can be constrained by the dominant culture beyond the university as well as within it. Thus, even in cases where a black woman is accorded the power of social agency by virtue of the particular position she is appointed into, she may be constrained by the ways in which she is constructed by those around her. She may well be expected to 'perform' her expertise in ways not required by other colleagues working at the same level.

Now that we have outlined some of the social and cultural conditioning in place in the early years of democracy, we move to look at some of the ideas conditioning higher education globally as South African isolation came to an end in 1994. We therefore return to the conversation started at the beginning of this book.

New Public Management and managerialism

As we have indicated previously, the concept of 'New Public Management' began to gain traction from the late 1970s onwards. New Public Management attempts to make public service organisations more 'business-like' by drawing on management models from commerce and industry. Within the overall umbrella of managerialism, the provision of customer services is understood as requiring specific approaches to management in order to achieve efficiency. This usually involves the identification of goals, strategies to achieve those goals, and indicators of progress towards them. The idea of key performance indicators is then introduced in relation to an individual's execution of a particular role or job.

One implication of this for academic staff has been the introduction of appraisal systems assessing their performance against these indicators. These systems usually focus on metrics and outputs and can ignore the 'softer' sides of academic work involving, for example, pastoral care for students, which is typically overlooked in the system. As such work often falls to women in what has been termed 'academic housekeeping' (Bird et al. 2004), this can add to the gender imbalances that already exist. Appraisal systems are usually put in place to 'manage underperformance'. Ironically, they can often fail to do this whilst ignoring those who do work extra hard. There is no evidence that such systems increase efficiencies, while there is ample evidence (Newfield 2016; Shore 2010; Shore & Wright 2015) that they undermine the trust that has been integral to academic work particularly in some kinds of institutions (McKenna & Boughey 2014; Thaver 2010).

Also associated with managerialism is the idea that 'quality' needs to be assured, managed and enhanced. Taken together with the notion of customer service, on a practical level, the practice of assuring, managing and enhancing quality then involves eliciting feedback from consumers on an ongoing basis and, also, benchmarking against the performance of other organisations working broadly in the same area. The impact of such initiatives is that they can make staff members risk-averse, particularly in relation to their teaching where they can perceive the need to 'please' rather than challenge students because of the impact poor feedback could have on their careers, as discussed in Chapter Four. Nixon et al. (2018) provide evidence of the way the privileging of the 'student as customer' can impact on the structure of the curriculum and on the kind of knowledge students are required to engage with in ways that can be seen to be questionable at least. While student feedback is valuable, the need to defend what we described in Chapters Five and Six as 'powerful knowledge' is important because, ultimately, this will benefit students who can have a very limited view of what they need to learn based only on their own experience and preferences. As academics are increasingly employed on a precarious basis with 66% of academics in South Africa working on contract (CHE 2020), the need to conform and meet expectations can become stronger. Eliciting positive student feedback can also introduce elements of 'performativity' where academics are pushed towards 'entertaining' students rather than focusing on criticality and challenge.

The term 'managerialism' infers that active management needs to be practised. The impact of such active management has been profound and is most clearly seen in the establishment of 'executive' positions with responsibility for managing different areas of academic life. It is now common to have executive deans who are not necessarily disciplinary leaders with the respect of their colleagues gained on intellectual grounds but, rather, individuals identified on the basis of their management skills to run a faculty (McKenna 2020). Furthermore, traditional deans are appointed by and primarily accountable to their faculty, whereas executive deans are appointed by and accountable to the executive and council, which shifts the balance of power in an institution in fundamental ways.

In a similar vein, it is common to find deputy vice-chancellors and directors with specific responsibility for managing areas such as teaching and learning, research and community engagement. In the case of teaching and learning, very few of those in senior positions have strong backgrounds in the scholarship of teaching and learning, with the result that the fall-back position is on the 'common-sense' approaches that we have critiqued throughout this book. The appointment of such key individuals to manage teaching and research corresponds to attempts to increase subsidy by, for example, increasing student throughput or research outputs. This is high-stakes work, given the poor South African performance data detailed throughout this book and what this actually means for the lives of students and the billions spent on grants earmarked for the improvement of teaching and learning. Ironically, however, initiatives introduced by such individuals to improve student performance often draw on 'common sense' rather than the research-based and carefully theorised approaches (Moyo 2018). (Trowler 2020 suggests that this is an international phenomenon.)

We argued in Chapter Five for different kinds of understandings to inform initiatives intended to enhance student success; understandings which acknowledge students as social beings and which see success as related to the ability to take on new academic identities. Sadly, although the need to recognise the impact of social context on teaching and learning has been cited for more than 20 years, efforts to get teaching and learning acknowledged as profoundly cultural, social and political endeavours have not managed to challenge dominant common sense in any significant way (see Boughey 2005a, 2005b, 2007, 2010a, 2012a, 2013, for a review).

Another effect of managerialist discourses, alluded to above, has been to weaken the power of the academics themselves. All South African universities have senates. As we have indicated, historically those universities which enjoyed more academic freedom had senates and faculty boards that were populated by the professors who held the power in determining the academic future of the university. Faculty boards and senates and their sub-structures approved curricula, oversaw assessment, approved proposals for research and so on and, thus, were intensely involved in the oversight of the academic project. Obviously, this was not entirely positive as it allowed a relatively small group of individuals, and the beliefs and intellectual positions they espoused, to hold sway over an entire institution. Nowadays, the power of senates and faculty boards has been reduced with the advent of other corporate agents as universities have opened up these bodies to such constituencies. It is now usual, for example, for trade union members and students to have representation on senate.

Furthermore, in many universities, key decisions are made by 'top managers' without being deliberated by institutional structures such as faculty boards and senates. When this happens, the council often becomes more directly involved in running the university rather than playing an oversight function on decisions taken within academic structures. Institutional governance thus becomes overtaken by management processes. There have then been a number of instances where seats on councils were highly contested as they open up opportunities for members to promote their own business interests within the institution. All this leads to a more general disempowerment of academic staff.

The growth of managerialism has also resulted in the establishment of very powerful institutional positions such as directors of quality assurance, risk management, intellectual transfer, equity, internationalisation and other functions that have arisen as a result of widening conceptions of the purpose of universities and the claimed need for active management of all areas of academic life. Many of these directorates have relatively large numbers of staff, which has impacted on the ratio of support staff to academics at institutional level, skewing it in favour of support in spite of the rapid increase in student numbers experienced over the years. These directorates exist in addition to those that have been part of institutional life for many years, such as Human Resources, which have also seen extensive growth in scope and numbers.

The power of these institutional managers is often experienced by academics in negative ways as they feel a shift of focus away from the academic project. To add insult to injury, the salaries of the managers usually exceed those paid to academic staff. One result of this lack of parity in salary scales can be a sense that academic work, central to the life of the university, is not as valued. This situation is then exacerbated by the shift towards what is often termed the 'casualisation' of academic work, which sees the tenured positions valued by academics replaced by short-term contracts and, even 'zero-hours' contracts. What we have described here is not peculiar to South Africa as accounts of the same phenomena abound in the international literature (see, e.g. Barnett & Peters 2018; Fabricant & Brier 2016; McCowan 2018; Newfield 2016).

As the impact of managerialism has been felt, directors and other support staff have also been allocated seats on senates and their key sub-committees. The extent to which institutions are now guided primarily by concerns for the academic project, however it is understood, is worthy of consideration given the many different constituencies represented on governance and management structures.

This is not to say that more representation of different constituencies is undesirable but rather that the nature and purpose of our universities and the academic projects which sustain them need to be held as paramount. In our experience, though, there is generally little articulation of what the academic project of the institution is and so there is little direct engagement in the domain of culture as to how these varied constituencies support it. The extent to which the academic project can be ensured when managers who are not academics hold considerable influence in running the institutions therefore needs to be questioned, especially when the structures in the institution are complemented by a culture of managerialism.

Critical theorists (see Gibson 1986, for an overview) have long been sceptical of 'instrumental rationality', or a focus on the means rather than the ends. In the university we have argued that the end is the academic project, which is the primary end towards which all means should be directed. The focus on means is often achieved by drawing on discourses privileging the need for efficiency and effectiveness. Arguably, one of the results of this focus on 'means' in our universities is that that bigger questions about 'ends' are ignored.

To return to the research that provided the impetus for this book, our work showed that the first cycle of institutional audits resulted in what Archer (1995) terms 'elaboration' of the structural system (Boughey & McKenna 2017). For example, complex quality assurance systems were set up, run by quality managers or quality officers. Although the definition of quality used by the HEQC is that of 'fitness for purpose', our research showed little consideration being paid to big questions about what the purpose of teaching or the purpose of learning might be in a newly democratic society. The focus was on the quality systems themselves (i.e. on the means) rather than on the ends. Academics were kept busy following and complying with quality assurance procedures and were thus distracted from the concerns which had long been central to the identities of many of them (Henkel 2005).

In many respects, this critique can also be applied to research. Executive positions and research offices intended to drive research have been created partly because of the benefits that accrue from research in the funding formula for public institutions in South Africa (DoE 2004) and the status attached to research, especially in global ranking systems.

The use of funding, through the allocation of subsidy in South Africa, as a steering mechanism has inevitably impacted on decisions regarding the academic project. Decisions related to the introduction of new programmes, for example, are now often driven by considerations of the amount of subsidy that will accrue, regardless of the quality of the programme, since some areas of study attract more subsidy than others. Moreover, and as we have indicated above, the push for research outputs in most universities has not necessarily been driven by understandings of the centrality of knowledge-production in a university per se but rather by funding benefits. For staff, this can mean that more esoteric intellectual interests which might previously have been reflected in curricula are now ignored, and research interests that are less likely to result in publications in the short term are set aside (Nash 2013).

Nonetheless, academics have not entirely succumbed to the demands of managerialism as small victories have been won along the way. For example, as the South African national qualifications framework was introduced there was a call for unit standards to be used to define small chunks of learning. Academics in some institutions were able to resist this call by insisting on all universities being allowed to register 'whole qualifications' on the framework. The battle was not only about registration, however, as it was also about the right and power of academics to make decisions about the what and how of academic teaching. That this call came largely from one group of institutions, those that had traditionally had more freedom from the state, while others were much more willing to comply, can be seen to relate to historical conditioning in the system overall.

Staffing in a global structure

The centrality of the concept of 'new knowledge' and call for workers who can generate and apply it in the global economy, as discussed previously, has increased demand for higher education across the world. In many countries in Africa, higher education systems are under pressure from students whose home countries in other parts of the continent cannot accommodate them (Oanda & Ngcwangu 2018). In this context, it is becoming increasingly important to understand any university as part of a global higher education structure. As we noted in Chapter Three, possibly the way this is most evident is in the ranking systems. The criteria used by these systems have an impact on the work of academics who are expected to perform in ways rewarded by them.

Writing of the QS/Times Higher Education (THE) world university rankings, Marginson (2007: 138–139) notes, 'in the Times Higher universe, higher education is primarily about reputation for its own sake, about the aristocratic prestige and power of the universities as an end in itself, and also about making money from foreign students'. As Badat (2010) points out, rankings serve to maintain the social, and one could also argue economic, status of some universities while keeping others out of the game.

In spite of numerous critiques of ranking systems (and, to those of Badat 2010 and Marginson 2006, 2009, one can also add those of, inter alia, Amsler & Bolsmann 2012; Harvey 2008; Taylor & Braddock 2007; Teferra 2017), many African universities have taken up the concept of ranking with vigour. For some universities, attaining a position in the 'top 100' of the Shanghai ranking system has become a strategic goal with concomitant impacts on staff members. For example, research counts more in ranking systems than teaching and learning, and community engagement is often entirely absent. Staff employed at a university seeking a ranking may thus be pressured to produce research at the expense of other areas of academic endeavour. If a university chooses to chase a prestigious academic for employment by offering an inflated salary, what impact might this have on its ability to employ others at the chalkface of teaching and learning where staff–student ratios may not be favourable? And how might the protection of prolific researchers from teaching duties then affect the careers of more junior members of staff who are left to cope with huge classes and the resultant marking loads? In South Africa, the goal of achieving a ranking can also mean that the transformation agenda is neglected as ranking systems do not include criteria to drive it. As a result, many institutions pursuing both ranking and demographic transformation of the academic staff body have sought to employ academics with prestigious reputations as researchers from the rest of Africa.

Like many other countries, South Africa is facing an academic staffing crisis as the number of young people choosing an academic career dwindles. One response to the general shortage of academics has been for South African universities to recruit academics from countries across the continent. Sadly, this structural response is often confronted by xenophobic discourses in the domain of culture. Unpleasant incidents and even violence at some institutions are compounded by the difficulty of getting the necessary permissions to work and study in the first place, with work and study visas often taking many months to secure. Government departments in South Africa often adopt opposing positions in this regard, with some drawing on discourses of pan-Africanism or Southern African Development Community (SADC) relations and others focused on protection of local employment and development opportunities. These all play out in the day-to-day experiences of staff.

The emergence of compliance

For Archer (1995, 1996, 1998), no one is completely free to make choices, but rather individuals are always conditioned by social and cultural mechanisms prevalent at any one time. It is probably fair to say, given our analysis above and the research projects that provided the basis for this book, that, in some South African institutions, academics have been conditioned into compliance in relation to instructions from management and other external stakeholders. In some places, quality managers and quality officers had drawn on the structural and cultural conditions prevalent at the time to garner significant power. The result was the introduction of quality systems involving, amongst other things, programme reviews, departmental reviews and benchmarking. These systems inevitably required a response from academics. In one institution we studied (Boughey 2010b), a 23-point checklist for academics had been introduced. Academics did not respond in the way the designer of the list had envisaged, as the complaint in the data was that they had simply 'ticked the boxes', indicating that required actions had been completed without necessarily doing anything.

The need for quality assurance is often balanced by the concept of quality enhancement, and different national processes may shift between emphasising one over the other at different times. As indicated earlier, in South Africa, a project focusing on quality enhancement followed a cycle of institutional audits intended to *assure* quality. As we write, the pendulum is arguably swinging back towards quality assurance. When shifts such as this take place, we need to consider how agents are using their personal powers and properties to protect the projects with which their offices are associated at institutional levels. The often-impenetrable nature of quality discourses can contribute to the protection of power, as the difficulty in understanding terminology can constrain engagement with what the processes actually involve.

What might be perceived to be our negativity towards quality assurance should not be taken to indicate that we believe that all staff are hugely committed to their work and that quality already exists everywhere. Rather, our point is that the introduction of quality assurance in South Africa overwhelmingly led to compliance and a focus on processes and systems without a concomitant effect on quality itself. The assumption is that the introduction of quality assurance processes (and in some cases performance-management systems) will improve quality and address inefficiencies in the system but, as Archer (1995, 1996, 1998, 2000) argues, unless there is complementarity with the ideas and values in the domain of culture, then the newly introduced structures may result in unintended consequences, such as bureaucracy and compliance.

Ever-increasing demands on academic life

For the last half century, the number of students enrolled in African universities has increased enormously. This has not been accompanied by a sufficient increase in the number of academics employed to teach them. As a result, and in combination with other phenomena such as increased diversity and austerity in the wake of falling state support for higher education, university teaching has become more and more demanding.

Throughout this book we have identified the way the perceived need for 'knowledge workers' in the global economy has impacted significantly on the roles assigned to universities in recent years. Students increasingly see a qualification from an institution of higher education as a means of securing work. This understanding very much focuses on the idea of higher education as a 'private good' which brings benefit to individuals. Universities have long valued another function, however, of contributing to the 'public good' through research which is beneficial to humankind in general and the production of graduates who can contribute to a critical citizenry. Balancing these purposes of higher education with the so-called 'three pillars' of academic work (teaching and learning, research and community engagement) is a decidedly complex task.

Community engagement, long specified as the 'third pillar' of academic endeavour, is sometimes cited as one means of correcting the balance between the focus on the private good that has emerged since the 1990s and the needs of society more generally (see, e.g. Subotzky 2003). Community engagement spans a continuum of activities from volunteerism to formally-curriculated service-learning courses where students take their learning to communities and, in return, challenge and refine what they have learned by engaging with those communities.

Community engagement also has a critical role to play in allowing universities to identify a niche for themselves in a differentiated higher education system. In South Africa, at least, institutional vision and mission statements often draw on the notion of serving communities, particularly in the case of universities located in impoverished rural areas. However, in the research that underpins this book, we identified little thought having been given to what this might mean for other core functions. How does community engagement link to research? How is so called 'engaged research' promoted in strategic planning for research production and capacity development? The potential for the community engagement–research nexus to be a central aspect of a university's identity has perhaps not been conceptualised as thoroughly as it could have been (Boughey 2012a; Muthama & McKenna 2017). In a similar vein, if service learning is seen as a means of incorporating community engagement into the formal curriculum, how does a university manage and monitor this? The 'living out' of mission and vision statements has profound implications for all activities of a university, yet we could see few attempts to make this happen.

Community engagement clearly has much to offer higher education and countries as a whole. The idea that universities should put their learning at the service of communities and, in return, learn from community members is important in developing countries with histories of inequality. Community engagement contributes to universities serving the 'public good' in significant ways. But it does increase the ambit of the university and adds to the workload of academics.

The pressure on staff to perform across the entire spectrum of academic endeavour has increased steadily over time. In promotion procedures, academics at many institutions need to demonstrate that they work across the three pillars. Academics thus need to look *inwards* to disciplinary concerns and to their own position in disciplinary structures by, for example, researching, publishing, reviewing and serving on editorial boards and the committees of professional or disciplinary organisations as well as *outwards* to communities.

As universities have increased in size, concerns about the performance of diverse student bodies have also arisen. Popular discourses tend to attribute poor performance to a variety of reasons including the lack of preparedness on the part of students, as noted in Chapter Four. Other discourses have offered very different reasons, including the lack of readiness of the universities themselves to engage with diverse groups of students (see, e.g. Vilakazi & Tema 1985). This has been taken up by a field known as Academic Development or Educational Development, which often encompasses the development of academic staff as educators (see, e.g. Boughey 2007; Volbrecht & Boughey 2005; Walker & Badsha 1993).

The fact that academics do not need any sort of professional training to teach in higher education has more recently been associated with the poor performance of a system overall, and efforts to 'manage' teaching and learning have included attempts to introduce staff development. To a large extent, just as naive thinking locates problems related to poor student performance in deficiencies at an individual level (see Chapter Five), many discourses calling for academics to be qualified as professional educators do the same thing.

As Behari-Leak (2017) shows, the privileging of academics' agency in the assumption that all that is needed is a course which will allow them to 'teach better' is flawed because of the way other cultural and structural conditions enable and constrain practice. She makes clear that the status of some individuals as black women or as foreign nationals means they do not have the authority to impose change. At departmental levels, academic hierarchies come into play, with new ideas proposed by junior members of staff stifled by more authoritative voices resistant to change. The capacity of individuals to bring about change is limited, given the conditions in which they work, which is why such programmes are most effective when they enjoy institutional support and when the focus is not only on the development of cognitive processes of individual academics or on sharing classroom strategies but rather on well-theorised accounts of how curriculum structures and teaching and learning events emerge from the interplay of multiple mechanisms (Quinn & Vorster 2014, 2015, 2017; Vorster & Quinn 2017). The generic nature of some staff development courses means that disciplinary difference as well as social and cultural differences are not sufficiently considered, with the result that their potential to bring about change is unfailingly overestimated.

In spite of these critiques, individual academics are increasingly being required not only to gain some sort of qualification in academic teaching but also to demonstrate their capacity in this area in order to gain promotion or tenure. In making this point, it is not that we are objecting to the idea of staff development in respect of teaching, but rather observing that the potential of individual academics to bring about change, and thus to impact on poor performance, is limited. In terms of the theory which holds this book together, what we are saying is that although an individual might be able to draw on a set of new ideas to inform practice as a result of completing a course on teaching, the extent to which they will be able to implement new practices will also be enabled or constrained by prevailing social and cultural conditions at classroom, departmental, institutional and, even, system-wide levels.

Alongside the need to demonstrate their competence as teachers, academics also need to show that they are productive as researchers. Pressure on academics to publish is often driven by reward systems such as payment for publication and the role played by research in personal promotion processes. In many places, this has led to a number of unintended consequences including 'salami slicing' whereby research findings are divided as thinly as possible, ghost authorship and publications in questionable journals (Muthama & McKenna 2020). In South Africa, Mouton and Valentine (2017) identify a huge increase in the number of papers published in journals categorised as 'predatory', a phenomenon common to the entire continent. According to Xia et al. (2014), those who publish in predatory journals are predominantly young and from developing countries. Institutions with a research-rich culture and significant history of producing research are less susceptible to such problems. The history of colonialism has meant that many institutions on the continent have not developed such cultures, a phenomenon exacerbated by previous World Bank policies downplaying the importance of higher education in national development in Africa.

The call for all countries to focus on research production in the knowledge-economy discourse has resulted in enormous pressures being placed on all academics to do research regardless of the institutional contexts in which they find themselves, and also in spite of the fact that many have not yet even qualified as researchers by attaining at least a master's degree. Academic inflation also means that it has become difficult to attain even an entry-level university position without a doctorate. For example, in 2014, the Commission for University Education (CUE 2014) in Kenya issued a directive that all assistant lecturers must acquire a doctorate by October 2019 to be qualified to teach.

The need to research is also complicated by the nature of knowledge in some disciplines, as discussed in Chapter Five. Areas such as somatology, defined as an interest in assisting people to improve 'their general wellness and aesthetic appearance through information and practice of healthy lifestyle habits, product use and clinic treatments' (Durban University of Technology 2018), or dental technology, which 'trains students to become dental technicians who fabricate removable intra-oral dental appliances in a dental laboratory' (Vahed et al. 2016), draw on multiple disciplines such as physiology, anatomy and chemistry. However, as we argue in Chapter Five, the knowledge base developed within these subject areas is often very context-specific, and professionals appointed to teach in them have not always had access to the foundational principles needed to undertake research.

As we write, in many institutions across the world there is a drive to produce research in pursuit of what is broadly known as the 'Scholarship of Teaching and Learning' (SoTL). While scholarship in teaching and learning is critical if we are to enhance our understandings of what it means to teach and learn in a university, there is a danger in privileging this particular direction at the expense of scholarship in the disciplines, not least because academic teaching is located in the disciplines. Unlike school teachers, academic teachers have much greater control over the curriculum (Bernstein 2000, 2003b). Universities are sites of knowledge production, and understanding the beliefs, values and processes involved in creating knowledge drives academic teaching (Boughey 2012b). If academic staff are diverted away from pursuing postgraduate study in the disciplines and, thus, from deepening their own understandings of the way knowledge is created in their own fields, what does this mean for their ability to understand what it is students actually need to know and learn?

This is not to say that work in the scholarship of teaching and learning should not be pursued, but rather that it cannot be pursued at the expense of an individual's development in the home discipline. Even more pertinently, the pursuit of SoTL should not be based on the belief that achieving 'outputs' (e.g. articles in subsidy-earning publications) is, in some way, easier to attain than in the home discipline. This is not the case as the field of SoTL has its own values, norms, theories and practices in which adepts need to be well versed. The ability to produce work that can be published in high-quality journals requires immersion in the field, as newcomers engage with theories and develop understandings of values, and is not a 'quick fix' to the need to produce outputs. The rise of the understanding that SoTL presents an easy way of increasing research outputs is deeply troubling (Muthama 2019).

As we have argued in Chapter Four, the wealth of literature in the field of SoTL, much of it coming from South Africa, provides us with a stockpot of understandings that can enhance higher education by challenging the common-sense approaches so prevalent in the sector, and yet there has been very little engagement with this literature. The rush to contribute publications in SoTL needs to be located in this context of few academics reading extensively in the field. Academics are striving to meet new structural arrangements in the form of personal promotions policies that require them to produce research without the necessary capacity development. While many universities now offer workshops and other initiatives designed to support research capacity, the Archerian framework underpinning this book reminds us that structures require complementary cultures to be effective. The development of a strong research culture takes time but sadly is often not the focus of those who are tasked with increasing institutional outputs.

Staff demographics

In South Africa, issues of race remain a major problem in the staffing of universities. The nuances of the way this plays out may be specific to South Africa, but across the rest of the continent, racial, tribal and linguistic differences impact on how individuals can build an academic career (Kisaka et al. 2019).

In 2017, only 44% of academic staff members employed in South African universities were black Africans (CHE 2020) although this group makes up the vast majority in the population overall.[7] If these numbers were to be scrutinised in greater detail, we would see that the majority of these black staff members were clustered in the lower academic ranks with very few comprising the professoriate.

Academic cultures and hierarchies often work to make staff from social groups not well represented at institutional levels feel alienated. This alienation can be experienced in relation to myriad practices, some of which are as mundane as coming together in staff rooms to drink tea in the middle of the morning (Tabensky & Matthews 2015). Given higher education's ascribed role in the development of a critical citizenry, it is particularly distressing that institutional contexts are experienced by many academics as places permeated by structural racism, sexism, xenophobia and other forms of exclusion. In this regard, it is useful to look at how Kumalo (2021) calls the decolonial movement 'the desire for ontological legitimacy'.

We needed some of the analysis we have provided in preceding sections of this chapter to argue a particular point about demographics: namely the lack of attraction of an academic career to many young people and, in particular, young black people in South Africa, where black individuals with qualifications are in high demand in almost all sectors of the economy. An academic career can lead to almost overwhelming pressure to publish in institutions where the number of subsidy units against a person's name can count much more than the quality of those publications. It means pushing to research and publish whilst, at the same time, dealing with ever-growing student numbers and facing demands to perform in the sphere of community engagement.

All this happens in the context of low rewards since academic salaries usually cannot compete with those offered in the corporate sphere. At the same time, the freedoms that have made academic life fulfilling over the years are increasingly being constrained by encroaching managerialism. The autonomy to craft one's own intellectual project, which may entail building scholarship over a number of years, is being attacked by performance-management systems looking for contributions to targets in strategic plans and other documents. In addition, the precariousness of much academic work now offered on a contract basis also works against the attraction of an academic career.

Attempts to increase equality in the demographic profile of institutions in South Africa and further afield need to take the full context of an academic career into account. Teaching, research and community engagement can be enormously fulfilling, but these positive aspects of an academic life are constrained if the context is one of precarity and performativity.

---

7   The 2011 South African census identifies 76% of the total population as Black African (Statistics SA 2012).

Concluding thoughts

In this chapter we have looked at ways in which global, national and institutional contexts enable and constrain the agency of academics. In terms of the framework structuring this book, we have attempted to interrogate how social and cultural conditioning in our universities impacts on the extent to which individuals can exercise their personal powers and properties to bring about change. What we have seen is a re-positioning of academics in institutions in ways which, arguably, have left them less powerful than before and subject to demands on their time and energy, both intellectual and otherwise, which were not prevalent 25 years ago. It is in this context that the agency of academics in explicitly stewarding the academic project is more important than ever.

7

Evaluating change, looking forward

Introduction

In this book we have reflected on the rapid growth in higher education around the world in a period of increased divides between rich and poor and the resilience of structural inequalities within society and our institutions. We used a framework derived from the work of Roy Bhaskar and Margaret Archer in order to produce a theorised response to questions about the relationship between teaching and learning in higher education, and its role in reproducing the status quo.

We began this book by looking at the forces of globalisation and neoliberalism; as we draw it to a close, we need to point out that many of the claims we have made and the conclusions we come to, rest on a larger project of challenging the everyday assumptions that emerge from these forces.

As we have indicated and as we tell our postgraduate students, theory functions like a pair of glasses. Without them, you see the world in one way. Put the glasses on and you can see things you didn't see before or you see them differently. As in real life, putting on theoretical spectacles involves choices. Anyone who has visited an optometrist to get a pair of prescription lenses will be aware of the array of 'finishes' available which will cut out glare, react to light and so on. Just as we can choose how we want to be able to see through the lenses of our glasses, so can we choose what and how we want to 'see' through theory.

We had originally chosen the framework using the work of Bhaskar and Archer to complete a piece of commissioned research looking at the impact of the first cycle of institutional audits on teaching and learning in South African higher education. Our theoretical choices in this case were informed by our desire to account for the enormous difference we could see across the system in South Africa and beyond. We believe that institutional differentiation is necessary and beneficial in a higher education system; however, the differences we have reflected upon are not always beneficial. In our own country, in spite of the fact that we were 25 years on from the first democratic election in South Africa, many differences still resulted from the constraints of apartheid and colonialism; systems which deliberately and consciously tried to shape higher education to serve some more than others. As we have argued, the legacies of colonialism emerge in very similar inequalities across the continent. The framework developed from the work of Bhaskar and Archer allowed us to account for difference structurally, in respect of the way access to resources was organised, and culturally, in respect to the world of ideas. It did this by allowing us to explore the world through three 'layers' of reality, the Empirical, the Actual and the Real.

As we explained in Chapter Two, the Empirical and Actual layers are transitive and relative as they are accessed via the senses. Individuals experiencing and observing these two layers then 'make sense' of what they see and experience using what they already know. In contrast, the deeper layer of reality, the Real, is comprised of relatively enduring mechanisms which interact together to allow for the emergence of events at the level of the Actual and observations and experiences of these events at the level of the Empirical. Our aim was to explore this layer of relatively enduring mechanisms in order to account for what we could see.

Importantly, the framework (and more specifically, Archer's morphogenetic cycle) allowed us to explore the way the interplay of mechanisms led to events and experiences *over time* whilst, at the same time, accounting for agency, or human action. Archer accords all individuals the personal powers and properties to draw on mechanisms and this leads to emergence. However, she is insistent that all individuals are conditioned by their own histories and, thus, that we are not completely free. We will all act in ways which are impacted by what we have previously experienced, what we already 'know' and what surrounds us in our present contexts. In the book, therefore, we have explored the social and cultural conditioning in place in a number of areas as individuals tried to bring about change in one higher education system. We then explored the ways they were able to act given the existence of the multiple mechanisms at play.

In this final concluding chapter, we arrive at what Archer terms T_4, a point where we assess whether or not change, termed 'morphogenesis', has emerged or whether things are much the same, a state Archer calls 'morphostasis'.

The landscape at T_4

While the main focus of the book has been on teaching and learning, in this chapter we attempt this evaluation by looking at what are usually called the three core functions, or pillars, of the university: teaching and learning, research and community engagement.

Teaching and learning

Our argument in this book has focused on the need for what we call 'social' understandings of teaching and learning. In Chapter Four we posited a continuum of theoretical positions drawn on to understand student success in higher education. At one end of the continuum is what we call 'the model of the student as a Decontextualised Learner'. This position holds that knowledge is unitary, that learning is uniform regardless of context, and that successful learning is dependent on factors inherent to the individual, such as intelligence, motivation and aptitude. The model allows us to absolve learning institutions of any bias towards particular groups of learners since failures are attributed to inborn characteristics about which the institution can do very little. The problem with this position which, admittedly, exists at the extreme end of the continuum of positions, is that it will not allow us to make sense of, for example, South African student performance data without going into very horrible places, since black students bear the burden of failure in universities much more heavily than their white peers. While this position may be at the extreme end, 'softer' variations of it dominate accounts of higher education success across the continent and beyond. Common-sense explanations of student success consistently suggest that higher education is a meritocracy where hard work and intellectual capacity triumph. Despite a plethora of research that challenges this position, the everyday assumption is that students succeed or fail primarily on their own merits.

The alternative to this position, 'the model of the student as a social being', which exists at the other end of the continuum, holds that there are many ways of knowing and, thus, many ways of learning. One way of knowing, for example, is craft knowledge. Craftspeople cannot necessarily explicate what they know as a set of principles. Some may be able to, but, in the main, the knowledge is 'in their hands'. Another form of knowledge is academic knowledge, which, as we explained in Chapter Four, is specialised, principled, and often abstract.

Academic knowledge, like all other forms of knowledge, is value driven. It is acquired through formal instruction and also through immersion in academic contexts where the values underpinning it are prevalent and can be acquired. Nonetheless, these values are not always made explicit to learners, with the result that some of the practices can be meaningless to those who have not been privy to this 'inside' information. Academic knowledge and knowing is not necessarily the same as school-based knowing since, in schools, knowledge is generally taught as uncontested, unlike in the universities, where the understanding is that knowledge is always open to challenge and is constantly subject to change and development.

The point about the model of the student as a social being is that it acknowledges that only some students have been exposed to ways of knowing that have similarities to those privileged in universities. Students who have had experience of these ways of knowing, generally by virtue of their upbringing in homes where at least one person has benefited from higher education, come into our universities with a significant advantage. The ways of knowing, and indeed the very ways of being, in the university are more familiar to them so they may not feel as alienated from their learning identities. In contrast, students who have only had experience of very different ways of knowing encounter the university as an enormously confusing place and may even feel invalidated as individuals as the ways of learning that have brought them so far now appear to fail them in the new context. It is this, we would argue, that leads to a great deal of depression and anxiety for students.

We would argue that it is possible to teach *towards* epistemological access. We can learn to make the familiar strange to ourselves such that we, as academics, see exactly what it is that we are asking of students, how it is that knowledge is made in our fields, and what peculiar literacy practices are the means of communicating this. As we come to understand the extent to which our fields 'work' and as we teach in ways that make this explicit, so will we also see the need to curriculate opportunities for modelling, practice and formative feedback. Taking on the social practices of the academy entails potential identity shifts and students need to be given ample opportunities to engage with these practices and their underpinning values and figure out what it will mean for them to become knowers in their fields of study.

We would also argue that simply acknowledging that becoming a successful learner requires many students to take on new identities would go a long way towards understanding what they say to us as individuals and in groups. The social, cultural and political struggles an increasing number of our students need to engage with are often ignored as their experiences are couched in psychologised terms or using understandings of higher education as meritocratic (Sobuwa & McKenna 2019). Acknowledging students' experiences is but a first step but is, nonetheless, one that has the potential to open the way for change.

Crucial to this argument is a call for a critique of the values embedded in the academy. Those who battle to access the practices deemed necessary for success may feel unwelcome. The normalised nature of these practices keeps them opaque and obscure and thereby provides protection from accusations that many expected practices may be racist, sexist and so on. Making the practices explicit would not only enhance opportunities for success, it would also open the practices and underpinning values to scrutiny and, in some cases, to dismantling. The call for epistemological access must be held alongside the call for epistemic justice.

Our analysis of the impact of the first cycle of institutional audits in South Africa was that, although they resulted in changes to management of teaching and learning in the form of policies, committees, teaching and learning centres, and so on, and also in the appointment of key agents (deans, directors and even deputy vice-chancellors responsible for this management), the 'domain of culture' did not change sufficiently. In other words, people in specific roles sitting on committees, writing policies and working in teaching and learning centres often relied on the same ideas and theories (located towards the 'student as a Decontextualised Learner' end of the continuum), in spite of the fact that student performance data in South Africa and elsewhere, as we have indicated, simply does not support this position. At the same time, massification of higher education around the world means that the student demographics of universities continue to change, requiring more nuanced understandings of learning than those we saw in the data we analysed.

Changes in student demographics are not new. The reliance on the model of the student as a Decontextualised Learner endures, however, because of the allure of common-sense accounts of failure located in factors inherent to the individual. These accounts surround us on a daily basis, and those who draw on them are overwhelmingly unconscious of their implications and consequently are often well-meaning in their actions. The preponderance of these discourses and the practices associated with them means that they are very difficult to resist.

Regardless of all efforts to improve teaching and learning, the dominance of the Decontextualised Learner model means that structural inequality continues to be ignored.

By this, we mean that no cognisance is taken of the way inequality is structured into what we do as teachers and what we expect of learners and which is 'hidden' because of the normalisation of those expectations. For example, in some disciplines we think it is normal for students to write academic essays where they are expected to draw on multiple sources to take a position and thereby to build an argument, without any thought being given for the way the language and structuring of this form of text is more familiar to some than to others. This is not only because of the demands of learning in English but also because the form of the academic essay and its underlying value system has not been encountered in students' previous experiences. When students cannot write such essays very well, we then attribute this to their status as speakers of English as an additional language and introduce courses, often bearing the misnomer 'academic literacy', that focus on the grammar and vocabulary of the language as well as on generic study skills.

When other mechanisms are introduced to try to improve teaching and learning, such as funding via the Development Grants in South Africa, individuals may draw on ideas associated with the model of the Decontextualised Learner when they use such funds. As a result, the grants are not consistently as effective as they could have been.

The dominance of the Decontextualised Learner model also means that even when academics are introduced to more productive ways of understanding students' experiences in staff-development courses, they are not always able to apply those ideas because of the response of others in the university more widely. The huge focus on the development of staff as professional educators in higher education in recent years has been such that staff development runs the risk of being positioned as the panacea for all ills related to student learning. Making new academics aware of the ways they could contribute to change is but one mechanism, however, and it cannot make a difference without complementary changes elsewhere. Alongside staff development, what is needed is capacity to rethink teaching and learning at institutional levels to see student, staff and institutional development coherently by drawing on understandings of the 'social model'.

As we have argued, the construction of students as 'Decontextualised Learners' is complementary to other discourses dominating our thinking about higher education. One such discourse involves the construction of students as clients. 'Student as client' discourses, characteristic of what could be termed the 'corporate university', construct higher education as an entity to be bought and sold anywhere in the world and, thus, as neutral. From this perspective, anyone who has the money can buy higher education and use it to gain access to more resources in the form of better employment and greater social status.

In South Africa, the subject of graduate unemployment is contentious, with some (see, e.g. Van Broekhuizen 2016) arguing that unemployment amongst graduates is relatively low and is, in any case, skewed when the institution awarding the qualification is considered. According to Van Broekhuizen (2016: 27), it is clear that attending a less prestigious institution 'is negatively associated with employment prospects and positively linked to the probability of unemployment'. This observation, if nothing else, points to continuing inequality in the system overall and to the problematic nature of the focus on understanding higher education as a private good in a hyper-capitalised world, especially since the 'private good' argument is often used to defend increases in tuition fees.

As we write, South Africa came very close to reaching the 35% unemployment in the general population forecast for December 2020 by the International Monetary Fund (IMF) with an unemployment rate of 32.5% for the last quarter of 2020, albeit in the context of a global pandemic. Chances of accessing meaningful employment without further education are limited (Organisation of Economic Cooperation and Development 2019). Young people perceive the need to enter universities for future employment but are 'tricked' in doing so by discourses constructing success as equally open to all. The idea that, regardless of the amount spent on it, higher education success may be more accessible to some than to others, as we have argued in Chapter Four, is not taken into account. Rather, in a hyper-capitalist world it is simply something to be bought and sold, whilst at the same time students are constructed as 'clients' purchasing their tickets to great wealth and improved social status. In this context, the discourse of the student as a Decontextualised Learner makes sense. If higher education is a private good, in that it is understood to bring increased wealth and social status for the successful individual, it is uncomfortable to admit that the goods it provides are not particularly accessible to some because of the way society is structured. Sadly, in spite of all the efforts to transform South African higher education into a system that would serve all citizens, developments have drawn on globalised discourses with the result that the dream of equality, at least in relation to teaching and learning, continues to evade us.

This is not to say that no changes have occurred and that all spaces draw on such problematic understandings at all times. There are indeed a number of initiatives, in South Africa and further afield, which have attempted to address the concerns raised here, but they have often failed to be taken up in ways that bring about systemic change. As Badat (2016: 8) argues:

> It is not that prior to the student protests there had not been critical voices that had raised issues of epistemology, curriculum and the like, but that they have gained little traction at universities and in higher education and have remained largely marginal concerns. It is also not the case that there has been either a uniform unwillingness or no efforts to tackle colonial, racist, patriarchal discourses and the culture of whiteness. The reality is that for reasons that are important to understand, initiatives to date have yet to succeed in uprooting inherited cultures and practices, and bringing about the far-reaching transformations that are necessary and long overdue.

But for system-wide shifts to occur, we argue that we have to call on more sophisticated understandings of teaching and learning in more coherent ways than we have done to date.

We believe that this is eminently possible but it will require an acknowledgement of the social nature of the university and the political nature of teaching and learning. Structural mechanisms such as the University Capacity Development Grant (Moyo &

McKenna 2021) and cultural mechanisms such as the strong student call for epistemic justice can enable significant shifts but only if they are harnessed and if constraining mechanisms, such as the three discourses of the Decontextualised Learner, the student as client, and higher education as a meritocracy, are directly identified and countered.

Research

The critiques we have offered in relation to teaching and learning can also be applied to research. With the emergence of the so-called 'knowledge economy' there has been a drive to increase postgraduate education and research-production. In many countries, including South Africa, research is especially rewarded in promotion systems and in national funding processes. Although research production has grown, with steady year-on-year increases across the entire continent of Africa, this success has not been unproblematic.

We would never argue that a university should not do any research even if the teaching of undergraduates is what occupies the time of the majority of staff. One reason for needing some form of research in *all* universities is that it is through research that academics become more and more aware of the disciplines they teach; awareness that is needed for the development of the curricula for which they are responsible. Unlike schoolteachers, who work with a curriculum that is typically centrally developed, all academics are responsible for curriculum development. Without an in-depth understanding of the norms, values and nature of knowledge in their fields, and the way it is changing, how can academics develop curricula which 'open up' that discipline to students in the ways we have argued are necessary?

Drivers in the form of international ranking systems, personal promotion and even individual cash incentives (Muthama & McKenna 2020) have pushed all institutions towards prioritising research regardless of their histories, their locations or their particular missions and visions. Although the various international, national and institutional incentives for publication have undoubtedly had an effect on the number of overall publications in South Africa, the impact has also been a privileging of quantity over quality (Mouton & Valentine 2017; Muller 2017; Thomas & De Bruin 2015). The focus is therefore often on the means, publication, rather than the ends, the dissemination of knowledge.

Many academics in universities across Africa are minimally qualified to conduct research. According to the Council on Higher Education (2020), about 48% of permanent academic staff in South African universities are qualified at doctoral level. This varies according to the university with some, in the small group producing the bulk of South Africa's research outputs, now employing up to 60% of staff with doctorates. At other universities, the number of staff with doctorates is almost pitifully low. Alarmingly, data for 2018 (CHE 2020: 50) shows that nearly 1637 academics are permanently employed with only a certificate or undergraduate diploma or degree. The National Development Plan 2030, in recognition of the importance of research to economic productivity, sets the goal of 75% of all academic staff having doctorates by 2030. As indicated previously, in Kenya, given the directive from the Commission for University Education that all assistant lecturers should have doctoral degrees by 2019 or lose their jobs, the goal appears to be 100%.

The South African funding formula is blunt in the way that it rewards research activity, with no nuances to take institutional difference into account in South Africa, which brings about problems of academic drift (Essop 2020). Universities with large undergraduate populations and relatively little research activity also tend not to attract students at postgraduate level. This means that more senior students who are able to act as tutors and mentors to their undergraduate peers are not available in sufficient numbers. As a result, undergraduate development can also suffer in those places where, arguably, there is the most need for increased efficiency and outputs. As the funding formula in South Africa also rewards outputs at undergraduate level, these institutions often bear a double burden. They cannot benefit from research funding in any significant way, even though it is lucrative, and at the same time they cannot maximise on funding for their work at undergraduate level.

A differentiated higher education system requires institutions to develop their own conceptualisation of the academic project that will drive them. Analysis of the mission and vision statements of all institutions showed that the nebulous idea of 'excellence' was a goal for many (Behari-Leak & McKenna 2017). The construct of excellence has been problematised by many, most notably Readings (1996: 32), who notes that:

> [e]xcellence is invoked ... as always, to say precisely nothing at all: it deflects attention from the questions of what quality and pertinence might be, who actually are the judges of a relevant or a good university, and by what authority they become those judges.

Barnett (2004: 64) follows up on Readings' observation by noting that excellence stands 'for no purpose, no ideal and no concept in particular'. Nash (2013) goes further to argue that the focus on excellence can be antithetical to being an ethical university.

Formal differentiation in the South African system has always been resisted because of the apartheid past, but it is also a problem in other countries as differentiation can rapidly translate into a hierarchy. Without a clear consideration of how differentiation can serve the multiple demands placed on higher education and attend to the varied desires of students, countries will not be able to foster the strong higher education systems required by the knowledge economy. In South Africa, until we summon the political will to genuinely engage with the issue of differentiation and develop a funding mechanism that equitably supports a variety of endeavours, institutions will be driven towards those activities that carry the biggest financial reward (Essop 2020).

Throughout this book, we have argued for what we have termed 'social' understandings of learning, learners, academics and the university. The model of the Decontextualised Learner we have cited so often in relation to teaching and learning can also be seen to apply to research, as people are inducted into understandings of knowledge-making in much the same way as they are inducted into understandings of learning, depending on the contexts to which they have access (Boughey 2018). Values related to the need for and excitement of generating new knowledge all contribute to the emergence of practices conducive to research production. If an academic is immersed in contexts where such values are common and where research-based practices can be observed on a daily basis, it is more likely that she will access those values and develop mastery of those practices than someone whose work environment is very different.

While universities might try to increase research production by, for example, running research-design workshops or holding retreats for academics to go away and write for publication, such initiatives can be seen to be akin to the adjunct efforts to improve students' skills that we have criticised in Chapter Four. Our argument would be that these initiatives need to be complemented by the development of research environments at departmental and faculty levels, if the conditions necessary for research production are to emerge. Versions of such environments already exist in the universities where research production is high. In others, they tend to exist only in pockets, with concomitant effects on academics' own sense of who they can be and what they can do.

As we have indicated throughout this book, universities across the world have been affected by globalisation and the thinking around their role in the new knowledge-based economy. As producers of knowledge, much in the same way as manufacturers of material goods, universities are constructed as having the means of creating income for themselves. If a university can make money by doing research, then the need for the state to fund knowledge-making activities is less important. This sort of thinking may work for applied knowledge, though as we will argue below that is still problematic, but it does not work for 'blue sky' knowledge or knowledge aimed at making society a better place for all. Not all kinds of knowledge can be commercialised yet all kinds of knowledge are essential for the development and well-being of society.

Furthermore, it must be noted that many of the most readily commercialised knowledge products are 'public bads' in that they function to harm the planet and people for improved profit for industry and its shareholders. There is a certain irony that the university is simultaneously tasked with making knowledge that plunders the planet *and* making knowledge that can resolve the problems emerging from such plundering (McKenna 2021). We need to be willing to discuss the ethical implications of the knowledge we produce and to consider taking a stance that is explicitly planet and people focused and which rejects being party to knowledge production which is explicitly harmful. In some cases, harmful knowledge projects are self-evident, such as developing accounting and legal models to allow multi-nationals to work outside of any nation state and thereby avoid paying tax or being accountable for human rights violations. In other cases, deliberations about whether the knowledge project is a public good or public bad will be far more complex. But in all cases, we would argue, the university has a role to play in nurturing researchers who take on, as a fundamental part of their identities, a commitment to work for the good of people and the planet.

The privileging of such knowledge with commercial value and the emphasis on higher education as a 'private good' which developed from the early 1990s onwards has been a particular threat to the humanities. Given the history of colonialism and apartheid, the potential to produce commercialised research is highly skewed. The small group of universities producing the majority of South African research outputs are more likely to be able to leverage such research. The universities of technology are potentially at an advantage as their key role is in producing research that is industry-focused and which thus can bring in income. However, their lack of capacity often constrains them, and traditional universities without strong research backgrounds are also unlikely to be able to benefit from the value of commercial research, yet these are the very institutions which tend to struggle the most financially and would thus most benefit from such an income stream.

In the second core function, research, globally we see that the universities that are least likely to have strong research cultures serve larger proportions of working-class students. The net effect is that such students have limited access to postgraduate studies and are less likely to be able to join in processes of knowledge-making.

It is very possible for universities to strengthen their research environments but we would argue that many current approaches try to insert performance management metrics and financial rewards to drive research at the cost of a focus on the inherent purpose and value of research. This may bring about short-term increases in outputs but might not bring about sustained knowledge creation. We argue that what is needed are consistent initiatives focused on the development of a public-good focused academic identity and institutional culture.

Community engagement

The final core function, community engagement, spans a range of activities as the following diagram, adapted from Furco (1996), shows:

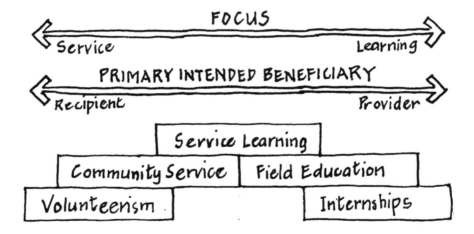

Activities on the left of the continuum are intended to serve communities; those on the right are directed at furthering students' learning. Key to understandings of community engagement is that activities should be *reciprocal*, in the sense that it is not simply that students serve communities and enhance their learning as a result of applying it in practical situations, but rather that the universities should *learn from* the communities with which they interact. This learning can involve the challenging of theory as well as practice. Given the decolonisation debates that have dominated higher education systems in recent years, the understanding of community engagement as *reciprocal* is key to taking the knowledge project further.

Our analysis of teaching and learning in all universities in South Africa found evidence of uneven engagement with wider communities. Commitment to community engagement was strong in some institutions within the cultural domain, particularly among rurally based institutions, with explicit references to the social and geographical context within which the university is embedded (Boughey 2011; Muthama & McKenna 2020). If community engagement is to be used to provide learning experiences for students and services to communities, however they are defined, it needs to be structured into institutional life through the development of policy and systems which recognise it. Policy, for example, could identify a minimum number of credits in a qualification which comprise service learning. Reward systems for academics could set criteria in relation to community engagement activity for the confirmation of appointment and personal promotion. In the data we studied for the research underpinning this book, such structures were in place in some institutions, while in others there was a contradiction between the references to community engagement in interviews and vision and mission statements on the one hand, and an absence of reference to community engagement in strategic plans, promotion policies, and budgeting on the other. Without complementary structures and cultures, community engagement remains ad hoc and dependent on the personal projects of individual academics.

Community engagement can take on many different forms in keeping with each university's mission and vision and geographical location. We would argue that it holds enormous potential to strengthen an institution's teaching and research. It would be possible to suggest that it is in the nexus between the university and the broader community within which it exists to serve that the African university could best take up its mantle.

Bundling and unbundling the university

Throughout this book we have reflected on numerous competing imperatives facing universities. Universities are being pulled by managerialist discourses towards performance management, and strategic decisions are increasingly undertaken outside of a concern for the academic project. At the same time, universities are being expected to take on roles that were not previously part of their mandate. For example, in a number of countries, the inability of the state to provide functional health systems and mental health support has resulted in universities having to increase their health and counselling services. As the state has failed to address the need for job creation, affordable housing and efficient public transport, so universities are increasingly being expected to pick up the bill for bus tickets, meals and more. Providing meals and toiletries for students who are in desperate need is now an urgent and ongoing concern for universities in South Africa despite the need for economic cuts (Habib 2019). As the university is being expected to provide a range of resources and services that were once far beyond its mandate, it is possible to argue that more is being 'bundled' into the university's realm of responsibility than ever before.

In such a context, the allure of unbundling is not surprising. Unbundling is a process whereby university programmes and experiences are disaggregated and outsourced (McCowan 2017; Czerniewicz 2018). Partnerships between universities and the private sector have proliferated in the last decade, with the emergence of a number of high-profile online programme-management companies. The outsourcing of materials development, assessment, course evaluations, institutional marketing, student admissions, and more has occurred in a number of universities around the world and many are in evidence in South Africa (unbundleduni.com).

Those in favour of this process point to the cost efficiency and the expertise brought to various tasks by external companies, particularly in regard to technology. Those opposed to it point out that the distinction between what is and what is not central to the academic project is difficult to judge, and that unbundling forces universities into a marketised context which does not serve its public good mandate well at all. We would argue that our universities are highly susceptible to the glitzy promises of online programme-management companies and their ilk because we have not sufficiently articulated for ourselves what the academic project is. Also of concern is the extent to which unbundling will privilege some institutions and some students over others. External companies are motivated by profit and therefore seek alliances with institutions and students who are most likely to be able to pay for their services. The affordances of technology need to be considered in relation to the growing marketisation of higher education within a highly unequal sector.

What is arguably needed is resistance to many of the globalised discourses which have resulted in many if not most of the universities in South Africa and beyond following what we have called hyper-capitalist models. We call for the espousal of what we will describe as the developmental university along with greater degrees of structured differentiation.

A differentiated and developmental system

As we have tried to indicate throughout this book, attempts to transform higher education on the continent have been conditioned by ideas related to globalisation in a worldwide system of universities. While it was always acknowledged in policy and other documents produced from the early 1990s onwards that South Africa needed to deal with equity in order to address the wrongs of apartheid, *as well as* to achieve efficiency in the sense of needing to join the global economy and thus, to some extent, a global worldview, in many respects the balance can be argued to have swung towards efficiency in that much of what has happened has moved us closer to global models of a hyper-capitalist university.

As a result, students are increasingly pushed towards understanding higher education as a private good because it appears to be the one way of ensuring social mobility. Much of this situation does, of course, result from the wider economic environment characterised by high levels of unemployment. As this understanding of higher education as a private good has grown, and partly in response to it, state funding has decreased, which means that students have been increasingly required to contribute more to the cost of their education.

At the same time, however, higher education has not served students equally well; slow throughput and drop-out rates are experienced by some social groups far more than others. As participation in higher education has increased, so too has the number of graduates employed in low-paid work in, for example, call centres or, possibly even worse, forced to take numerous postdoctoral fellowships and unpaid internships in order to have any chance of gaining more permanent employment. A lack of career guidance and family networks means that these outcomes are experienced by some more than others (Case et al. 2018). These patterns have been observed in countries even with high participation levels, such as the United Kingdom, Australia and the United States of America, but they are also becoming more and more evident in South Africa in particular. The situation is generally explained away by discourses that essentially blame the universities for not producing graduates who are 'work ready'. As we have argued throughout the book, however, vocational qualifications are not necessarily the answer, because if they are designed without sufficient conceptual coherence, they 'lock' graduates into specific contexts by denying them access to powerful disciplinary knowledge (Muller 2000). Such powerful knowledge allows movement across contexts and, even more importantly, provides the abstractions and theories to imagine a future world which is different to the present.

The focus on work readiness is thus, we would argue, largely misplaced. As Allais (2014) and Ashwin (2020) point out, the construct of the knowledge economy has resulted in a narrowing of the purpose of higher education to the provision of skilled labour. According to the Universum Talent Research Report 2018 (Universum Communications 2018), the top career goal identified by all South African students was 'to be dedicated to a cause or to feel that I am serving a greater good'. The second goal was 'to be secure or stable in my job' and the third, 'to have work/life balance'. Nowhere does the private good in the sense of the accrual of personal wealth feature. While employability of graduates is key this cannot be at the cost of attending to the university's role in furthering the public good.

Of even more concern, however, many students encounter the time spent in the university not as a time of growth but one of pain. As one student noted in a meeting we attended, 'The universities are places of self-doubt, not self-development'. Over and over in our work, we have heard testimonies of suffering both because of the economic circumstances experienced by students and also because of their alienation from the academic project and from the very life of the university itself, an alienation which has been explained as the imposition of whiteness.

One of the problems with the notion of transformation is that it has arguably been used to mask other things. We have had the experience, for example, of calls for transformation being used to introduce regimes of accountability and monitoring which are linked with managerialism. Yet another problem is that meanings of the terms are not always shared and not sufficiently interrogated. We may all assume that we know what the term 'transformation' means, but do we? Determining what counts as powerful, decolonised knowledge and how best to produce and teach it becomes even more difficult because of a lack of definition of the academic project itself in many universities and then the failure to implement activities fit for the purpose of serving such a project.

What would seem to be the case, therefore, is that, in spite of the very best efforts of policy makers and many others working to transform the higher education system so that it truly is one that serves all, in South Africa we have arrived at a position where a combination of a very fractured past and an apparent lack of political will to achieve more clarity around differentiation has led to the creation of a complicated territory where universities, and the academics who work in them, are trying to be all things to all people and competing as they do so. Sadly, our reading of the literature, much of which is cited in this book, suggests that many of these problems characterise other countries on the continent too.

This book has been a reflection on our research in teaching and learning in higher education, mainly in South Africa, over the past two decades. The book is rooted in a belief that higher education has the potential to contribute to the well-being of societies through the production of research and of graduates who can contribute to critical discourse and, thus, to democracy itself. It is through a social understanding of the complexity of higher education that this might become possible.

As we have indicated in this chapter, it is our view that much needs to be done in the university sector. But if we are able to take up some of the alternative perspectives on offer, we can ensure that higher education offers knowledge and knowers who are committed to people and the planet. We are optimistic about the role that higher education plays and can play as a key structure in developing a more just society.

A Covid Postscript

In the time since we finished the first draft of this book, a great deal has happened. In early 2020, the first cases of Covid-19 began to appear and by March of that year large portions of the world had 'locked down' in an attempt to limit transmission of the virus. For higher education, lockdowns meant that face-to-face teaching was suspended and a rapid move to online teaching took place.

Online teaching has long been touted as a panacea for many ills in higher education including, amongst other things, the need to teach larger numbers of students as systems massified and universities grew in size (Dutton, Ryznar & Long 2018), the need for flexibility (Dhawan 2020) and the need to accommodate the preferences of so called 'Generation Z', who, we are informed by Wikipedia, 'have grown up with the internet and portable digital technology from a young age' and who are thus deemed to be 'digital natives'. The arrival of Covid-19 has provided the impetus for universities to draw on the use of technology at a pace and in ways that those arguing for it could never have imagined possible.

In the context of all this change, we need to ask: is the position we have taken in this book still relevant? This short postscript added to the book just before publication aims to argue that what we have said in the preceding chapters is even more important, even more relevant, now than the day we finished writing it in late 2019.

In the book, we adopt what is essentially a socio-cultural view of learning which acknowledges the way dominant forms of both knowledge and knowing can serve to privilege some and marginalise others. At the same time, we argue for what theorists such as Wheelahan (2010) term 'powerful' knowledge-coherent, structured bodies of knowledge which allow knowers to move across contexts and to imagine worlds that do not yet exist. These bodies of powerful knowledge *need not* be the same as the knowledge of the powerful although, at the moment, it is the knowledge developed in the north and west which dominates in the academy at the cost of other forms of knowledge which have been side-lined, ignored or deemed illegitimate.

Our position draws on what we term a 'model of the learner as a social being' which we contrast with that of the 'Decontextualised Learner' and the belief that it is factors inherent to the individual which lead to access to and success in higher education.

As African universities began to draw on technology more extensively than ever before as Covid-19 swept across the world, two concerns came to occupy the minds of university leaders: (i) the need to provide students with access to devices and to data and (ii) the need to train staff to teach online. For many students in Africa, access to technology was usually possible thanks to the availability of computer laboratories on campus because ownership of a personal device is a dream beyond their means. While enormous strides were made in providing students with both devices and data in South Africa at least, and many institutions quickly made plans to develop the capacity of their academic teachers to work with online learning platforms such as Moodle and Blackboard, arguably not much attention was paid to what the inability to access face-to-face teaching would mean beyond these immediate practical and technical considerations.

A recent call for papers for a colloquium hosted by the South African Council on Higher Education with the theme of *Safeguarding the Quality of Provision with the Shift to Online Teaching and Learning in the Times of Covid-19* (CHE 2021) notes an Association of Commonwealth Universities (ACU) policy brief which shows that 'the continuing digital divide poses a major threat to equitable access to higher education and lifelong learning globally'.

The same document (CHE 2021) goes on to cite Pedro and Kumar (2020) who identify the following requirements for high-quality online teaching:

- Appropriate and updated technology for supporting synchronous and asynchronous activities for online programs/courses.
- Efficient technical support, help-desk activities and online related facility manage-ment services.
- Online access to self-help technical support materials.
- Allocation of administrative staff specifically prepared to support online programmes and courses.
- Sufficient and well-qualified instructional design services.
- Access to diversified and high-quality media support services.
- Appropriate support for online teaching staff by providing e-tutors and other support services to ensure a reasonable faculty workflow in online programs.
- Availability of online library services as well as library staff, specifically for supporting online programs/courses.
- Availability of other student-related services for online education (career guidance, writing centres).

All but two of these requirements relate to the technicalities of online learning. In those two that do not directly relate to technicalities, one notes 'the provision of e-tutors and other support services' and another 'the availability of other student related services'. All of these requirements, we would argue, draw on what we have termed 'the model of the Decontextualized Learner'.

It is important to note, moreover, that these requirements are identified as relating to the provision of 'high-quality online teaching' where the definition of quality is understood to be 'fit for purpose'. From the perspective we have advanced in this book that teaching and learning is profoundly social, cultural and political, the question which needs to be asked, therefore, is whether the technicalities identified above are sufficient to make online teaching fit for purpose in the wide range of contexts that characterise higher education in Africa.

As we have noted throughout this book, as higher education systems massify they also diversify (Trow 1973). What this means is that an increasing number of 'first generation' students, young people from homes where they are the first to experience higher education, have entered and will continue to enter universities. The arrival of Covid-19 meant that these students were forced to return home and engage with the online learning provided by their universities. For some students this meant returning to crowded environments with no quiet study space. Even more significantly, it involved returning to environments where reading and writing were not the dominant practices and where other activities were privileged in order to maintain the family home economically, socially and culturally. In some cases, returning home impacted on women in particular as they were called upon to take up childcare, housework and cooking responsibilities which impacted in no small measure on the time available to study. Regardless of the extent to which the requirements for 'high-quality online teaching' were met, it is unlikely that students from homes not headed by educated middle-class caregivers would readily be able to achieve the sort of meaningful engagement with learning materials necessary for high-quality learning.

The social, cultural and political view of teaching and learning we have offered in the book also leads to another understanding of why the focus on technicalities offered in Pedro and Kumar's (2020) identification of the requirements for 'high-quality teaching' is inadequate. In Chapter Four, we drew on the work of Gee (2008) who argues that being 'literate' in any particular context involves taking on a related 'way of being' or social role. This idea is also taken up in the work of Maton (2014) who argues that curricula construct different kinds of 'knowers'. Many of the more diverse groups of students now entering African universities draw on social roles and understandings of what it means to know that are far removed from those which are privileged in academia. For these students, developing the roles required to be successful in higher education depends on accessing values and practices around what can count as knowledge within the field and how it can be known. Gee (2008) is insistent that a literacy is acquired through immersion in the contexts in which it is practiced and cannot be developed through direct teaching (for example, in 'study skills' courses). This means that, for many students immersion in the life of a contact university is highly beneficial. Typically, universities with face-to-face teaching on physical campuses allow for this immersion. Students are exposed to peer-learning as more senior students demonstrate ways of doing things, many extra-curricula learning spaces are open to them and they interact with lecturers on a day-to-day basis.

The task of developing these literacies or social roles is made all the more difficult by the fact that literacy practices differ across different knowledge fields. In Chapter Five, we drew on the concept of knowledge structures, such as Bernstein (2000), who argues that, in some knowledge areas, knowing involves using a particular 'language of description' to see the world. These languages of description differ according to the particular theoretical lens being used by researchers to 'see' the world. Access to these languages of description comes from engagement with those who use them, with the academics teaching courses and modules, with technicians running the laboratories and the texts communicating the knowledge of the field. Throughout this book, we have been critical of the extent to which access to such languages of description is often provided tacitly rather than explicitly but nonetheless, these ways of being are modelled to students in their interactions with academics in the field and through the feedback they receive on their work. It is unlikely that a generic 'e-tutor' or those working in student support structures (i) are able to identify this specialist understanding and (ii) are able to model it for students.

In the book, we problematise the way current approaches to teaching fail to take account of the social and cultural in teaching and learning, arguing that, if only academic teachers were more aware and more explicit about the differences in performance we see between different social groups might be eased. The current system of face-to-face campus-based education is poor enough at introducing students to the practices they need to succeed but we very much doubt that online learning can even begin to compensate for the loss of the 'social' and 'cultural' that face-to-face teaching can model. This is even more the case if the shift to online teaching is understood simply as needing to meet sets of technical requirements.

There is a distinction to be made between, on the one hand, carefully designed online teaching that takes issues of student interaction and epistemological access seriously, and, on the other hand, the rapid move to emergency remote learning that all of us were thrust into in 2020. While we will always be proponents of the benefits of face-to-face teaching, our concern is not with online education per se but rather with the rise of technicist understandings that taking classes online is a simple matter or a solution to many of the financial and logistical constraints being faced by our universities. The call we have made throughout this book for more social, critical deliberations about curricula, students, epistemological access and epistemic justice, and higher education generally are intensified for the online environment and we note with despair some of the more simplistic accounts of what emergency remote education has meant for our students.

Furthermore, our concern that the rapid shift to online learning is often understood in purely technicist ways is accompanied by our concern that the pedagogical changes in the face of the pandemic are often discussed as if they are neutral rather than inherently political (Czerniewicz 2020). Questions about the datafication and unbundling of higher education need careful attention as do issues of escalating marketisation made possible through uncritical adoption of technology (Giroux 2021).

In short then and as, hopefully, vaccine programmes kick in across the continent and begin to lessen the impact of the Covid-19 pandemic, we challenge all those who argue that the past year or so has resulted in a fundamental shift to the way universities go about doing things through movement to online learning *unless we can find ways of online teaching acknowledging and accommodating the social, cultural and political we have argued so passionately for.* From this perspective, Covid-19 has not impacted on the relevance of the chapters we wrote before those first cases of disease emerged in December 2019. If anything, it has just made them even more significant and relevant to what we need to do as we move forward.

References

Achadu O, Asfour F, Chakona G, Mason P, Mataruse P, McKenna S & Oluwole DO (2018) Postgraduate writing groups as spaces of agency development. *South African Journal of Higher Education* 32(6): 370–381

Allais S (2007) Education service delivery: The disastrous case of outcomes-based qualifications frameworks. *Progress in Development Studies* 7(1): 65–78

Allais S (2010) *The Implementation and Impact of National Qualifications Frameworks: Report of a Study in 16 Countries.* Geneva: International Labour Organisation

Allais S (2014) *Selling Out Education: National Qualifications Frameworks and the Neglect of Knowledge.* Dordrecht: Springer

Altbach P, Reisberg L & Rumbley L (2009) *Trends in Global Higher Education: Tracking an Academic Revolution: A Report Prepared for the UNESCO 2009 World Conference on Higher Education.* Paris: Unesco

Amsler S & Bolsmann C (2012) University ranking as social exclusion. *British Journal of Sociology of Education* 33(2): 283–301

Amutabi MN (2002) Crisis and student protest in universities in Kenya: Examining the roles of students in national leadership and the democratization process. *African Studies Review* 45(2): 157–177

Archer A & Richards R (2011) *Changing Spaces: Writing Centres and Access to Higher Education.* Stellenbosch: African SUN Media

Archer M (1995) *Realist Social Theory: The Morphogenetic Approach.* Cambridge: Cambridge University Press

Archer M (1996) *Culture and Agency: The Place of Culture in Social Theory.* Cambridge: Cambridge University Press

Archer M (1998) Introduction: Realism in the Social Sciences. In: M Archer, R Bhaskar, A Collier, T Lawson & A Norrie (eds) *Critical Realism: Essential Readings.* Abingdon: Routledge. pp. 189–203

Archer M (2000) *Being Human: The Problem of Agency.* Cambridge: Cambridge University Press

Archer M (2002) Realism and the problem of agency. *Alethia* 5(1): 11–20

Archer M (2003) *Structure, Agency and the Internal Conversation.* Cambridge: Cambridge University Press

Archer M (2007) *Making Our Way through the World: Human Reflexivity and Social Mobility.* Cambridge: Cambridge University Press

Armstrong E & Hamilton L (2013) *Paying for the Party: How College Maintains Inequality.* Cambridge, Mass.: Harvard University Press

Armstrong M (2019) Learning to learn: A Critical Realist exploration into the home established learning practices of a marginalised community in Port Elizabeth. Unpublished doctoral dissertation, Rhodes University, Makhanda

Ashton D & Green F (1996) *Education, Training and the Global Economy.* Cheltenham: Edward Elgar

Ashwin P (2020) *Transforming University Education: A Manifesto*. London: Bloomsbury Academic

Atteh S (1996) The crisis in higher education in Africa. *Journal of Opinion* 24(1): 36–42

Badat S (2010) Global rankings of universities: A perverse and present burden. In: E Unterhalter & V Carpentier (eds) *Global Inequalities and Higher Education*. Basingstoke: Palgrave Macmillan

Badat S (2016) Deciphering the meanings, and explaining the South African higher education student protests of 2015–16. *Pax Academica* 1&2: 71–106

Bangeni B & Kapp R (2017) *Negotiating Learning and Identity in Higher Education: Access, Persistence and Retention*. London: Bloomsbury

Barnett R (2004) The purposes of higher education and the changing face of academia. *London Review of Education* 2(1): 61–73

Barnett R & Peters A (2018) *The Idea of the University: Contemporary Perspectives*. New York: Peter Lang

Bartolomé L (1994) Beyond the methods fetish: Toward a humanizing pedagogy. *Harvard Educational Review* 64(2): 173–195

Bass G (2008) An investigation of the perceptions of learners and staff in respect of the Dental Technology extended first year programme. Unpublished Master's of Technology dissertation, Durban University of Technology, Durban

Bathmaker A, Ingram N, Abrahams J, Hoare A, Waller R & Bradley H (2016) *Higher Education, Social Class and Social Mobility: The Degree Generation*. New York: Springer

Becher T (1989) *Academic Tribes and Territories: Intellectual Enquiry and the Culture of Disciplines*. Buckingham: Open University Press

Becher T & Trowler P (2001) *Academic Tribes and Territories: Intellectual Enquiry and the Culture of Disciplines*. 2nd edn. Buckingham: Open University Press/SRHE

Behari-Leak K (2015) Conditions enabling or constraining the exercise of agency among new academics in higher education, conducive to the social inclusion of students. Unpublished doctoral dissertation, Rhodes University, Makhanda

Behari-Leak K (2017) New academics, new higher education contexts: A critical perspective on professional development. *Teaching in Higher Education* 22(5): 485–500

Behari-Leak K & McKenna S (2017) Generic gold standard or contextualised public good? Teaching excellence awards in post-colonial South Africa. *Teaching in Higher Education* 22(1): 1–15

Bernstein B (1981) Codes, modalities, and the process of cultural reproduction: A model. *Language In Society* 10(3): 327–363

Bernstein B (2000) *Pedagogy, Symbolic Control, and Identity: Theory, Research, Critique*. Lanham, Maryland: Rowman & Littlefield

Bernstein B (2003a) *Class, Codes and Control: Theoretical Studies towards a Sociology of Language*. Abingdon: Routledge

Bernstein B (2003b) *Structuring of Pedagogic Discourse*. Abingdon: Routledge

Bernstein B (2006) Vertical and horizontal discourse: An essay. *British Journal of Sociology of Education* 20(2): 157–173

Bertram C (2004) Exploring informal student study groups in a South African teacher education programme. In: A Tait & R Mills (eds) *Rethinking Learner Support in Distance Education: Change and Continuity in an International Context*. London: Taylor & Francis. pp. 14–27

Bharuthram S & McKenna S (2006) A writer–respondent intervention as a means of developing academic literacy. *Teaching in Higher Education* 11(4): 495–507

Bharuthram S & McKenna S (2012) Students' navigation of the uncharted territories of academic writing. *Africa Education Review* 9(3): 581–594

Bhaskar R (1979) *The Possibility of Naturalism: A Philosophical Critique of the Contemporary Human Sciences*. Brighton, UK: Harvester Press

Bhaskar R (1998) Philosophy and scientific realism. In: M Archer, R Bhaskar, A Collier, T Lawson & A Norrie (eds) *Critical Realism: Essential Readings*. Abingdon: Routledge. pp. 16–47

REFERENCES

Bhaskar R (2000) Introducing transcendental dialectical critical realism. *Alethia* 3(1): 15–21

Bhaskar R (2002) The philosophy of meta-reality. *Journal of Critical Realism* 1(1): 67–93

Bhaskar R (2008) *Dialectic: The Pulse of Freedom*. Abingdon: Routledge

Bhaskar R (2016) *Enlightened Common Sense: The Philosophy of Critical Realism*. Abingdon: Routledge

Biglan A (1973) Relationships between subject matter characteristics and the structure and output of university departments. *The Journal of Applied Psychology* 57(3): 204–213

Bird S, Litt J & Wang Y (2004) Creating status of women reports: Institutional housekeeping as 'women's work'. *NWSA Journal: A Publication of the National Women's Studies Association* 16(1): 194–206

Bloch G (2009) *The Toxic Mix: What's Wrong with South Africa's Schools and How to Fix It*. Cape Town: Tafelberg

Boughey C (2002) 'Naming' students' problems: An analysis of language-related discourses at a South African university. *Teaching in Higher Education* 7(3): 295–307

Boughey C (2005a) 'Epistemological' access to the university: An alternative perspective. *South African Journal of Higher Education* 19(3): 638–650

Boughey C (2005b) *Lessons learned from academic development movement in South African higher education and their relevance for student support initiatives in the FET College sector*. Commissioned research paper. Pretoria: Human Sciences Research Council

Boughey C (2007) Educational development in South Africa: From social reproduction to capitalist expansion? *Higher Education Policy* 20(1): 5–18

Boughey C (2009) *A meta-analysis of teaching and learning at five research-intensive South African universities*. Commissioned research paper. Pretoria: Council on Higher Education

Boughey C (2010a) *Academic development for improved efficiency in the higher education and Training System in South Africa*. Commissioned research paper. Johannesburg: Development Bank South Africa

Boughey C (2010b) *A meta-analysis of teaching and learning at four South African universities of technology*. Commissioned research paper. Pretoria: Council on Higher Education

Boughey C (2010c) Understanding teaching and learning at foundation level: A 'critical' imperative. In: C Hutchings & J Garraway (eds) *Beyond the University Gates: Provision of Extended Curriculum Programmes in South Africa*. Cape Town: Cape Peninsula University of Technology. pp. 4–7

Boughey C (2011) Institutional difference: A neglected consideration in the scholarship of teaching and learning? *International Journal of the Scholarship of Teaching & Learning* 5(2): Article 6

Boughey C (2012a) The significance of structure, culture and agency in supporting and developing student learning at South African universities. In: R Dhunpath & R Vithal (eds) *Alternative Access to Higher Education: Underprepared Students or Underprepared Institutions?* Cape Town: Pearson

Boughey C (2012b) Linking teaching and research: An alternative perspective. *Teaching in Higher Education* 17(5): 629–635

Boughey C (2013) What are we thinking of? A critical overview of approaches to developing academic literacy in South African higher education. *Journal for Language Teaching* 47(2): 25–41

Boughey C (2018) Learning to research: A 'social' account. In: P du Preez & S Simmonds (eds) *A Scholarship of Doctoral Education: On Becoming a Researcher*. Stellenbosch: SUN Media

Boughey C & McKenna S (2011a) *A meta-analysis of teaching and learning at five historically disadvantaged universities*. Commissioned research report. Pretoria: Council on Higher Education

Boughey C & McKenna S (2011b) *A meta-analysis of teaching and learning at four comprehensive universities*. Commissioned research report. Pretoria: Council on Higher Education

Boughey C & McKenna S (2016) Academic literacy and the Decontextualised Learner. *Critical Studies in Teaching and Learning* 4(2): 1–9

Boughey C & McKenna S (2017) Analysing an audit cycle: A critical realist account. *Studies in Higher Education* 42(6): 963–975

Bourdieu J (1990) *Homo Academicus*. London: Polity

Bourdieu P & Passeron J-C (1994) Introduction: Language and relationship to language in the teaching situation. In: P Bourdieu, J-C Passeron & J de Saint Martin (eds) *Academic Discourse*. Stanford, CA: Stanford University Press. pp. 1–34

Bowles S & Gintis H (1976) *Schooling in capitalist America*. New York: Basic Books

Bozalek V & Boughey C (2012) (Mis)framing higher education in South Africa. *Social Policy & Administration* 46(6): 688–703

Bozalek V & Boughey C (2020) (Mis)framing higher education in South Africa (updated version of Bozalek & Boughey 2012). In: V Bozalek, D Hölscher & M Zembylas (eds) *Nancy Fraser and Participatory Parity: Reframing Social Justice in South African Higher Education*. Abingdon: Routledge

Bradbury J (1993) The meta-language of cognition. In: C Criticos, R Deacon & C Hemson (eds) *Proceedings of the Kenton, Olwandle Conference, Scottburgh, Natal, 1993*

Bunting I (2002) Funding. In: N Cloete, P Maasen, R Fehnel, T Moja, H Perold & T Gibbon (eds) *Transformation in Higher Education: Global Pressures and Local Realities in South Africa*. 2nd edn. Dordrecht: Kluwer. pp. 73–94

Bunting I (2006) The higher education landscape under apartheid. In: N Cloete, P Maassen, R Fehnel, T Moja, T Gibbon & H Perold (eds) *Transformation in Higher Education: Global Pressures and Local Realities*. Dordrecht: Springer Netherlands. pp. 35–52

Bunting I, Cloete N & Van Schalkwyk F (2014) *An empirical overview of eight flagship universities in Africa 2001–2011. Report of the Higher Education Research and Advocacy Network in Africa (HERANA)*. Wynberg, Cape Town: CHET

Carpentier V, Lebeau Y & Välimaa J (2018) International perspectives on equality of higher education opportunities: Models and strategies for accessibility and availability. In: P Ashwin & J Case (eds) *Higher Education Pathways: South African Undergraduate Education and the Public Good*. Cape Town: African Minds. pp. 95–111

Carspecken (1996) *Critical Ethnography in Educational Research: A Theoretical and Practical Guide*. New York: Routledge

Case J (2011) Knowledge matters: Interrogating the curriculum debate in Engineering using the sociology of knowledge. *Journal of Education* 61: 51–72

Case J (2013) *Researching Student Learning in Higher Education: A Social Realist Approach*. Abingdon: Routledge

Case J (2016) Re-imagining the curriculum in a postcolonial space: Engaging the public good purposes of higher education in South Africa. *Journal for New Generation sciences* 14(3): 22–33

Case J, Marshall D, McKenna S & Mogashana D (2018) *Going to University: The Influence of Higher Education on the Lives of Young South Africans*. Cape Town: African Minds

Castells M (1996) *The Rise of the Network Society. The Information Age: Economy, Society, and Culture Vol. I (Information Age Series)*. London: Blackwell

Castells M (2001) Information technology and global capitalism. In: W Hutton & A Giddens (eds) *On the Edge. Living with Global Capitalism*. London: Vintage

Chidindi J (2017) Discursive constructions of quality assurance: The case of the Zimbabwe Council for Higher Education. Unpublished doctoral dissertation, Rhodes University, Makhanda

Chisholm L (2005) The making of South Africa's National Curriculum Statement. *Journal of Curriculum Studies* 37(2): 193–208

Chisholm L, Volmink J, Ndhlovu T, Potenza E, Mahomed H, Muller J & Lubisi C (2000) *A South African Curriculum for the Twenty First Century*. Pretoria: Department of Education

Christie F (1985) *Language Education*. Victoria: Deakin University Press

Clarence S (2014) Enabling cumulative knowledge-building through teaching: A legitimation code theory analysis of pedagogic practice in Law and Political Science. Unpublished doctoral dissertation, Rhodes University, Makhanda

Clegg S (2011) Cultural capital and agency: Connecting critique and curriculum in higher education. *British Journal of Sociology of Education* 32(1): 93–108

Cloete N, Maassen P, Fehnel R, Moja T, Gibbon T & Perold H (2006) *Transformation in Higher Education: Global Pressures and Local Realities*. Dordrecht: Springer

Cloete N, Bailey T & Maasen P (2011) *Universities and Economic Development in Africa: Pact, Academic Core and Coordination*. Cape Town: African Minds

Commission for University Education (CUE) (Kenya) (2014) *Harmonised Criteria and Guidelines for Appointment and Promotion of Academic Staff*. Nairobi: CUE

Cooper D (2015) Social justice and South African university student enrolment data by 'race', 1998–2012: From 'skewed revolution' to 'stalled revolution'. *Higher Education Quarterly* 69(3): 237–262

Cooper D & Subotzky G (2001) *The Skewed Revolution: Trends in South African Higher Education, 1988–1998*. Cape Town: Education Policy Unit, University of the Western Cape

Council on Higher Education (CHE) (2001a) *Higher Education Quality Committee Founding Document*. Pretoria: CHE

Council on Higher Education (CHE) (2001b) Reinserting the public good into higher education. *Kagisano* No. 1. Pretoria: CHE

Council on Higher Education (CHE) (2004) *Criteria for Institutional Audits*. Pretoria: CHE

Council on Higher Education (CHE) (2012) *Higher Education Qualifications Sub-Framework*. Pretoria: CHE

Council on Higher Education (CHE) (2013a) The aims of higher education. *Kagisano* No. 9. Pretoria: CHE

Council on Higher Education (CHE) (2013b) *The Higher Education Qualifications Sub-Framework*. Pretoria: CHE

Council on Higher Education (CHE) (2016) *South African Higher Education Reviewed: Two Decades of Democracy*. Pretoria: CHE

Council on Higher Education (CHE) (2020) *Vital Stats Public Higher Education 2018*. Pretoria: CHE

Council on Higher Education (CHE) (2021)

Crawford C, Dearden L, Micklewright J & Vignoles A (2017) *Family Background and University Success: Differences in Higher Education Access and Outcomes in England*. Oxford: Oxford University Press

Czerniewicz L (2018) Unbundling and rebundling higher education in an age of inequality. *Educause Review*. https://er.educause.edu/articles/2018/10/unbundling-and-rebundling-higher-education-in-an-age-of-inequality

Czerniewicz L (2020, 15 March) What we learnt from 'going online' during university shutdowns in South Africa. *PhilOnEdTech* [Blog]. https://philonedtech.com/what-we-learnt-from-going-online-during-university-shutdowns-in-south-africa/

Danermark B, Ekström M, Jakobsen L & Karlsson JC (2002) *Explaining Society. Critical Realism in the Social Sciences*. London: Routledge

Darvas P, Gao S, Shen Y & Bawany B (2017) *Sharing Higher Education's Promise beyond the Few in Sub-Saharan Africa*. Washington, DC: World Bank

De Bie G (2017) Analysis of a foundational biomedical curriculum: Exploring cumulative knowledge-building in the rehabilitative health professions. Unpublished doctoral dissertation, Rhodes University, Makhanda

De Kadt E & Mathonsi N (2003) Writing in English with an 'African voice': Ownership, identity and learning. *Journal for Language Teaching* 37(1): 92–103

De Sousa Santos B (2007) Beyond abyssal thinking: From global lines to ecologies of knowledges. *Review* 30(1): 45–89

De Sousa Santos B (2019) Information, understanding, transformation: The challenges of 4IR. Public address, University of Johannesburg, 3 October

Department of Education (DoE), South Africa (1997) *Education White Paper 3: A Programme for the Transformation of Higher Education*. Pretoria: DoE

Department of Education (DoE), South Africa (2004) *Creating Comprehensive Documents in South Africa: A concept document*. Pretoria: DoE

Department of Higher Education & Training (DHET) (2008) *Report of the Ministerial Committee on Transformation and Social Cohesion and the Elimination of Discrimination in Public Higher Education Institutions*. Pretoria: DHET

Department of Higher Education & Training (DHET) (2020) *Register of Private Higher Education Institutions*. Pretoria: DHET

Department of Higher Education and Training (DHET) (2017) Draft Policy Framework for Extended Curriculum Programmes. Developed by Ministerial Reference Group.

Dewey J (1900) *The School and Society*. Chicago: University of Chicago Press

Dhawan S (2020) Online learning: A panacea in the time of COVID-19 Crisis. *Journal of Educational Technology Systems* 49(1): 5–22

Dison L & Clarence S (2017) *Writing Centres in Higher Education*. Stellenbosch: African SUN Media

Du Pré R (2009) The place and role of universities of technology in South Africa. South African Technology Network. *Kagisano* No. 7. Pretoria: Council on Higher Education

Durban University of Technology (DUT) (2018) What is somatology? https://www.dut.ac.za/clinics/somatology/

Dutton YM, Ryznar M & Long K (2018) Assessing online learning in law schools: Students say online classes deliver. *Denver Law Review* 96: 493–534

Edwards D & McMillan J (2015) Completing university in Australia: A cohort analysis exploring equity group outcomes. *Joining the Dots Research Briefings* 3(3): 1–12. Melbourne: Australian Council of Educational Research

Edwards M (2017, 25 July) I quit! Why I am leaving UK academia. *Times Higher Education*. https://www.timeshighereducation.com/blog/uk-academia-has-gone-hell-handcart-and-i-quit

Elder-Vass D (2013) Re-examining Bhaskar's three ontological domains: The lessons from emergence. In: C Lawson, J Latsis & N Martins (eds) *Contributions to Social Ontology*. London & New York: Routledge. pp. 160–177

Ellery K (2016) Epistemological access in a science foundation course: A social realist perspective. Unpublished doctoral dissertation, Rhodes University, Makhanda

Ellery K (2017) Conceptualising knowledge for access in the sciences: Academic development from a social realist perspective. *Higher Education* 74(5): 915–931

Ensor P (2014) Neoliberalism, education and the 'neglect of knowledge'. *Journal of Education* 59: 115–125

Essop A (2020) *The changing size & shape of the higher education system in South Africa 2005-2018*. Johannesburg: Ali Mazrui Centre for Higher Education Studies, University of Johannesburg

Fabricant M & Brier S (2016) *Austerity Blues: Fighting for the Soul of Public Higher Education*. Baltimore: John Hopkins University Press

Fanon F (1961) *The Wretched of the Earth*. Tr. Constance Farrington. New York: Grove Weidenfeld

Finegold D (2006) The role of education and training systems in innovation. In: J Hage & M Meeus (eds) *Innovation, Science, and Institutional Change: A Research Handbook*. Oxford: Oxford University Press

Finegold D & Soskice D (1988) The failure of training in Britain: Analysis and prescription. *Oxford Review of Economic Policy* 4(3): 21–53

Fraser N (1999) Social justice in the age of identity politics: Redistribution, recognition, and participation. In: L Ray & A Sayer (eds) *Culture and Economy after the Cultural Turn*. London: Sage. pp. 25–52

Fraser N (2007) Re-framing justice in a globalizing world. In: T Lovell (ed.) *(Mis) Recognition, Social Inequality and Social Justice*. London: Routledge. pp. 17–35

Freire P (1970) *Pedagogy of the Oppressed*. New York: Herder & Herder

Fricker M (2007) *Epistemic Injustice: Power and the Ethics of Knowing*. Oxford: Oxford University Press

Fricker M (2013) Epistemic justice as a condition of political freedom? *Synthese* 190(7): 1317–1332

Friedman M (1970, 13 September) The social responsibility of business is to increase its profits. *New York Times Magazine*

Furco A (1996) Service-learning: A balanced approach to experiential education. In: B Taylor (ed.) *Expanding Boundaries: Serving and Learning.* Washington, DC: Corporation for National Service. pp. 2–6

Gamble J (2001) Modelling the invisible: The pedagogy of craft apprenticeship. *Studies in Continuing Education* 23(2): 185–200

Gamble J (2014) 'Approaching the sacred': Directionality in the relation between curriculum and knowledge structure. *British Journal of Sociology of Education* 35(1): 56–72

Garraway J & Winberg C (2019) Reimagining futures of universities of technology. *Critical Studies in Teaching and Learning* 7(1): 38–60

Gee J (1989) Literacy, discourse, and linguistics: Introduction. *Journal of Education* 171(1): 5–17

Gee J (2008) *Social Linguistics and Literacies: Ideology in discourses.* Abingdon: Routledge

Gee J (2012) *Situated Language and Learning: A Critique of Traditional Schooling.* London: Routledge

Gee J (2014) *Literacy and Education.* London: Routledge

Geisler C (1994) Literacy and expertise in the academy. *Language and Learning across the Disciplines* 1(1): 35–57

Gibson R (1986) *Critical Theory and Education.* London: Hodder and Stoughton

Ginsberg B (2011) *The Fall of the Faculty.* Oxford: Oxford University Press

Giroux H (2021) *Race, Politics, and Pandemic Pedagogy: Education in a Time of Crisis.* London: Bloomsbury Academic

Graham G (2013) The university: A critical comparison of three ideal types. *Kagisano* No. 9: 5–22

Grant C, Quinn L & Vorster J (2018) An exploratory study of heads of departments' responses to student calls for decolonised higher education. *Journal of Education* 72: 73–88

Guinier L (2007) *Meritocracy, Inc.: How Wealth Became Merit, Class Became Race and Higher Education Became a Gift from the Poor to the Rich.* Boston, Mass.: Harvard University Press

Guinier L (2015) *The Tyranny of the Meritocracy: Democratizing Higher Education in America.* Boston, Mass.: Beacon

Gumbi T (2017) An investigation into Dental Technology academics' discourses on the emergence of universities of technology in South Africa. Unpublished master's dissertation, Durban University of Technology, Durban

Gumbi T & McKenna S (2020) Reimagining academic identities in response to research demands in universities of technology. *Critical Studies in Teaching and Learning (CriSTaL)* 8(1): 96–110

Habib A (2019) *Rebels and Rage: Reflecting on #FeesMustFall.* Johannesburg: Jonathan Ball

Haggis T (2009) What have we been thinking of? A critical overview of 40 years of student learning research in higher education. *Studies in Higher Education* 34(4): 377–390

Halliday MAK (1985) Systemic background. *Systemic Perspectives on Discourse* 1: 1–15

Harley A (2017) Alienating academic work. *The Journal of Education as Change* 21(3): 1–14

Harvey L (2008) Rankings of higher education institutions: A critical review. *Quality in Higher Education* 14(3): 187–207

Harvey L & Green D (1993) Defining quality. *Assessment & Evaluation in Higher Education* 18(1): 9–34

Heath S (1983) *Ways with Words: Language, Life and Work in Communities and Classrooms.* Cambridge: Cambridge University Press

Henkel M (2005) Academic identity and autonomy in a changing policy environment. *Higher Education* 49(1/2): 155–176

Hibbert L & Van der Walt C (2014) *Multilingual Universities in South Africa: Reflecting Society in Higher Education.* Bristol: Multilingual Matters

Higher Education Quality Committee (HEQC) (2004) *Criteria for Institutional Audits.* Pretoria: Council on Higher Education

Higher Education South Africa (HESA) Experts in Higher Education Data and Analysis (n.d.) https://www.hesa.ac.uk/

Hlatshwayo M (2019) 'I want them to be confident, to build an argument': An exploration of knowledge and knower structures in Political Studies. Unpublished PhD thesis, Rhodes University, Makhanda

Hlengwa A (2013) An exploration of conditions enabling and constraining the infusion of service-learning into the curriculum at a South African research led university. Unpublished doctoral dissertation, Rhodes University, Makhanda

Hlengwa A & McKenna S (2017) Dangers of generic pedagogical panaceas: Implementing service-learning differently in diverse disciplines. *Journal of Education* 67: 129–148

Hlengwa A, McKenna S & Njovane T (2018) The lenses we use to research student experiences. In: P Ashwin & J Case (eds) *Higher Education Pathways: South African Undergraduate Education and the Public Good*. Cape Town: African Minds. pp. 149–162

Hollingsworth M & Lansey S (2009) *Londongrad*. London: Fourth Estate

Holloway J (2010) *Crack Capitalism*. London: Pluto

Jacobs C (2007) Mainstreaming academic literacy teaching: Implications for how academic development understands its work in higher education. *South African Journal of Higher Education* 21(7): 870–881

Jacobs C (2009) Teaching explicitly that which is tacit: The challenge of disciplinary discourses. In: B Leibowitz, A Van der Merwe A & S Van Schalkwyk (eds) *Focus on First-Year Success: Perspectives Emerging from South Africa and Beyond*. Stellenbosch: SUN Media. pp. 241–252

Jacobs C (2013) Academic literacies and the question of knowledge. *Journal for Language Teaching* 47(2): 127–140

Janks H (2000) Domination, access, diversity and design: A synthesis for critical literacy education. *Educational Review* 52(2): 175–186

Janks H (2009) *Literacy and Power*. Abingdon: Routledge

Jansen J (1998) Curriculum reform in South Africa: A critical analysis of Outcomes-Based Education. *Cambridge Journal of Education* 28(3): 321–331

Jansen J (2001) Rethinking education policy making in South Africa: Symbols of change, signals of conflict. In: A Kraak & M Young (eds) *Education in Retrospect: Policy Implementation since 1990*. Pretoria: Human Sciences Research Council

Jansen J (2012) National senior certificate results belie conceptual and skill limitations of school-leavers. *South African Journal of Science* 108(3/4): 1–2

Jansen J & Christie P (1999) *Changing Curriculum: Studies on Outcomes-Based Education in South Africa*. Cape Town: Juta

Kisaka L, Jansen E & Hofman A (2019) Workforce diversity in Kenyan public universities: An analysis of workforce representativeness and heterogeneity by employee, gender and ethnic group. *Journal of Higher Education, Policy and Management* 41(1): 35–51

Klemenčič M (2017) From student engagement to student agency: Conceptual considerations of European policies on student-centered learning in higher education. *Higher Education Policy* 30(1): 69–85

Kolb D (1981) Learning styles and disciplinary differences. *The Modern American College* 1: 232–255

Kraak A (2000) *Changing Modes: New Knowledge Production and its Implications for South Africa*. Pretoria: Human Sciences Research Council

Kraak A (2006) High skills and joined-up policy: An introduction to the debate. In: A Kraak, H Lauder, P Brown & D Ashton (eds) *Debating High Skills and Joined-up Policy*. Pretoria: HSRC Press. pp. 1–30

Kraak A (2009) South African technikons and policy contestation over academic drift. In: R Maclean & D Wilson (eds) *International Handbook of Education for the Changing World of Work: Bridging Academic and Vocational Learning*. Dordrecht: Springer. pp. 961–975

Kumalo S (ed.) (2021) *Decolonisation as Democratisation: Global Insights into the South African Experience*. Pretoria: Human Sciences Research Council

REFERENCES

Lange L (2017) 20 Years of higher education curriculum policy in South Africa. *Journal of Education* 68: 31–58

Leibowitz B & Bozalek V (2015) Foundation provision – A social justice perspective. *South African Journal of Higher Education* 29(1): 8–25

Lesteka M & Maile S (2008) *High University Dropout Rates: A Threat to South Africa's Future.* Pretoria: Human Sciences Research Council

Lück J (2014) Knowledge and knowing in the Public Management and Public Administration programmes at a comprehensive university. Unpublished doctoral dissertation, Rhodes University, Makhanda

Luckett K (2007) Methodology matters: Possible methods to improve quality. *Perspectives in Education* 25(3): 1–11

Luckett K & Luckett T (2009) The development of agency in first generation learners in higher education: A social realist analysis. *Teaching in Higher Education* 14(5): 469–481

Luescher TM, Webbstock D & Bhengu N (eds) (2020) *Reflections of South African Student Leaders, 1994 to 2017.* Cape Town: African Minds

Madra Y & Adaman F (2018) Neoliberal turn in the discipline of economics: Depoliticization through economization. In: D Cahill, M Cooper, M Konings & D Primrose D (eds) *SAGE Handbook of Neoliberalism.* Melbourne: Sage. pp. 113–127

Malan L (1996) Literacy learning and local literacy practice in Bellville South. In: M Prinsloo & M Breier (eds) *The Social Uses of Literacy: Theory and Practice in Contemporary South Africa.* Amsterdam: John Benjamins. pp. 141–156

Mamdani M (1998) Is African studies to be turned into a new home for Bantu Education at UCT? *Social Dynamics* 24(2): 63–75

Mamdani M (2017) Decolonising the post-colonial university. TB Davie Memorial Lecture. University of Cape Town, 22 August

Manathunga C & Brew A (2012) Beyond tribes and territories: New metaphors for new times. In: P Trowler, M Saunders & V Bamber (eds) *Tribes and Territories in the 21st Century: Rethinking the Significance of Disciplines in Higher Education.* London: Taylor & Francis

Mann M (2013) *The Sources of Social Power: Volume 4, Globalizations, 1945–2011.* Cambridge: Cambridge University Press

Marginson S (2006) Dynamics of national and global competition in higher education. *Higher Education* 52(1): 1–39

Marginson S (2007) The public/private divide in higher education: A global revision. *Higher Education* 53(3): 307–333

Marginson S (2009) University rankings, government and social order: Managing the field of higher education according to the logic of the performative present-as-future. In: M Simons, M Olssen & M Peters (eds) *Re-Reading Education Policies. Studying the Policy Agenda of the 21st Century.* Rotterdam: Sense

Marginson S & Considine M (2000) *The Enterprise University: Power, Governance and Reinvention in Australia.* Cambridge: Cambridge University Press

Marginson S & Rhoades G (2002) Beyond national states, markets, and systems of higher education: A glonacal agency heuristic. *Higher Education* 43: 281–309

Marshall D (2018, 15 April) A more flexible curriculum approach can support student success. *The Conversation Africa.* https://theconversation.com/a-more-flexible-curriculum-approach-can-support-student-success-92751

Marton F & Säljö R (1976) On qualitative differences in learning: I—Outcome and process. *The British Journal of Educational Psychology* 46(1): 4–11

Masehela L (2015) An exploration into the conditions enabling and constraining the implementation of quality assurance in higher education: The case of a small comprehensive university in South Africa. Unpublished doctoral dissertation, Rhodes University, Makhanda

Maton K (2004) The wrong kind of knower: Education, expansion and the epistemic device. In: J Muller, B Davies & A Morais (eds) *Reading Bernstein, Researching Bernstein*. Abingdon: Routledge

Maton K (2009) Cumulative and segmented learning: Exploring the role of curriculum structures in knowledge-building. *British Journal of Sociology of Education* 30(1): 43–57

Maton K (2014) *Knowledge and Knowers*. Abingdon: Routledge

Maylam P (2017) *Rhodes University 1904-2016: An Intellectual, Political and Cultural History*. Makhanda: Institute of Social and Economic Research, Rhodes University

Mbembe A (2016) Decolonizing the university: New directions. *Arts and Humanities in Higher Education* 15(1): 29–45

McCowan T (2017) Higher education, unbundling and the end of the university as we know it. *Oxford Review of Education* 43(6): 733–748

McCowan T (2018) Quality of higher education in Kenya: Addressing the conundrum. *International Journal of Educational Development* 60: 128–137

McKenna S (2003) Changing discourses of academic development at a South African technikon 1991 to 2002: Perspectives on higher education. *South African Journal of Higher Education* 17(2): 60–67

McKenna S (2004a) Lecturers' discourses about the interplay between language and learning. *South African Journal of Higher Education* 18(2): 278–286

McKenna S (2004b) The intersection between academic literacies and student identities: Research in higher education. *South African Journal of Higher Education* 18(3): 269–280

McKenna S (2010) Cracking the code of academic literacy: An ideological task. In: C Hutchings & J Garraway (eds) *Beyond the University Gates: Provision of Extended Curriculum Programmes in South Africa*. Cape Town: Cape Peninsula University of Technology

McKenna S (2012a) The context of access and foundation provisioning in South Africa. In: R Dhunpath & R Vithal (eds) *Alternative Access to Higher Education*. Cape Town: Pearson

McKenna S (2012b) Interrogating the academic project. In: L Quinn (ed.) *Reimagining Academic Staff Development: Spaces for Disruption*. Stellenbosch: SUN Media

McKenna S (2013) The dangers of student-centered learning: A caution about blind spots in the scholarship of teaching and learning. *International Journal for the Scholarship of Teaching and Learning* 7(2): 1–5

McKenna S (2017, 21 April) Unmasking the doctorate. *University World News*. https://www.universityworldnews.com/post.php?story=20170421113152878

McKenna S (2020) The rise of the executive dean and the slide into managerialism. *Educational Research as Social Change* 9(1): 76–89

McKenna S (2021) Supervising postgraduate scholarship in a troubled world. *The Global Scholar: Implications for Postgraduate Studies and Supervision*. Stellenbosch: SUN Media

McKenna S & Boughey C (2014) Argumentative and trustworthy scholars: The construction of academic staff at research-intensive universities. *Teaching in Higher Education* 19(7): 825–834

McKenna S & Quinn L (2016) Lost in translation: Transformation in the first round of institutional audits. *South African Journal of Higher Education* 26(5): 1033–1044

McKenna S & Quinn L (2020) Misconceptions and misapplications of student-centered approaches. In: S Hoidn & M Klemenčič (eds) *The Routledge International Handbook of Student-Centered Learning and Teaching in Higher Education*. Oxford: Routledge. pp. 109–120

McKenna S & Sutherland L (2006) Balancing knowledge construction and skills training in universities of technology. *Perspectives in Education* 24(3): 15–24

Mettler S (2005) 'The only good thing was the G.I. Bill': Effects of the education and training provisions on African-American veterans' political participation. *Studies in American Political Development* 19(1): 31–52

Mettler S (2014) *Degrees of Inequality: How the Politics of Higher Education Sabotaged the American Dream*. New York: Basic Books

Mignolo W (2000) *Local Histories/Global Designs.* New Jersey: Princeton University Press

Millar B (2014) Becoming and being: A critical realist study into the emergence of identity in emergency medical science students, and the construct of graduate attributes. Unpublished doctoral dissertation, Rhodes University, Makhanda

Ministry of Education (MoE), South Africa (2001) *National Plan for Higher Education.* Pretoria: MoE

Ministry of Education (MoE), South Africa (2002) *The Restructuring of the Higher Education System in South Africa: Report of the Working Group to the Minister of Education.* Pretoria: MoE

Ministry of Education (MoE), South Africa (2004) *A New Funding Framework: How Government Grants are Allocated to Public Higher Education Institutions.* Pretoria: MoE

Mintz S (2019, 4 February) Educating versus training and credentialing. *Inside Higher Ed.* https://www.insidehighered.com/blogs/higher-ed-gamma/educating-versus-training-and-credentialing

Mitchell L (2009) The oppression of non-human animals: A critical realist account. Unpublished doctoral dissertation, Rhodes University, Makhanda

Mkhize D (2018) The language question at a historically Afrikaans university: Access and social justice issues. *Southern African Linguistics and Applied Language Studies* 36(1): 13–24

Mkhize T (2015) An analysis of the Certificate of the Theory of Accounting knowledge and knower structures: A case study of professional knowledge. Unpublished doctoral dissertation, Rhodes University, Makhanda

Monnapula-Mapesela M (2017) Developing as an academic leader in a university of technology in South Africa: Dealing with enabling and constraining teaching and learning environments. *Critical Studies in Teaching and Learning* 5(2): 69–85

Moremi M (2018) Factors shaping higher education in Botswana: A recipe for policy formulation and implementation? *International Journal of Learning and Teaching* 4(1): 64–69

Morrow W (1993) Epistemological access in the university. *AD Issues* 1(1): 3–4

Morrow W (2009) *Bounds of Democracy: Epistemological Access in Higher Education.* Pretoria: HSRC Press

Mose PN (2017) Language-in-education policy in Kenya: Intention, interpretation, implementation. *Nordic Journal of African Studies* 26(3): 215–230

Mouton J & Valentine A (2017) The extent of South African authored articles in predatory journals. *South African Journal of Science* 113(7): 1–9

Moyo T (2018) An analysis of the implementation of the teaching development grant in the South African higher education sector. Unpublished doctoral dissertation, Rhodes University, Makhanda

Moyo T & McKenna S (2020) Constraints on improving higher education teaching and learning through funding. *South Africa Journal of Science* 117 (1/2): 1–7

Mphahlele A (2019) Conceptualisations of and responses to plagiarism in the South African higher education system. Unpublished doctoral dissertation, Rhodes University, Makhanda

Mphahlele A & McKenna S (2018) Plagiarism in the South African higher education system: Discarding a common sense understanding. In: S Razi, I Glendinning & T Foltýnek (eds) *Towards Consistency and Transparency in Academic Integrity.* Bern: Peter Lang. pp. 31–41

Mphahlele A & McKenna S (2019) The use of turnitin in the higher education sector: Decoding the myth. *Assessment and Evaluation in Higher Education* 44(7): 1079–1089

Mtombeni T (2018) Knowledge practices and student access and success in General Chemistry at a large South African university. Unpublished doctoral dissertation, Rhodes University, Makhanda.

Muller J (1998) NQF and Outcomes-Based Education: Pedagogic models and hard choices. *Proceedings of the Reconstruction, Development, and the National Qualifications Framework Conference.* Johannesburg: Centre for Education Policy Development

Muller J (2000) *Reclaiming Knowledge: Social Theory, Curriculum and Education Policy.* Abingdon: Routledge Falmer

Muller J (2001a) Responsiveness and innovation in higher education. Paper commissioned as support material for N Cloete, P Maassen, R Fehnel, T Moja, T Gibbon & H Perold (eds) *Transformation in Higher Education: Global Pressures and Local Realities* (2006). New York: Springer

Muller J (2001b) Connectivity, capacity and knowledge. In: J Muller & N Cloete (eds) *Challenges of Globalisation: South African Debates with Manuel Castells*. Cape Town: Maskew Miller Longman

Muller J (2009) Forms of knowledge and curriculum coherence. *Journal of Education and Work* 22(3): 205–226

Muller J & Taylor N (1995) Schooling and everyday life: Knowledges sacred and profane. *Social Epistemology* 9(3): 257–275

Muller J & Young M (2014) Disciplines, skills and the university. *Higher Education* 67(2): 127–140

Muller S (2017) Academics as rent seekers: Distorted incentives in higher education, with reference to the South African case. *International Journal of Educational Development* 52(1): 58–67

Mungungu-Shipale S (2016) Lecturers' and students' perceptions and preferences about ESL corrective feedback in Namibia: Towards an intervention model. Unpublished PhD thesis, University of Namibia

Muthama E (2019) Conditions constraining and enabling research production in historically black universities in South Africa. Unpublished PhD Thesis, Rhodes University, Makhanda

Muthama E & McKenna S (2017) The contradictory conceptions of research in historically black universities. *Perspectives in Education* 35(1): 129–142

Muthama E & McKenna S (2020) The unintended consequences of using direct incentives to drive the complex task of research dissemination. *Education as Change* 24(1): 1–23

Naidoo R & Ranchod R (2018) Transformation, the state and higher education: Towards a developmental system of higher education in South Africa. In: P Ashwin & J Case (eds) *Higher Education Pathways: South African Undergraduate Education and the Public Good*. Cape Town: African Minds

Nampota T (2015) Emergent governance practices in the University of Malawi following reform implementation from 1997 to 2013. Unpublished doctoral dissertation, Rhodes University, Makhanda

Nash A (2013) Excellence in higher education: Is there really no alternative? *Kagisano* No. 9: 42–62

Ndimele O (2016) *Studies in Nigerian linguistics*. Lagos: M & J Grand Orbit Communications

Ndlovu-Gatsheni S (2013) *Coloniality of Power in Postcolonial Africa: Myths of Decolonisation*. Dakar: Codesria

Neves J & Hillman N (2018) *2018 Student Academic Experiences Survey*. Oxford: Higher Education Policy Institute (HEPI)

Newfield C (2016) *The Great Mistake: How We Wrecked Public Universities and How We Can Fix Them*. Baltimore: Johns Hopkins Press

Nichols P (2011) Student culture and cultural change: A manifesto for writing praxis in a South African writing centre. In: A Archer & R Richards (eds) *Changing Spaces: Writing Centres and Access to Higher Education*. Stellenbosch: SUN Media. pp. 19–31

Nichols P (2016) Heeding the corpse in the cargo: The writing centre and the need to listen. *South African Journal of Higher Education* 28(3): 894–906

Niven P (2012) Narrating emergence in the curious domain of academic development research: A realist perspective. Unpublished doctoral dissertation, Rhodes University, Makhanda

Nixon E, Scullion R & Hearn R (2018) Her Majesty the student: Marketised higher education and the narcissistic (dis)satisfactions of the student–consumer. *Studies in Higher Education* 43(6): 927–943

Nkinyangi JA (1991) Student protests in sub-Saharan Africa. *Higher Education Journal* 22(2): 157–173

Nudelman G (2018) A social realist study of employability development in Engineering education. Unpublished doctoral dissertation, Rhodes University, Makhanda

Nussbaum M (1998) *Cultivating Humanity*. Boston, Mass.: Harvard University Press

Nyerere J (1967) Education for self-reliance. *The Ecumenical Review* 19(4): 382–403

Nyinondi O, Mhandeni A & Mohamed HI (2016) The use of communicative language teaching approach in the teaching of communication skills courses in Tanzanian universities. *International Journal of Research Studies in Language Learning* 6(3): 89–99

REFERENCES

Oanda I & Ngcwangu S (2018) Destination and outcome trends for graduates from sub-Saharan African countries. In: P Ashwin & J Case (eds) *Higher Education Pathways: South African Undergraduate Education and the Public Good.* Cape Town: African Minds. pp. 260–273

Odhiambo G (2016) Higher education in Kenya: An assessment of current responses to the imperative of widening access. *Journal of Higher Education and Management* 38(2): 196–211

Office for Students (2020) *What We Do.* London: Office for Students

O'Keeffe P (2013) A sense of belonging: Improving student retention. *College Student Journal* 47(4): 605–613

Organisation of Economic Cooperation and Development (OECD) (2019) *Education at a Glance: Indicators.* Paris: OECD

O'Shea C (2017) Understanding the reading practices of Fort Hare students. Unpublished doctoral dissertation, Rhodes University, Makhanda

O'Shea C, McKenna S & Thomson C (2019) 'We throw away our books': Students' reading practices and identities. *Linguistics and Education* 49(February): 1–10

Pedro NS & Kumar S (2020) Institutional support for online teaching in quality assurance frameworks. *Online Learning* 24(3): 50–66.

Pereira L (2012) A critical realist exploration of the implementation of a new curriculum in Swaziland. Unpublished doctoral dissertation, Rhodes University, Makhanda

Powell P & McKenna S (2009) 'Only a name change': The move from Technikon to University of Technology. *The Journal of Independent Teaching and Learning* 4(1): 37–48

Prah K (2017) The centrality of the language question in the decolonization of education in Africa. *Alternation* 24(2): 226–252

Prinsloo M & Breier M (1996) *The Social Uses of Literacy: Theory and Practice in Contemporary South Africa.* Amsterdam: John Benjamins

Quinn L (ed.) (2012) *Re-Imagining Academic Staff Development: Spaces for Disruption.* Stellenbosch: SUN Media

Quinn L & Boughey C (2009) A case study of an institutional audit: A social realist account. *Quality in Higher Education* 15(3): 263–278

Quinn L & Vorster J (2014) Isn't it time to start thinking about 'developing' academic developers in a more systematic way? *International Journal for Academic Development* 19(3): 255–258

Quinn L & Vorster J (2015) Pedagogy for fostering criticality, reflectivity and praxis in a course for lecturers on teaching. *Assessment and Evaluation in Higher Education* 41(7): 1–13

Quinn L & Vorster J (2017) Connected disciplinary responses to the call to decolonise curricula in South African higher education. In: B Carnell & D Fung (eds) *Developing the Higher Education Curriculum. Research-based Education in Practice.* London: UCL Press. pp. 131–144

Rata E (2012) *The Politics of Knowledge in Education.* Abingdon: Routledge

Rata E (2017) Connecting knowledge to democracy. In: B Barrett, U Hoadley & J Morgan (eds) *Knowledge, Curriculum and Equity: Social Realist Perspective.* Abingdon: Routledge

Readings B (1996) *The University in Ruins.* Boston, Mass.: Harvard University Press

Reay D & Vincent C (2016) *Theorizing Social Class and Education.* Abingdon: Routledge

Reddy S (2011) Experiences of clinical practice in a problem-based learning medical curriculum and subsequent clinical environments. Unpublished doctoral dissertation, University of KwaZulu-Natal, Durban

Republic of Kenya (2007) *Kenya Vision 2030.* Nairobi: Vision 2030 Delivery Secretariat

Republic of South Africa (RSA) (1983) University Amendment Act No. 83 of 1983. Pretoria: Government Printers

Republic of South Africa (RSA) (1995) South African Qualifications Authority Act No. 58 of 1995. Pretoria: Government Printers

Republic of South Africa (RSA) (1996) The Constitution of the Republic of South Africa No. 108 of 1996. Government Printers: Pretoria

Republic of South Africa (RSA) (1997) Higher Education Act (Act No. 101). Government Printers: Pretoria

Richardson J (2005) Students' approaches to learning and teachers' approaches to teaching in higher education. *Educational Psychology Review* 25(6): 673–680

Rogers C & Freiberg J (1994) *Freedom to Learn*. New York: Maxwell Macmillan International

Russell SG & Carter PL (2018) When the past is in the present: Unintended consequences of non-racialization/de-ethnicization in South Africa and Rwanda. *Sociology of Race and Ethnicity* 5(4): 547–561

Said E (1978) *Orientalism: Western Representations of the Orient*. New York: Pantheon

Salazar M (2013) A humanizing pedagogy: Reinventing the principles and practice of education as a journey toward liberation. *Review of Research in Education* 37(1): 121–148

Samuelson B (2013) Rwanda switches to English: Conflict, identity and language-in-education policy. In: JW Tollefson (ed.) *Language Policies in Education: Critical Issues*. New York: Routledge. pp. 211–232

Scott I, Ndebele N, Badsha N, Figaji B, Gevers W & Pityana B (2013) *A Proposal for Undergraduate Curriculum Reform in South Africa: The Case for a Flexible Curriculum Structure*. Pretoria: Council on Higher Education

Scott I, Yeld N & Hendry J (2007) *A Case for Improving Teaching and Learning in South African Higher Education*. Pretoria: Higher Education Monitor, 6. Council on Higher Education

Shay S (2012) Educational development as a field: Are we there yet? *Higher Education Research & Development* 31(3): 311–323

Shay S (2013) Conceptualizing curriculum differentiation in higher education: A sociology of knowledge point of view. *British Journal of Sociology of Education* 34(4): 563–582

Shay S & Mkhize T (2018) Curriculum transformation: Looking back and planning forward. In: P Ashwin & J Case (eds) *Higher Education Pathways: South African Undergraduate Education and the Public Good*. Cape Town: African Minds. pp. 192–203

Shay S, Oosthuizen M, Paxton P & Van der Merwe R (2011) Towards a principled basis for curriculum differentiation. In: E Bitzer & N Botha (eds) *Curriculum Inquiry in South African Higher Education: Some Scholarly Affirmations and Challenges*. Stellenbosch: SUN Media. pp. 93–112

Shay S & Steyn D (2014) Enabling knowledge progression in vocational curricula: Design as a case study. In: K Maton, S Hood & S Shay (eds) *Knowledge-Building: Educational Studies in Legitimation Code Theory*. Abingdon: Routledge. pp. 138–157

Shore C (2010) Beyond the multiversity: Neoliberalism and the rise of the schizophrenic university. *Social Anthropology* 18(1): 15–29

Shore C & Wright S (2015) Governing by numbers: Audit culture, rankings and the new world order. *Social Anthropology* 23(1): 22–28

Singh M (2008) Valuing differentiation as a qualified good: The case of South African higher education. *Higher Education Policy* 21(2): 245–263

Sobuwa S & McKenna S (2019) The obstinate notion that higher education is a meritocracy. *Critical Studies in Teaching and Learning* 7(2): 13–28

Soudien C, Michaels W, Mthembi-Mahanyela S, Nkomo M, Nayenda G, Nyoka N et al. (2008) *Report of the Ministerial Committee on Transformation and Social Cohesion and the Elimination of Discrimination in Public Higher Education Institutions*. Pretoria: Department of Education of Higher Education & Training (DHET)

Spivak G (1988) Can the subaltern speak? In: C Nelson & L Grossberg (eds) *Marxism and the Interpretation of Culture*. Champaign, Illinois: University of Illinois Press. pp. 271–315

Statistics South Africa (2012) *Census 2011: Census in Brief*. Pretoria: Statistics SA

Statistics South Africa (2020) *Quarterly Labour Force Survey June 2020*. Pretoria: Statistics SA

Street B (1984) *Literacy in Theory and Practice*. Cambridge: Cambridge University Press

Subotzky G (2003) Public higher education. In: A Kraak & H Perold (eds) *Human Resources Development Review.* Pretoria: HSRC

Tabensky P & Matthews S (eds) (2015) *Being at Home: Race, Institutional Culture and Transformation at South African Higher Education Institutions.* Pietermaritzburg: UKZN Press

Tamrat W (2018) Private higher education in Africa: Old realities and emerging trends. *International Journal of African Higher Education* 4(2): 17–40

Taylor P & Braddock R (2007) International university ranking systems and the idea of university excellence. *Journal of Higher Education Policy and Management* 29(3): 245–260

Teferra D (2017) Tempest in the rankings teapot: An African perspective. *International Higher Education* 91(Fall): 18–20

Teferra D & Altbach P (2004) African higher education: Challenges for the 21st century. *Higher Education* 47(1): 21–50

Tehan D (2020) Address to the National Press Club, Canberra, Australia

Thaver B (2010) The transition to equity in South African higher education: Governance, fairness, and trust in everyday academic practice. *International Journal of Politics, Culture, and Society* 23(1): 43–56

The Education Commission (2016) *The Learning Generation: Investing in Education for a Changing World.* www.educationcommission.org

Thesen L & Cooper L (2013) *Risk in Academic Writing: Postgraduate Students, their Teachers and the Making of Knowledge.* Bristol: Multilingual Matters

Thesen L & Van Pletzen E (eds) (2006) *Academic Literacy and the Languages of Change.* London: Bloomsbury

Thomas A & De Bruin GP (2015) Plagiarism in South African management journals. *South African Journal of Science* 111(1/2): 1–3

Tight M (2004) Research into higher education: An a-theoretical community of practice? *Higher Education Research & Development* 23(4): 395–411

Tight M (2018) *Higher Education Research: The Developing Field.* London: Bloomsbury Academic

Tomas L (2013) What works? Facilitating an effective transition into higher education. *Widening Participation and Lifelong Learning* 14(1): 4–24

Tronto J (1994) *Moral Boundaries: A Political Argument for an Ethics of Care.* New York: Routledge

Trow M (1973) *The Transition from Elite to Mass to Universal Higher Education.* Berkeley, CA: Carnegie Commission on Higher Education

Trowler P (2008) *Cultures and Change in Higher Education: Theories and Practice.* Hampshire: Palgrave MacMillan

Trowler P (2014) Academic tribes and territories: The theoretical trajectory. *Osterreichische Zeitschrift fur Geschichtswissenschaften* 25(3): 17–26

Trowler P (2020) *Accomplishing Change in Teaching and Learning Regimes: Higher Education and the Practice Sensibility.* Oxford: Oxford University Press

Tuck R (2007) *An Introductory Guide for National Qualifications Frameworks: Conceptual and practical issues for policymakers.* Geneva: International Labour Office (ILO)

Tuhiwai Smith L (2012) *Decolonising Methodologies: Research and Indigenous Peoples.* 2nd edn. London: Zed

United Nations Educational, Scientific and Cultural Organisation (Unesco) (1953) *The Use of Vernacular Languages in Education.* Monographs on Fundamental Education, VIII. Paris: Unesco

United Nations Educational, Scientific and Cultural Organisation (Unesco) (2020) Gross enrolment rate by level of education. www.data.uis.unesco.org

Universum Communications Sweden (2018) Universum talent report: South Africa. Stockholm: Universum Communictions

Vahed A (2014) Ensuring the quality of pedagogy through games in Dental Technology at a selected university of technology. Unpublished doctoral dissertation, Durban University of Technology, Durban

Vahed A, McKenna S & Singh S (2016) Linking the 'know-that' and 'know-how' knowledge through games: Evolving the future for Science and Engineering education. *Higher Education* 71(6): 781–790

Van Broekhuizen H (2016) *Graduate Unemployment and Higher Education Institutions in South Africa.* Working Paper 08/2016, Department of Economics, Stellenbosch University

Veblen TB (1899) *The Theory of the Leisure Class.* New York: MacMillan

Venter-Hildebrand M (1996) *Framework for Transformation of Higher Education in South Africa: National Commission on Higher Education Ministry of Education.* Pretoria: Ministry of Education, National Commission on Higher Education

Vilakazi HB & Tema B (1985) White universities and the black revolution. *ASPects* 6: 18–40

Volbrecht T & Boughey C (2005) Curriculum responsiveness from the margins? In: H Griesel (ed.) *Curriculum Responsiveness: Case Studies in Higher Education.* Pretoria: SAUVCA

Vorster J & Quinn L (2017) The 'decolonial turn': What does it mean for academic staff development? *Education as Change* 21 (1): 31–49

Walker M (2008) Widening participation; widening capability. *London Review of Education* 6(3): 267–279

Walker M (2018) Dimensions of higher education and the public good in South Africa. *Higher Education* 76(3): 555–569

Walker M & Badsha N (1993) Academic development: The 1990s. *South African Journal of Higher Education* 7(1): 59–62

Walpole M (2003) Socioeconomic status and college: How SES affects college experiences and outcomes. *The Review of Higher Education* 27(1): 45–73

Wheelahan L (2007) How competency-based training locks the working class out of powerful knowledge: A modified Bernsteinian analysis. *British Journal of Sociology of Education* 28(5): 637–651

Wheelahan L (2009) The problem with CBT (and why constructivism makes things worse). *Journal of Education and Work* 22(3): 227–242

Wheelahan L (2010) *Why Knowledge Matters in Curriculum: A Social Realist Argument.* Abingdon: Routledge

Wheelahan L (2015) Not just skills: What a focus on knowledge means for vocational education. *Journal of Curriculum Studies* 47(6): 750–762

Whitchurch C (2015) The rise of third space professionals: Paradoxes and dilemmas. In: U Teichler & W Cummings (eds) *Forming, Recruiting and Managing the Academic Profession.* Dordrecht: Springer. pp. 79–99

White K, Carvalho T & Riordan S (2011) Gender, power and managerialism in universities. *Journal of Higher Education Policy and Management* 33(2): 179–188

Wilkinson K (2015, 25 March) Checked: 80% of South African schools indeed 'dysfunctional'. *Mail & Guardian*

Wilmot K & McKenna S (2018) Writing groups as transformative spaces. *Higher Education Research & Development* 37(4): 868–882

Winberg C (2005) Continuities and discontinuities in the journey from Technikon to University of Technology. *South African Journal of Higher Education* 19(2): 189–200

Winberg C, Engel-Hills P, Garraway J & Jacobs C (2013) Professionally oriented knowledge and the purpose of professionally oriented higher education. *Kagisano* No. 9. Pretoria: Council on Higher Education

Wolff K & Luckett K (2013) Integrating multidisciplinary engineering knowledge. *Teaching in Higher Education* 18(1): 78–92

Xia J, Harmon J, Connolly K, Donnelly R, Anderson M & Howard H (2014) Who publishes in predatory journals? *Journal of the Association for Information Science and Technology* 66(7): 1406–1417

Young M (2007) *Bringing Knowledge Back in: From Social Constructivism to Social Realism in the Sociology of Education.* Abingdon: Routledge

Young M (2008) From constructivism to realism in the sociology of the curriculum. *Review of Research in Education* 32(1): 1–28

Young M (2013) Overcoming the crisis in curriculum theory: A knowledge-based approach. *Journal of Curriculum Studies* 45(2): 101–118

Young M & Muller J (2010) Three educational scenarios for the future: Lessons from the sociology of knowledge. *European Journal of Education* 45(1): 11–27

Young M & Muller J (2013a) Context and implications document for: On the powers of powerful knowledge. *Review of Education* 1(3): 251–253

Young M & Muller J (2013b) On the powers of powerful knowledge. *Review of Education* 1(3): 229–250

Zembylas M (2015) 'Pedagogy of discomfort' and its ethical implications: The tensions of ethical violence in social justice education. *Ethics and Education* 10(2): 163–174

Zembylas M, Bozalek V & Shefer T (2014) Tronto's notion of privileged irresponsibility and the reconceptualisation of care: Implications for critical pedagogies of emotion in higher education. *Gender and Education* 26(3): 200–214